Layman's
BIBLE
Commentary

Isaiah thru Ezekiel

Volume
6

Contributing

JOHN HANNEMAN
REV. STEPHEN C. MAGEE
DOUG MCINTOSH
DR. ROBERT RAYBURN

Consulting Editor:
DR. TREMPER LONGMAN

BARBOUR
PUBLISHING

Produced with the assistance of Christopher. D. Hudson & Associates. Contributing writers include: Gordon Lawrence, Heather Rippetoe, Laura Coggin, Stan Campbell, and Carol Smith.

Published by Barbour Publishing, Inc., P.O. Box 719, Uhrichsville, Ohio 44683, www.barbourbooks.com

Our mission is to publish and distribute inspirational products offering exceptional value and biblical encouragement to the masses.

Member of the
Evangelical Christian
Publishers Association

TABLE OF CONTENTS

ISAIAH

INTRODUCTION TO ISAIAH

The book of Isaiah is a potentially intimidating challenge for novice Bible readers, but it is a rich and rewarding pursuit for those willing to delve into it. Its sixty-six chapters comprise the fifth longest book of the Bible in terms of word count. But even more daunting than its sheer length is the prophetic nature of the writing. The author (or perhaps authors) writes of events that cover centuries, and it can be difficult in places to tell if he speaks of the present, the near future, or the long-range future. Yet while the prophet's narrative can be a bit confusing in places, large portions are quite clear in presenting a merciful God who does not give up on His people even though they have been repeatedly rebellious and wayward.

AUTHOR

The name *Isaiah*, "Salvation of Yahweh," is closely related to that of *Joshua* ("Yahweh is salvation"), which is the Old Testament equivalent of *Jesus*. However, not much is known about the prophet other than what he reveals in his book. He is identified as "the son of Amoz" thirteen times. He also writes that he has a wife and two children (7:3; 8:3). Little more is known about his personal life. Justin Martyr recorded the tradition that Isaiah died a martyr's death at the hands of King Manasseh, sawed in two (possibly the source of the reference in Hebrews 11:37).

A debate has raged for more than a century now as to whether the book of Isaiah was written by a single person or more than one author. Most scholars agree the book has distinctive sections. Chapters 1–39 comprise one unit and chapters 40–66 another. (Many purport that 40–55 should be a second unit and 56–66 a third, and that a different Isaiah wrote each section. Still others suggest the existence of an Isaiah "school," where disciples carried on the work of the original Isaiah.) If a single author wrote the entire book, he was given extremely precise insight into Judah's future, including the name of the ruler who would release the people after their captivity (44:28–45:1). Yet Cyrus wouldn't come to power for more than a century, after the Medes conquered Babylon, which was the rise of Babylon and fall of Assyria. However, the oldest available scrolls have no breaks between the different sections, recording Isaiah as a single book. And numerous New Testament figures, including Jesus Himself, quote from various portions of Isaiah as if the writing is from a single author. So the debate will continue, but for purposes of this commentary, references to the author throughout the entire book will be, simply, "Isaiah."

PURPOSE

Isaiah's purpose in writing is described during a vision in which he receives his calling from God (6:6–10). He is instructed to speak to his people, even though most are spiritually rebellious and disobedient and will not listen to him. (Jesus later quotes this very passage to explain why He uses parables to teach the people [Matthew 13:13–15].) Isaiah faithfully brings God's word to the people, warning anyone who will listen of what is to come.

THEMES

God's sovereignty is evident throughout Isaiah. The Lord maneuvers great empires to accomplish His will, including the chastisement of His people, and then brings those "powers" to nothing in judgment of their arrogance and sin. He allows His people to be dispersed throughout the world but then promises to call them back to Jerusalem, bringing their captors with them to worship together. Even in the turbulence and violence of the ancient world, the supremacy of God was always certain.

The book of Isaiah repeatedly emphasizes the sinfulness of humanity as well as the holiness, mercy, and grace of God, creating an overarching theme of redemption. In one section are four "Servant Songs" that describe a special servant God will provide to suffer for and deliver His people.

HISTORICAL CONTEXT

During Isaiah's lifetime in the eighth century BC, the Near East was already a political miasma. Nations continually struggled for dominance. Egypt was still a major power, yet she could no longer hold her own against a more recent contender: Assyria. As the surrounding nations grew in power, thus jostling to control more and more territory, the small nation of Judah was caught in a crossfire. Assyria conquered the northern kingdom of Israel in 721 BC. It appeared that Judah would follow quickly, but Isaiah assured the people that Assyria would not, in fact, take Judah. Jerusalem and the southern kingdom stand until 586 BC, when Nebuchadnezzar's Babylonian forces destroy the city and carry away most of the productive population. The people remain in Babylon for seventy years until the empire falls to the Persians, who allow the Jewish people to return to their homeland. Isaiah covers this entire span of history in his writing.

CONTRIBUTION TO THE BIBLE

Isaiah is sometimes called the evangelist of the Old Testament (or even "the Paul of the Old Testament"). The influence of his writing is reflected by its frequent citations in the New Testament. (Isaiah is quoted more than all the other prophets combined.) The prophet is identified by name twenty-one times and is cited in numerous other places without direct attribution.

OUTLINE

ISAIAH 1:1–5:30
AN OMINOUS INTRODUCTION

Setting Up the Section

It can be disheartening to read the opening of Isaiah without context, yet even providing the historical background doesn't help much. Israel and Judah, having deserted God for the gods and customs of surrounding nations, find themselves powerless pawns in an international struggle. Assyria, Babylon, and Egypt are all attempting to establish and/or maintain empires. Israel's and Judah's loyalties, which should have been to God, have been bouncing from one power to another in an attempt to persevere. But Israel will soon fall to Assyria, followed more than a century later by Judah's overthrow at the hands of Babylon.

1:1–31

AN OPENING WARNING

In verse 1, Isaiah's vision is primarily in regard to the southern kingdom of Judah because the kings he lists are all from the south. Most of the other Old Testament prophets spoke of bringing *the word* of the Lord to the people. Isaiah is unusual in stating that what he is presenting is a *vision*, although there are a few other exceptions (see Obadiah 1:1). Isaiah's father, Amoz (who is not the same person as the prophet Amos), is mentioned several times.

Isaiah doesn't pull any punches as he begins his writing. His presentation is essentially an arraignment, a legal accusation argued before the judges of heaven and earth (Isaiah 1:2). Immediately he compares the people of God (unfavorably) to a dumb ox or donkey that would at least have the sense to recognize its master (1:3). Soon he will be comparing them to the iconic cities best known for wickedness: Sodom and Gomorrah (1:9–10).

Critical Observation

Isaiah receives his calling in the year that King Uzziah [Azariah] died (6:1), which was 740 or 739 BC. King Hezekiah took the throne no later than 716 BC and ruled until 686 BC. Therefore, based on Isaiah 1:1, the prophet's ministry could have been no less than twenty-three years and may well have lasted fifty years or longer.

The accusations against Judah continue: sin, guilt, evil, rebellion, rejection of God, defeat, and desolation (1:4–8). Although the people have a pretense of religious commitment, their prayers and offerings are devoid of meaning, and God is not pleased with them (1:11–15).

Jerusalem (the faithful city) has become corrupt, along with the values of its inhabitants. The rulers take bribes and do not defend the helpless (1:21–23). Still, there is hope for the people as Isaiah presents God's exhortation to start doing right and to repent (1:16–18). If the people choose to submit to God in obedience, they can prosper. If not, they will not survive the coming judgment (1:16–20). Jerusalem will again be faithful, but it will come after a purging from God (1:24–31).

📖 **2:1–22**

THE DAY OF THE LORD

Isaiah can see plainly what has gone wrong with Judah and Jerusalem, even though the people appear oblivious to their sinful actions and attitudes. In addition, Isaiah is given great insight into what will happen later. In verse 2, he writes of the last days. Some debate the time frame of the last days with much speculation, but all that can be safely presumed is that the reference is to a period of time after Jesus' incarnation (when some believe the "last days" began) that will culminate with His second coming.

More important than *when* this will occur is *what* the people of God can expect. Isaiah describes an elevation of the mountain of the Lord's temple (2:2). The temple of Solomon had been built on the spot where Abraham had attempted to offer Isaac. The entire area was later known as Zion, a designation Isaiah uses many times throughout his prophecy.

In the Bible, *mountain* often symbolizes stability and is often associated with divinity. Isaiah's description indicates that one day the kingdom of the Messiah will be preeminent over all the kingdoms of the earth. The nations (Gentiles) will desire to know God's truth and will stream to the house of God, resulting in an unprecedented time of peace (2:3–4). Although the Messiah is not named in this passage, later portions of Isaiah (chapters 7, 9, 11, 53) will be quite specific about His character and the role He will play. In this instance, He fulfills the role of judge. In light of what God will eventually accomplish in the Gentile world, Isaiah challenges the house of Jacob (Judah and Jerusalem) to walk in the light of the Lord (2:5).

Demystifying Isaiah

This portion of Isaiah (2:2–4) regarding the Messiah's future kingdom is repeated almost verbatim in Micah 4:1–3. We don't know if one writer borrowed from the other or if they both drew from the same source.

The existing situation in Judah, however, is bleak. Isaiah's account of God's people might have described any of the surrounding unbelieving nations. In fact, they have adopted various superstitions, idolatry, and occult practices from numerous places.

Isaiah's reference to the East in verse 6 could be to the Assyrians or Syrians. The Philistines were in the southwest. Their practice of divination could be either an attempt to foretell the future or to maneuver people and situations to their advantage. In their pursuit of the futile practices of other nations, God's people have turned away from the only One who knows the future and is in complete control. They have wealth and resources, but rather than seeing such things as blessings, those assets further turn the hearts of the people away from God (2:6–10).

But Judah is about to be humbled. The people's arrogance will be destroyed along with their dependence on wealth and idols, and it will be a turbulent transition. Isaiah warns that people will flee to caves and hide among the rocks. They will again acknowledge God, but their change of attitude will begin with a sense of great dread. The result, however, will be the disappearance of all idols and their exaltation of God alone (2:11–22).

📖 **3:1–4:1**

A CHANGE IN GOVERNMENT

God alone is good. God alone cares for His creation. God alone is beneficent. Yet God's people reject the government of their good, caring, beneficent God, so He removes all supply and support from Judah and Jerusalem through a series of foreign invasions (3:1–3). Included in their losses will be food, water, all leadership of any consequence, honor, skill, and respect. Within a hundred years of the death of Isaiah, this prophecy is fulfilled when Babylon breaches the walls of Jerusalem, destroys the city, and carries off most of the people.

In place of qualified leadership, Judah will get leaders who are boys and mere children (3:4). The reference is usually less in regard to physical age than the person's maturity level. *Boys* refers to those without wisdom and experience. However, this prophecy comes true literally when Manasseh succeeds his father Hezekiah as king at age twelve. During Manasseh's fifty-five-year rule, he acquires the designation of the most wicked ruler in the history of Judah.

Isaiah describes a terrible breakdown of social order: young against old, crude against honorable, neighbor against neighbor, and individual against individual. People will be desperate for leadership, but no one will be qualified (3:5–7). Yet even in their confusion and disarray, the people will remain arrogant, plundering the poor and continuing to parade their sin (3:8–9, 11–14).

The problem will be widespread, but there will be exceptions. Isaiah assures righteous people that things will end well for them (3:10). God certainly does not fail to see what is happening, and He will soon expose the arrogant population for what they are. The description in 3:15–4:1 is brutal in its honesty. As the men of Judah fall in battle, the women will lose every pretense of arrogance and symbol of finery, reduced to desperation and groveling.

God's warning that He is about to remove supply and support from Judah (3:1) is initially confirmed by the Assyrian invasion but is demonstrated even more emphatically by the subsequent Babylonian domination.

A BRANCH AND A VINEYARD

At this point, Isaiah's writing takes a sudden shift. He moves abruptly from talking about the nation of God as ruins (3:6) to a section where every phrase seems to insist on a meaning that moves the reader toward the future fulfillment of the kingdom of God. Something has happened. There is a new day beyond the disgrace of the people of the old covenant, and Isaiah is serving as a herald of that coming day.

The difference is the appearance of the branch of the Lord—Israel's Messiah. Those who come to the kingdom by His name are holy in Him. Their names have been duly recorded. God has washed away their filth (4:2–4). It is not the trappings of wealth that ensure survival (3:18–23) but the purifying fire of God in the judgment poured out on His Messiah (4:4). Eventually the day will come when God's divine presence will be evident to the senses. God will be the ever-present light, with no need for artificial lighting (4:5–6). Believers know this in their best moments, but someday they will recognize God's presence clearly and continually.

Demystifying Isaiah

Some people believe that in this case the *branch* of the Lord signifies believers—the remnant of humanity who repent and are therefore beautiful and glorious (4:2). However, in chapter 11 Isaiah will use a branch analogy where the indication is clearly in reference to God's Messiah, Jesus.

Vineyards were important commodities in ancient Judah. When someone went to the trouble of planting a vineyard, he expected to eventually reap fruit from his labor. So the song of the vineyard in Isaiah 5:1–7 is a prophetic parable, and there is no doubt as to its meaning.

Verse 7 clarifies that the vineyard of the Lord represents the house of Israel. God has taken great care of His vineyard. He has done all He can, but still the vineyard does not yield fruit as it should. God looks for the fruit of justice but finds bloodshed. He desires righteousness but hears instead an outcry from the oppressed, poor, and powerless. Therefore, God will remove His protection, and what had once been a beautiful vineyard will be trampled and destroyed. With no further blessing (rains) or cultivation, it will become a wasteland.

Critical Observation

Throughout Isaiah are instances (as in 5:7) where *Israel* refers to the southern kingdom (rather than the more traditional *Judah*). After the northern kingdom's fall to the Assyrians, Israel continued to refer to the people of God wherever they were.

📖 5:8–30

AN INDICTMENT OF JUDAH

From the parable, Isaiah moves into a more direct pronouncement of woe upon his people. They have ignored God in many ways, including failure to acknowledge that He owns their land and established laws to protect the poor throughout the generations. Families could legally lease their land to others for income, but it was supposed to eventually revert to the original family. The people of Judah, however, disregarded God's instructions and joined house to house and field to field. People live in large homes with extensive vineyards, but the land will become unproductive and the homes will soon be empty (5:8–10).

With no regard for the concerns of God, the people are devoting themselves to late-night drinking and feasting. They are content with falsehood and darkness and are quite proud of themselves. Meanwhile, guilty people are being acquitted by paying bribes, while innocent people are deprived of their rights (5:11–12, 18–23).

Since so many refuse to exercise justice and righteousness, God Himself will enact those standards—beginning with His people! His righteous judgment will include exile, hunger and thirst, the death of many, and the humbling of the rest (5:13–15). And through His demonstration of justice, God will be exalted (5:16–17).

God is the one who pronounces judgment, but the means of affliction will be nations that are far away. Isaiah is clear on the matter: God is angry, and His anger is not easily diffused (5:24–25). The Lord is portrayed as whistling for distant nations to come, and when they do they roar as lions, growling as they seize their prey. The once-prosperous land of Judah will be a site of darkness and distress (5:26–30).

Yet in the wake of God's anger is His great mercy. If God only wanted to demonstrate His justice, He could have destroyed the world immediately after the sin of Adam. He is able to also show His mercy without sacrificing His great holiness and justice.

Take It Home

Have you ever given serious thought to how God can exact justice and still show mercy on those who are guilty? Justice demands that wicked people be punished, and *all* people are lawbreakers in the sight of God (Romans 3:23). Mercy allows those people to be forgiven and blessed. How can God possibly accomplish both justice and mercy without negating one or the other? Isaiah will later speak to this conundrum, foretelling an eternal substitute who will bring mercy to those who deserve God's judgment. Today God's people can give thanks for the assurance of their eternal security. Still, they should quake at the discipline of the Lord in this world of sorrow.

ISAIAH 6:1–12:6

ISAIAH'S CALL, GOD'S SIGN, AND ISRAEL'S FAILURE

Setting Up the Section

In this section Isaiah describes his distinct calling and begins to provide some hope-inspiring prophecies about Immanuel. The people certainly need hope because of conflict with the Assyrians that is devastating their nation. It is a desperate and miserable time, so the anticipation of God's Messiah is especially welcome.

📄 **6:1–13**

ISAIAH ANSWERS GOD'S CALL

When Old Testament priests and kings were invested with the authority of their offices, it was traditional for them to have oil poured onto their heads. The anointing was symbolic of the Holy Spirit's designating and empowering the person for a specific job. Kings were often referred to as "the Lord's anointed."

Prophets, however, tended to bypass human ceremony. They were anointed by God's Spirit as they were commissioned for service. The work of a prophet was not an easy calling. Isaiah records his own experience as God calls him and speaks to him about the difficult ministry before him.

During a vision, Isaiah is shown the throne room of God (6:1–4). He sees the Lord on the throne, surrounded by mysterious fiery angelic creatures. (This is the only biblical mention of seraphs ["burning ones"], or seraphim, although some of the heavenly beings mentioned in Revelation have a similar description [Revelation 4:6–8].) Some consider the seraphim to be the angels closest to God since that is how they are described here.

Critical Observation

Many people seem to have a fascination with angels, but where angels appear in the Bible they almost always insist that people focus on God. The interest of heaven is the Lord God Almighty, as it should be for God's people on earth.

As soon as Isaiah witnesses the glory of God, he senses that he is in mortal danger. Even Moses, when he had asked to see God, had been told that no one could see God's face and live (Exodus 33:20). Isaiah immediately acknowledges his sin and the sin of the community in which he lives (Isaiah 6:5). In response, one of the angels takes a burning coal from the altar and touches it to the prophet's mouth (6:6–7).

The coal is a symbol. When God established the Day of Atonement ceremony, one duty of the high priest was to take coals from the altar into the Most Holy Place and burn incense there (Leviticus 16:11–14). The altar was where sacrificial animals were slaughtered, and their blood ceremonially took away guilt and atoned for sin. But Isaiah is witnessing the actual heavenly temple.

Isaiah must have experienced an immediate inner change. When he hears the invitation of God, he volunteers at once to go and serve (6:8). God's response is also immediate. God does not provide many specifics, but the severity of Isaiah's mission is clear. He is being sent to people who will not listen or respond to him, yet he is to continue his work until their nation is destroyed (6:8–13). Israel and Judah have been like a mighty oak, but eventually they will fall and only a stump will remain. Still, the stump will be the holy seed—the remnant of believers from which the tree will grow again (6:13). All is not lost, but the near future will not be pleasant.

Demystifying Isaiah

Though it may seem that Isaiah's calling comes after he had already started to prophesy, since it is placed in chapter 6, it is doubtful that Isaiah worked as a prophet for a time prior to receiving his heavenly calling. He probably simply waited until this point in his narrative to relate the events of his call. The despair of the first five chapters is somewhat offset by this unmistakable experience with the Lord God Almighty, still on the throne and enlisting people to do His work, even during times of national peril and failure.

7:1–25

AN UNMISTAKABLE SIGN

Ahaz is not one of Judah's better kings. He brings much trouble on the nation by encouraging false worship. In this section he is shown as weak and frightened (7:1–2), and for good reason. The northern kingdom of Israel has formed an alliance with the Syrians (Arameans), and they are bearing down on Jerusalem.

Sometimes the nation of Israel was called *Ephraim*, because that particular tribe was large and centrally located among the others. Consequently, the battle described in this section came to be known as the Syro-Ephraimite War. The alliance of Syria and Ephraim had been formed to defend against the expanding empire of Assyria—a useless action since Assyria will be God's instrument in executing His judgment.

God speaks to Ahaz through Isaiah, telling him not to fear. Israel and Syria are only "burned-out embers" (7:4 NLT). In fact, both of these nations are facing impending disaster and will fall. God draws attention to the head of Israel and the head of Syria. The implication is that Ahaz may be the king of Judah, but God is ultimately the head of the house of David in Jerusalem.

God emphasizes the certainty of His message in two ways. First, He encourages Ahaz to strengthen his spiritual commitment—he must stand firm in faith or not at all (7:9). Then He gives Ahaz permission to ask for a sign to confirm that the word of Isaiah is the true promise of God. Ahaz expresses reluctance to make such a request, claiming that he does not want to test the Lord. Actually, it is his lack of commitment that is testing God's patience, so God chooses a sign: A virgin will conceive and bear a son named *Immanuel* ("God with us" [7:10–16]).

Demystifying Isaiah

Many modern believers are familiar with Isaiah's prophecy in 7:14 because of its long-range application to the birth of Jesus, cited in Matthew 1:22–23. This is the first of several messianic prophecies in Isaiah. However, most Old Testament prophecies also have a more immediate fulfillment, as is evident from Isaiah 7:15–16. While opinions vary, a likely explanation is that Isaiah refers to a young unmarried woman—a virgin at the time—who will marry and raise a child. The time frame for the initial fulfillment of the prophecy, then, will require a minimum of nine months for the pregnancy and another couple of years or so until the young child is eating solid food and beginning to make moral decisions. Centuries will then pass before Isaiah's words will be understood to also apply to the Virgin Mary and her son, Jesus.

Although Judah will not fall to the Assyrians, they will suffer from the presence of such a powerful enemy (7:17). The Assyrians will arrive like swarms of flies and bees. The Assyrian king will humiliate Judah like a razor shaving off a warrior's hair and beard (7:18–20). The glut of milk and honey (7:21–22) might sound promising at first, but it actually predicts a shortage of young animals to nurse and flowers being pollinated in fields that should have been growing crops. This less flattering scenario is confirmed by the prediction of briers and thorns in verses 23–25.

📄 8:1–22

RIGHT AND WRONG REASONS TO FEAR

Next Isaiah receives an interesting assignment from God. He is to father a son and give the child a Hebrew name that designates the coming of an invading army (8:1–2). It is an intriguing name and the longest personal name in the Bible: *Maher-shalal-hash-baz*. The name is a battle cry, meaning "quick to the plunder, swift to the spoil." Some people try to make the case that this child of Isaiah's is the child predicted in 7:14, but the name is a far cry from Immanuel. And unless Isaiah has a second wife, the child-of-a-virgin requirement is out of the question because the prophet already had one child (7:3).

Before this new child of Isaiah can develop any significant speech patterns, the Assyrians will have defeated both the armies that are threatening Judah: Aram and Israel. Judah will not be unscathed; Assyria is portrayed as a large devouring bird of prey. But God will be with Judah, and Assyria will not prevail (8:5–10).

Unbridled fear can lead to various problems. But such problems can be prevented if one's source of fear is properly placed. Those who fear God—who regard Him as holy and live to do His will—can be spared many other fears (8:11–17). Even the powerful Assyrian Empire is no threat for those who place their trust in God. But those without God exhibit a pathetic existence. Without the genuine source of truth, they seek advice from mediums. When they get distressed and hungry, they curse their leaders and their God. And still, they perceive only distress, darkness, and gloom (8:18–22).

📖 9:1–7

A COMING RULER

Isaiah, like other Old Testament prophets, has two major roles that are very different. One of his responsibilities is corrective in nature, as he prosecutes God's case against the Lord's own people for their unfaithfulness. His other major function is celebratory: to herald a coming day of blessing and connect the people with the approaching new covenant era. These two aspects of prophetic ministry do not conflict with each other, yet the alternating sections of disciplinary and celebratory messages can seem quite jarring to the reader.

For example, the gloom Isaiah warns of in 8:22 is temporarily offset in 9:1–2 by his foretelling of a great light to come. This great light will accompany the birth of a child (9:6), and the reader immediately recalls Isaiah's recent promise of Immanuel (7:14).

This is another case where, in retrospect, it becomes clear what Isaiah means in these prophecies. Yet for his original audience, Isaiah's words in verses 6–7 must have sounded almost too good to be true, and most likely confusing as well. The Wonderful Counselor is to be a descendant of Adam, yet He is also Mighty God and Everlasting Father. And His other title, Prince of Peace, must have been puzzling in light of the war and destruction Isaiah had been predicting. Clearly Isaiah is bringing good news, yet it must have been a bit mystifying to his generation.

📖 9:8–10:34

THE SAD STATE OF ISRAEL

After a short passage about this person who will reign on David's throne, Isaiah goes right back to why God's anger against Israel has not relented. The people have simply refused to turn to the Lord (9:13). The nation is beginning to deteriorate, but in their pride they presume they will rebuild it even better than before (9:8–12). Wickedness is pervasive among young and old, rich and poor (9:16–18). So God is about to deal with both the head (elders and the well-to-do) and tail (false prophets) of Israel (9:14–15).

The land is about to be scorched by God's wrath, and the people will begin to turn on one another (9:18–21). Those who have been preying on others will be brought to justice. Their options are limited: be taken captive or be included among those who will be killed (10:1–4).

Israel has a false sense of strength that is exposed when a mightier adversary (Assyria) threatens. But Israel's greatest adversary is God Himself. Isaiah makes it clear that in this case God's anger is not quickly turned away (9:12, 17, 21; 10:4). Assyria only *appears* to be the threat to Israel; that powerful nation is actually the hand of God (10:4).

Yet even though God chooses to use Sennacherib and the formidable military might of the Assyrians, Assyria will also be judged. They have no respect for the things of God, and they take it for granted that Jerusalem will be next on their list of easy conquests (10:6–11). God will allow them to trouble Judah, but only to a point. When God completes His work of judgment against His own people, Assyria will find itself powerless against Him (10:12–19).

Critical Observation

The intensity and proximity of the Assyrian threat is better detailed in 2 Kings 19. Isaiah's assurances to King Hezekiah are confirmed when an angel of the Lord puts to death 185,000 Assyrian soldiers overnight, followed by the withdrawal of Sennacherib. Perhaps the deaths are connected to the disease mentioned in Isaiah 10:16.

The Assyrians will do ample damage to Judah before being miraculously repelled by the power of God. They barrel through many of the cities but only get close enough to Jerusalem to shake their fist before being cut down like a lofty tree (10:26–34). The remnant of God's people who survive and endure will have the opportunity to witness the end of God's anger and again learn to rely on Him alone (10:20–25).

📖 11:1–12:6

NEW GROWTH FROM A STUMP

During Isaiah's vision of his calling from God, he had been told that the nation will be destroyed like a large tree cut down, leaving only a stump (6:11–13). In 11:1 he again writes of a stump, but the imagery is a little different. In this case, the stump is of Jesse. The series of kings of Judah had all descended from Jesse's son, David, yet the time will come when it seems that the line has ended. But from that stump a branch will one day spring up. It is a marvelous fact that God's Son will be born from the line of the kings of Judah.

This prophetic section of Isaiah provides insight into the character of Christ as king. He will be filled with the Spirit of God (11:2–3). This most powerful of all kings will have no hint of corruption that seems to permeate human positions of power. Instead, the qualities of righteousness and faithfulness will be so clearly attributed to Him that they are called His belt. One day His righteousness will result in the frightening vengeance of God against the wicked (11:4–5).

The person and purpose of this Prince of Peace (9:6) are described in idyllic terms. Under His influence, fierce predators and their prey will become happy inhabitants of the kingdom. Children can safely play around cobra nests. All who are ruled by the king will have perfect security. This blessing is not just restricted to Judah and Israel: The whole earth will be full of the knowledge of the Lord (11:10). Through the knowledge of this ruler from the root of Jesse, peace will be extended far beyond the borders of Israel.

God's people will be called out of captivity, and all their adversaries will be overwhelmed (11:10–16). In response, people will offer widespread and unbridled praise to God (12:1–6). Praise seems especially meaningful after God's people have been delivered from a particularly difficult experience. Praise had been abundant after the Lord delivered the Israelites from Egypt and when David united the kingdom after the civil war between Israel and Judah. Later generations will praise God during the days of Ezra and Nehemiah, when they return to their homeland after several decades in captivity. How much more should today's believers praise God when they realize His Prince of Peace has removed all obstacles that previously stood in the way of complete and eternal fellowship with Him!

Take It Home

Israel had a harmful tendency to become lax in their praise and worship when things were going well. They would slide spiritually to a point where God would need to discipline them. Then only when they began to lose the blessings they had taken for granted did they turn back to God. Contemporary believers have the advantage of the incarnation of Jesus and the coming of the Holy Spirit, yet they may follow the same pattern. We're still a long way from the blissful state described by Isaiah. But as we wait for that day, how might you improve your worship and praise to become more devoted to God and grounded in your faith?

ISAIAH 13:1–23:18

PROPHECIES AGAINST OTHER NATIONS

Setting Up the Section

For the next several chapters, Isaiah presents a number of judgments concerning the nations around Israel and Judah. He has already been writing about Assyria and the crown jewel of its empire: Babylon. Eventually Babylon overtakes Assyria to form an empire of its own. In this section, Isaiah addresses Babylon and a number of other countries, delivering messages from God.

📖 13:1–14:27

A MESSAGE FOR BABYLON AND ASSYRIA

One of the challenges of great might, wisdom, or beauty is the danger of pride forming as a result. People quickly forget that God, the one in whom they live and move and have their being, is continually above them. If human pride is not resisted, it will lead to destruction. At times an entire society may be swimming in arrogance with the danger of God's wrath so near that it would seem that there is no way out.

Babylon is first on Isaiah's list. Ruthless and arrogant, Babylon is considered the "jewel of kingdoms" (13:19 NIV). But the might of Babylon at its pinnacle is no match for the power of the Lord God Almighty. Isaiah declares its certain destruction. He describes an army that God Himself is forming (13:1–6). The haughtiness and ruthlessness so prevalent in Babylon will be replaced by terror and anguish. Some of the actions taken against Babylon will be horrendous (13:7–16).

Demystifying Isaiah

The superpowers of Isaiah's day were the Assyrians and the Persians. There was not always a clear succession of one empire falling and being replaced by the next. Rather, various nations coexisted for periods and had numerous coalitions and conflicts. For example, there was an alliance between the Medes and Babylonians in the late 600s BC, but about fifty years later the Medes were absorbed by the Persians, who then conquered Babylon. Various opinions exist, but it is likely that Isaiah's reference in 13:17 is to an early conquest of Babylon by the Assyrians in 689 BC rather than its more notable defeat by the Persians in 539 BC.

There is general agreement that the *Babylon* in verse 19 refers to the city rather than the empire. The people's arrogance and sense of immortality will be shattered. After centuries of existence and influence, Babylon will come to an inglorious end. History confirms that Babylon does indeed become a ghost town by the seventh century AD, confirming Isaiah's prophecy in 13:19–22.

Yet for the time being, Babylon is one of the biggest threats to Israel and Judah. What a surprise and comfort it must have been to hear Isaiah's prediction that one day, thanks to God's great compassion, He will reestablish Israel and people will flock there from all nations (14:1–2). Israel will have the last word with Babylon. God will lift up His people even as their enemies are falling (14:3–23).

Critical Observation

Isaiah 14:12–17 is sometimes said to be a biblical account of Lucifer's pride that caused him to be cast out of heaven, but there is no basis for this in the text. This poetic description of the king of Babylon (14:4) stands as a warning for anyone who allows ambition to override commitment to the service of others.

Assyria is right up there with Babylon on the power scale. Yet they, too, are going to be crushed. God has planned it, so it is certain to happen (14:24–27).

📖 14:28–32

A MESSAGE FOR THE PHILISTINES

The Philistines had long been oppressors of Israel. The Israelites occasionally came out victorious, most notably during the rise and reign of David. But the Philistines had frequently been the victors, and when they were, they could be quite cruel.

Isaiah's oracle warns the Philistines against rejoicing so quickly at the demise of their enemies. Perhaps the reference in verse 29 is to Assyria. The fall of one enemy leader might be cause for celebration, but victory is tentative because others will arise to replace the fallen leader. The Philistines won't even have the honor of dying in battle. Instead they will be afflicted with famine (14:28–32).

A MESSAGE FOR MOAB

The Moabites were frequently at odds with the Israelites. During Israel's exodus from Egypt, Moabite King Balak had hired Balaam to curse the Israelites, but God didn't allow him to do so (Numbers 22). Moabite women had attempted to seduce the Israelites (Numbers 25:1–9). During the era of the judges, Moab had oppressed and financially burdened Israel until Ehud assassinated Moabite King Eglon (Judges 3:12–30). Saul and David had both defeated Moab, but Solomon had been persuaded by one of his wives to worship the Moabite god Chemosh (1 Kings 11:1, 7).

The origin of Moab can be traced back to the child conceived as a result of the incestuous relationship between Lot and his older daughter (Genesis 19:30–38). Moab is going to be destroyed, but not because of its ethnic heritage. The Lord despises the Moabites' false gods and high places of idolatry. He hates the way they have repeatedly turned against His people with violence. Yet Isaiah appears to demonstrate a heart of sympathy for Moab in distress (15:5). Entire cities (Ar and Kir) will fall in a single night. Even armed men trained for danger will be filled with fear in the face of a far more powerful enemy (15:1–4).

This is not the first time God's sympathy has been recorded for Moab. Israel had not been permitted to destroy Moab on the way to the promised land (Deuteronomy 2:9), nor was Moab among the nations that were to be dispossessed by Joshua and his generation during the conquest of Canaan. Ruth had been from Moab, returning to Israel with Naomi to eventually become the great-grandmother of David and be included in the genealogy of Christ (Ruth 4:13–22). It is clear that God's mercy extends beyond the borders of Israel.

Yet Moab remains a proud nation (Isaiah 16:6). They would have done well to unite with Judah (send lambs) because Judah will escape the conquest of the Assyrians (10:24–25). Instead, they will experience great suffering (15:6–9; 16:7–12). They have only three years remaining as a nation (16:13–14).

A MESSAGE FOR SYRIA

Syria was one of the great ancient nations. It was common for an entire nation to be referred to by the name of its leading city, so in Isaiah 17 Syria is called *Damascus*. (Similarly, Israel is called *Ephraim* [17:3] after its prominent tribe.) And when a key city falls, the entire nation feels the humiliation of the defeat.

At one time Israel and Syria (Aram) had been impressive nations. But here Isaiah compares them to a human body wasting away, a field that has already been harvested, and an olive tree picked clean except for a few remaining olives that can't be reached (17:4–6). Their devastation will be horrendous, but not total.

Demystifying Isaiah

Damascus is captured by Tiglath-pileser, a king of ancient Assyria, in 732 BC. Shortly afterward, the kingdom of Israel and her capital city of Samaria will also be subdued. All that will be left of Syria is just a small percentage of the fruitfulness that she once enjoyed, proving the accuracy of Isaiah's prophecies.

After trouble arrives, the people will forsake their idols and turn to God—something they could have done all along, but refused to do (17:7–14). Their once-popular fertility cults will no longer be a pleasant diversion. In such a time of great trouble, God alone is a rock of refuge.

📖 18:1–20:6

A MESSAGE FOR EGYPT AND CUSH

As Isaiah turns his attention to nations farther away from Israel, his description becomes more exotic: whirring wings (strange insects?), papyrus boats, tall and smooth-skinned (clean-shaven?) people, and strange-sounding dialects (18:1–2). The land of Cush, south of Egypt, was essentially the most remote portion of known geography for those living in the Near East.

Perhaps Cush had sent their envoys to Israel to broach the idea of forming an alliance against Assyria. No evidence of any such proposal exists, although they were, after all, described as an aggressive nation (18:2). The Cushites are not alone in their desire to resist Assyria, so Isaiah's message is directed to all people (18:3). The fall of Assyria is up to God's timing, and when it happens, everyone will be sure to hear of it. Indeed, judgment of all the nations is in the hands of God (18:4–6). In time, however, the people of Cush will be among those who stream to Mount Zion to offer their gifts to God.

Egypt has much more of a history with Israel. God had long ago removed His people from the idolatrous nation, but their idolatry had continued (19:1–4). Egypt remained a formidable power largely because of the Nile River that provides constant water in a land where such a resource is rare. The Nile allows Egypt to produce grain for much of the world, and Egypt takes great pride in the Nile.

But Isaiah warns that the Nile will one day dry up (19:5), causing many previously stubborn people to humble themselves before God in the midst of their great suffering. None of Egypt's leaders or presumed powerful idols can keep the mighty river flowing to deliver the nation from disaster (19:5–18). Yet, like Cush, the long-range prediction for Egypt is positive. God has a wonderful plan of grace that includes the Egyptians. It must have been quite shocking to hear that Assyria and Egypt will someday be embraced by God like Israel (19:18–25). They will all know and fear the Lord, and somehow they will all worship together.

But first Egypt and Cush must endure the wrath of Assyria. As the Assyrians move into Philistine territory, capturing the city of Ashdod, God gives Isaiah an unusual assignment: The prophet is to remove his clothing and sandals and minister three years this way (20:1–6). His actions are symbolic of what will happen to Egypt and Cush.

Their people will be led away to Assyria, naked and humiliated. Anyone who had looked to Egypt for support against Assyria (as Judah had been tempted to do) will be disappointed and frustrated.

Critical Observation

It is debated whether or not Isaiah was completely naked for this three-year period. The word used can certainly be interpreted that way. Still, some people presume a sense of propriety would be necessary and believe that the prophet was expected to remove his *outer* clothing. Either way, whether Isaiah was totally nude or only in his loincloth undergarment, it would have been both disconcerting for the prophet and attention-getting for those who saw him. For anyone who may have presumed him to be among the lunatics who run about scantily dressed, the fulfillment of his prophecy would be especially emphatic.

📖 21:1–10

ANOTHER MESSAGE FOR BABYLON

Isaiah's prophecies in chapters 13–20 may be difficult for modern readers to properly interpret and understand, yet they are reasonably clear and to the point. Chapters 21–23, however, are not as straightforward and can be even more difficult to comprehend.

In this section, for example, Babylon isn't mentioned by name until verse 9, which then helps explain the "desert by the sea" reference in verse 1. Babylon referred to their southern region as "the land of the sea," so Isaiah seems to indicate their impending defeat by the Assyrians. Babylon will eventually rise against Assyria and rule in glory for a short time, but then the Medes and Persians will rise to power.

Isaiah describes his vision of Babylon's destruction as a source of anguish, making him bowed over, dismayed, and appalled (21:2–4). What a contrast with the way others, oblivious to the coming destruction, live around him (21:5). But soon enough a messenger will arrive bearing the terrible news (21:6–9). Isaiah leaves no doubt that God is the source of his vision (21:10).

📖 21:11–17

A MESSAGE FOR EDOM AND ARABIA

Brief words of coming difficulties are addressed to Edom and to Arabia. Although Edom is not mentioned by name, its identity is known because of *Seir*, the residence of Esau's descendants and another name for Edom.

Perhaps one of Edom's citizens had approached Isaiah looking for a positive word, displaying the optimistic expectation of Scarlett O'Hara that, "tomorrow is another day." Isaiah agrees that another morning is coming but adds that another night will follow immediately afterward. In other words, their circumstances are not likely to improve (21:11–12).

The people of Arabia are also in a dire situation. They can expect harsh defeat within a year at the hands of the Assyrians. The people will attempt to flee, but only a few will survive (21:13–17).

📖 22:1–25

A MESSAGE FOR JERUSALEM

In this list of God's pronouncements directed at Assyria, Babylon, Edom, and other nations, it is unsettling to see one against Jerusalem as well. Jerusalem is literally a city on a hill, intended to be a place of great spiritual value. It is supposed to be a light to the surrounding Gentile world. But the people have rejected God, their source of spiritual strength and insight. Consequently, Isaiah addresses the city as a valley (rather than a hill [22:1]).

Because Jerusalem has persistently committed evil, their people will face discipline from the Lord. The leaders will attempt to flee the city to save themselves rather than stand firm in faith, but they will be captured (22:1–4).

Demystifying Isaiah

Isaiah is not speaking symbolically; his words in 22:3 are literally fulfilled. When the Babylonians siege Jerusalem, King Zedekiah and his entire army try to sneak out of the city, but they are pursued and captured. The Babylonians make Zedekiah watch as they kill his sons, and then they blind him (2 Kings 25:1–7).

God had long ago decreed a day of destruction, and it will soon arrive. God instructs His people to weep, mourn, put on sackcloth, and humble themselves. And although He is the one who will bring the day of disaster, the people will not respond to Him. They attempt to prepare for conflict but refuse to acknowledge God or repent (22:5–13).

Shebna (22:15) is a high-ranking official who was involved in dealing with the Assyrians when they threatened Jerusalem (2 Kings 18:17–19:37). But instead of a godly humility, Jerusalem's leaders appear to have a strange arrogance and even a hedonistic fatalism. Shebna attempts to establish the glory of his name in a potential day of disaster for the people of God. As a result, he is replaced by another man, Eliakim (Isaiah 22:20), who has more concern for the good of those who are looking for responsible leadership. Eliakim is an honorable and successful leader for a while, but even *his* time of influence will be limited (22:20–25).

📖 23:1–18

A MESSAGE FOR TYRE

Tyre was a location known for its ships and merchants at a time when many nations counted on trade with the Phoenicians. If Tyre was to fall, numerous other powers would suffer as well. Isaiah lists Tarshish (very likely located in Spain), Cyprus, and Egypt among those who will feel the effect of Tyre's destruction. Even the seas are personified as mourning the loss (23:1–5).

Tyre will face a generation or more of trouble, and its fall will create more than economic concerns for its allies. The description is similar to that of the death of a loved one. Egypt will be in anguish (23:5). Tarshish will wail (23:6). And for those seeking an explanation, Isaiah makes clear that God has planned the change of Tyre's fortune in response to the great pride that had resulted from their success (23:9). No matter how respected a person or nation may be in the opinion of humanity, a refusal to acknowledge God will result in failure and dishonor. No nation's security is assured. Even the Babylonians have been bested by the Assyrians (23:13).

Yet Babylon will again become a world power, and Tyre will also revive after seventy years (23:15). In the meantime, however, Tyre is portrayed as a forgotten prostitute in a pitiful journey through the cities of the world, singing songs of better days. And when Tyre *is* eventually reestablished, it will be to benefit the people of the Lord. Even this proud city will be used to accomplish God's purpose (23:16–18).

Take It Home

It is possible to read through this series of grim judgments on various nations and give little thought to the person who is called to deliver them. But put yourself in Isaiah's place for a moment. How would you like to confront influential people all around you with the severity and inevitable consequences of their sin? And what if God wanted you to do so in a hyper-conspicuous manner, as He did by having Isaiah remove his clothes? To what extent would you be willing to face personal embarrassment to take a stand for God and His truth?

ISAIAH 24:1–35:10

THE WORLD STRUGGLES, BUT GOD REIGNS SUPREME

Setting Up the Section

After delivering a series of judgments against numerous nations (chapters 13–23), Isaiah expands his focus to the world as a whole. Isaiah 24–27 is frequently called Isaiah's Apocalypse, although many argue that the term is a bit strong. The remaining chapters in this section (28–35) are more specific and develop a historical perspective for the reader, although they do so with a series of woes.

24:1–23

THE EARTH DEFILED, THEN DEVASTATED

From the opening verse of the Bible, it is clear that the rule of the God of Israel is not limited to the area around Palestine. God formed the heavens and the earth and created humanity in His own image. No power on earth or heaven is a threat to Him. Kings must answer to Him, and His salvation can reach the most humble sinner.

It might be supposed by some that only people who have been given God's law in written form will be judged by God's commandments. However, all the lands of the earth are aware of God and His majesty. Everyone has been given a conscience that is more or less informed concerning the ways of God (Romans 2:15). All should seek to further understand and experience God's presence because all are guilty before the Lord and without excuse for breaking the relationship with the Almighty Father. Eventually people in every territory will face the Lord's righteous wrath in judgment (24:1–4).

It is important to understand why God would do such a thing—completely lay waste and plunder the earth (24:3). It is because people have totally defiled the earth through disobedience and utter disregard for His laws. God established a covenant with His people, and they have broken it (24:5).

As a curse consumes the earth, the time for partying comes to an end. Wine loses its appeal, and the tambourines are put away. The singers, dancers, and merry-hearted people return to their homes as joy turns to gloom for those who do not know the Lord (24:6–13). There will be exceptions, although very few (24:6). However, those few who escape God's judgment on the wicked will respond with shouts of joy and praise (24:14–16).

People who remain disobedient will be so furious that the very pit of destruction will seem to swallow up all the inhabitants of the earth. Terror results from the earth splitting apart and being violently shaken. Once-powerful authorities and rulers in high places will be called to account. At long last the wicked oppressors, both in heaven and on earth, will be shut away for eternity as the Lord Almighty reigns on Mount Zion and in Jerusalem (24:16–23). It will be a day of great vindication for those who trust in the Lord's unfailing righteousness.

25:1–26:21

AN INTERLUDE OF PRAISE

It is always assuring to see the violent plans of a powerful force thwarted as it attempts to destroy a weak and vulnerable opponent. Some adversaries seem simply too strong to defend against, and what could be more demoralizing to the desperately weak guardians of Israel than the victory song of an overpowering enemy? But the Lord is capable of silencing that victory song in a moment and stopping the onslaught of the mightiest power. And when His people see such powerful demonstrations of God's protection, the result is spontaneous praise (25:1).

The destroyed city in 25:2 is probably representative of all the cities/nations that have defied God throughout the ages. Israel's victory is not just another instance of "the little guy" able to survive another day with a massive military force arrayed against him. This time those ruthless powers are facing utter defeat. God's victory will be world-changing and life-giving. The veil of misery and confusion will be lifted. Death will be defeated, and tears will all be wiped dry (25:3–8). The powerful enemies of God who want to see His plans thwarted will not succeed. They will be most soundly defeated in the hour of the Lord's choosing (25:9–12).

Isaiah records a song to the glory of the city of God (26:1), thus directing the reader's attention to the kingdom of heaven. Isaiah 26 provides a lens through which present-day believers can anticipate the ultimate victory of God on behalf of His people in the coming Day of the Lord. Believers need to live in the light of that event every day of their lives. As they become more steadfast, God provides perfect peace (26:3).

God *will* deliver His people (26:7–21). Someday the song of deliverance will be sung in earnest. Until then, God's people seek and find Him every day. Through His grace they follow in the journey of the righteous. The reality of sin may load their pathways with spiritual and physical land mines, but the Lord is their safety and His promises are sure. Not only shall the remnant of Israel and Judah be saved but also the inhabitants of the world will love the judgments of God and learn the way of righteousness. Even the righteous dead shall live, and their bodies shall rise because of the conquering Lord (26:19).

27:1–13

THE POWER OF THE LORD

In this section, Isaiah describes the Lord's ability to protect His people by portraying Him as holding a powerful sword with which He slays Leviathan (27:1). Many of the nations surrounding Israel had legends and mythologies that included their gods doing battle with sea monsters, of which Leviathan was one of the best known. But Isaiah uses the image of the great sea monster to symbolize the powerful nations that show more regard for such mythologies than for the God of Israel. When it comes down to a matter of conflict, no other power can rival the power of the Lord.

Critical Observation

From the opening chapters of the Bible, serpents have represented evil and opposition to God. Sin entered the world as Adam and Eve were deceived by the serpent and disobeyed God (Genesis 3). But no sooner did that take place than God announced that the seed of the woman would eventually crush the serpent's head. The slaying of Leviathan (Isaiah 27:1) is another portrayal of God's triumph over an evil serpent.

By slaying the serpent, God protects His kingdom, which is symbolized by a vineyard to which God devotes much personal attention (27:2–5; see 5:1–7). In that day of the Lord's deliverance, Israel's influence will be greatly expanded. Jacob will take root, growing to eventually fill the world with fruit (27:6).

The guilt of God's elect will be atoned for. People of God can be identified by their refusal to be involved with idols. However, that atoning will first involve war and exile. In 27:8, the fierce blast of the east wind may be a reference to the Babylonians. For a while, Jerusalem will be desolate and forsaken (27:10–11). But the day will come when the people of Israel will be again gathered one by one and return to worship God in Jerusalem (27:12–13).

📖 28:1–31:9

A SERIES OF WARNINGS

As Isaiah begins a series of pronouncements of woe to various places, the first is directed to *Ephraim*, another name to indicate Israel (the northern kingdom). The nation is portrayed both as a drunkard and a fading flower (28:1). It is a proud nation yet is past its prime and soon to be humbled by the Lord's hailstorm, destructive wind, and flooding downpour (28:2–4).

Demystifying Isaiah

Many of Isaiah's prophecies concerning Israel will be fulfilled with the invasion by Assyria in 722 BC, after which most of the population is carried away into captivity.

Yet even Israel will have a remnant of people who are protected by God. That holy remnant will turn to the Lord Almighty and find Him to be beautiful and glorious. In contrast, the drunken priest and prophet will find no help from the God they are supposed to represent (28:5–8). They will still claim to bring a prophetic vision, but since their own lives are covered with filth, who will believe them?

Verse 10 reflects the people's mocking of what Isaiah is trying to teach them. Perhaps the misguided priests and prophets feel they are being talked down to and respond with taunting. If so, Isaiah is not fazed. He acknowledges that they don't have to listen to him, but they will soon be forced to learn their lesson from foreign oppressors—the Assyrians (28:11). Instead of growing little by little in the way of righteousness, they will little by little fall away and eventually be utterly broken.

So Israel—the northern kingdom—does not learn the message of God. Lest the southern kingdom of Judah and capital city of Jerusalem presume the way will be smoother for them, Isaiah reveals that they will be scoffers. Their leaders will be grave disappointments, with false confidence in the religious practices they have learned from pagan nations. The covenant to cheat death (28:15) is something that they (mistakenly) imagine will protect them from the grave, but the truth is that their covenant with death will be annulled (28:18–19). No other gods or religions can save them. Consequently, it is appropriate for them to stop mocking Israel and realize their own peril (28:20–22).

Demystifying Isaiah

The *cornerstone* that Isaiah mentions (28:16) is a term that frequently applies to the Messiah, Jesus Christ (Zechariah 10:3–4; Acts 4:9–11; Ephesians 2:19–20; 1 Peter 2:4–8). It is unclear whether Isaiah intends this particular reference to be messianic. Perhaps he is simply affirming that God will ensure justice and righteousness in Judah.

However, Isaiah uses a number of analogies to assure his listeners that their coming troubles will only be temporary. Just as planting requires first breaking up the soil to be effective, and just as certain seeds must be beaten or ground to break the outer shell, God's people need to be broken in order for them to become useful and productive. Hard times will be necessary to effect positive change, but the difficulties will not be permanent (28:23–29).

After addressing Israel (28:1–13) and then Judah (28:14–29), Isaiah's narrative narrows to the city of Jerusalem, addressed here by the name *Ariel*. The name can mean either "lion of God" or "altar hearth" (29:2). In the context of Isaiah's message, perhaps the latter definition is more appropriate. Just as Jerusalem had been the place where people brought their animal offerings to be burned in sacrifice, the city itself will soon be a site of bloodshed and burning.

God is going to bring judgment on faraway nations and on the northern kingdom of Israel, and then He is going to judge the very center of His presence on earth during the days of the kings—the city of Jerusalem. Isaiah describes God as the one encamped and constructing siege works for the destruction of the holy city (29:3–4). His people have become haughty, and He is going to humble them.

God's people will suffer a period of disgrace, but their enemies will eventually be even more humiliated. When the Assyrians approach, it may seem that disaster is imminent for Jerusalem, but God will provide divine protection. The invaders will become like a bad dream that vanishes with the dawn of a new morning (29:5–8).

Experiencing such a miraculous delivery should capture the attention of God's people, yet it won't be long until they return to a spiritual daze. The prophets are a disgrace to their titles. Worship is not sincere but rather confused and hypocritical. What passes for wisdom is neither genuine nor lasting. It is a ludicrous situation: People who reject the leadership of God are like lumps of clay questioning the work of the potter (29:9–16).

Still, Isaiah again interjects a reminder that better days are ahead, when Zion will experience real joy. It will be a time of widespread divine healing. The deaf will hear and the blind will see. Even the land will have a vast increase in yield. Those previously subdued by the powerful will be vindicated, and the poor will celebrate their deliverance. All of the redeemed will glorify God. Even those who have gone astray in spirit will be brought back to an understanding and receptivity to spiritual instruction. This exciting announcement of hope stands out for the faithful remnant of God's people (29:17–24).

But Isaiah then immediately returns to his series of woes, now directed to rebellious children (30:1). God has a long history of delivering His people in times of trouble, but the Israelites are like children who never seem to learn to trust Him. This time Assyria is the outside threat—mighty, to be sure, but no match for the power of God.

Still, rather than turn to God for deliverance, the people of Judah seek help from Egypt (30:1–2). Egypt has tangible assets: chariots, horses, and soldiers. God is all-powerful, but invisible, and human beings frequently make the same mistake of trusting what can be seen. The people have a plan, but it isn't God's plan, so it will surely fail. Isaiah sees clearly that Egypt will be no help to Judah against the Assyrians (30:3–7).

Judah is like a child who will not listen to wise advice. The people resent the seers and prophets who pass along the message of God to them. So God instructs Isaiah to write down their words as a witness against them (30:8–14). Their only hope is in God. The wise course of action is to repent and wait quietly and faithfully for Him to act, but they are unwilling to hear. Instead, they run toward the clamor of Egyptian power, forgetting the God who created them and who had, on a previous occasion, rescued them from the hand of Egyptian oppressors (30:15–17).

The sad fact of the people's actions is that all the time they are seeking help from foreign human powers, God yearns to show them grace and compassion (30:18). The very reason for their adversity and affliction is to help them recognize truth. He wants them to acknowledge their prophets (teachers) again. He wants them to hear His voice and dispose of their idols. He wants to bless them with rain and food. He wants to bind up their injuries and heal their wounds (30:19–26).

It will be a while before the people experience such a significant turnaround. First, God will give them a reason to rejoice by delivering them from Assyria (30:27–33). The people will not need the help of Egypt.

Demystifying Isaiah

Topheth (30:33) was a location south of Jerusalem associated with fire and burning. It was where, on occasion, children were sacrificed to Molech, a god of the Ammonites. The Assyrians will be disposed of like a load of wood readily consumed by fire, except the source of heat in their case is the breath of the Lord.

Turning to Egypt is an offense to God (31:1–3). In Israel's history, Egypt was a place of bondage, a nation of idolatry, a symbol of commitment to the things of this world. God had done things through Moses that were far beyond the capabilities of just a man with a staff in his hand. Great waters had parted. Water had come from a rock. And a nation of God's people had been liberated from a great oppressor. Now those people are attempting to go back voluntarily rather than recall what God had done and trust Him to continue to deliver them.

God is not intimidated by any adversary. He will come down to fight on Mount Zion and shield Jerusalem from harm. Just as the angel of death had passed over homes in Egypt with the sign of blood on the doorposts, God will see that danger passes over Jerusalem in the days to come. Assyria certainly appears to be the stronger power by far, yet they will fall as Jerusalem stands (31:4–9).

RIGHTEOUSNESS, JUDGMENT, AND JOY

In his writing, Isaiah moves back and forth between his present time and the messianic age ("that day"). Israel and Judah had recently known very few good kings, so Isaiah again looks to the future to describe a different kind of leader yet to come. Much good can come from an excellent king. A ruler who leads in righteousness provides stability and protection even during a time of shifting circumstances. And God's future king does more than that. He gives sight and hearing. He helps people discern what really matters. He showers them with gifts from heaven. When such a leader arrives, it will become clear how incompetent previous leaders have been (32:1–8).

One danger of poor leadership is complacency among the people. Isaiah singles out the women of Jerusalem who use drinking to foster a false sense of security (32:9–15). He offers people a happiness that does not turn to panic when the grape harvest fails. No amount of wine can produce fruit among God's people that is available from the Spirit of God (32:15). Once people get beyond complacency in their lives, they open themselves to the possibilities of justice, righteousness, peace, and other blessings (32:16–20).

At this point Isaiah comes to his sixth and final woe in this section (28:1; 29:1; 29:15; 30:1; 31:1; 33:1), this time directed toward the destroyers (this is probably speaking of Assyria). The destroyer will eventually be destroyed, and the betrayer will be betrayed. According to the sovereign plan of the Lord, Assyria will have its day, but like all the powers that have come before, it will then fall.

The righteous remnant of people realizes that the God of Israel controls all their affairs with His mighty hand. They can be happy as they wait for the Lord and His grace to be their salvation in times of trouble (33:2–6).

But the sinners in Zion will have a completely different experience. The nearness of destruction will terrify them. Brave men will weep. Highways will be empty as people fear to travel. Once-plush areas of land will become like deserts. The people who have made plans apart from God will be subject to burning and consumption (33:7–13).

As always, God will see to the welfare of righteous people. Those who continue to place their faith in God will behold His great beauty in a land that stretches to the horizon. The humble servant of the Lord will find refuge, but the proud can not dwell there. The Lord Himself will be king, judge, and lawgiver. For the time being, however, Jerusalem is like a ship in disrepair, nowhere near ready to go to war. Its future might be glorious and secure, but it will first experience additional strain and conflict (33:14–24).

One day all the nations of the world will face the judgment of God. The destruction described in this section is massive and vivid. The coming of the Lord's mighty vengeance will go beyond the destruction of the peoples of the earth and will include the very heavens being rolled up like a scroll as stars seem to fall from the sky (34:1–4).

Edom is singled out in this passage as representative of all the nations who will face the sword of the Lord on that day (34:5–17). Why Edom? One likely possibility is that Edom took great joy at the harsh discipline of God against His covenant people. Those descendants of Esau had long shown disdain for the chosen status of God's people who descended from Jacob.

Critical Observation

The Lord God has a jealous love for His people (Exodus 20:5; 34:14). He may discipline them and even use unbelieving nations to do so. But those nations dare not celebrate the shame of the people of God. The Lord will not stand for their pride, their boasting in their idols, their unbelief, and their immorality. They will discover that He is an enemy who knows how to rescue His own beloved ones when they call out to Him for aid. They are likely to end up as Edom does in this passage: destroyed, desolate, deserted, and never to rise again.

Then, in abrupt juxtaposition, Isaiah brings marvelous news. A day is coming when people will be able to see what they now know only by faith. Land that is currently parched and dry shall be fruitful, with refreshing streams of clear water for thirsty lips. People will be strengthened, encouraged, and healed. A road—the Highway of Holiness— will be made available for the redeemed and those the Lord has ransomed who travel to Jerusalem. Dangers will be removed, and the general atmosphere will be one of gladness and joy (35:1–10).

Take It Home

It is important to note in this section how intent God is that His people not rely on the strength of the world for their survival. The world He created contains not only many things that are visible but also a number of invisible spiritual realities. Preeminent among those realities is God Himself. Yet most people can relate to the insecurities (and perhaps even desperation) of the Israelites. What are some of the things you tend to rely on in threatening situations? How can you prepare to more readily reach out to God in faith the next time those situations arise?

ISAIAH 36:1–39:8

A HISTORICAL VERIFICATION

Setting Up the Section

This section of Isaiah is quite different from what precedes and follows it. For a few chapters, Isaiah provides a historical narrative with specific dates, names, and events.

📖 36:1–37:38

JERUSALEM IN PERIL

Prior to this point, Isaiah has been prophesying that God is going to use the Assyrians to serve both as a means of punishing Judah's sins and as a motivation for the people to once more turn to the Lord in faith. Yet Isaiah has also said that Jerusalem will not fall to the mighty Assyrians. Just as God will certainly discipline His own people, He will also punish the Assyrians for their arrogance.

As the events in this section begin to unfold, the king in Judah is Hezekiah—definitely one of the better kings of the southern kingdom. The nation has watched the Assyrians get nearer and nearer in their conquests—seemingly unstoppable. Now these powerful enemies are at the threshold. The northern kingdom of Israel has fallen, and much of Judah already suffered from Assyrian domination. It looks as if Hezekiah and Jerusalem will be next.

Critical Observation

Another description of these events is found in 2 Kings 18–20. Isaiah's account was written first and may have been the source for the author of 2 Kings. It is also possible that both writers drew from yet another (unknown) source.

The king of Assyria at the time is named Sennacherib. After he captures a number of Judah's well-defended cities, he sends a message to Hezekiah by way of his field commander. The Assyrian official goes to a public place where the leaders of Jerusalem and the populace as a whole can hear his message (36:1–3). Speaking in the language of the common people (36:11–12), he delivers a frightening warning that contains much truth interlaced with lies and half-truths, all designed to inspire fear among the Judahites and make them less likely to support Hezekiah in resisting the Assyrians.

Sennacherib has a well-deserved reputation as a powerful leader in Assyria. He will not be stopped by the empty words of an enemy attempting to negotiate out of a confrontation (36:4–6). The people of Judah had a tendency to place their trust in foreign alliances and considered going to Egypt for help against Assyria, but Sennacherib knows that not even Egypt can stand up to Assyria. (God had told Isaiah as much.) The Assyrians greatly outnumber those in Jerusalem, and the people might even feel more insecure than usual because Hezekiah has removed many of the idolatrous high places and altars where they tended to go instead of worshiping God at the temple (36:6–7). If the people cannot depend on Egypt, or their God, or even the other gods they seek out, then what hope do they have against the Assyrians?

Another realistic consideration is what was likely to occur if the Assyrians conducted a lengthy siege against Jerusalem. It wouldn't be just the leaders who suffered, but everyone within the city. The Assyrian field commander makes sure the people of Judah are aware that they might soon be forced to consume their own body wastes for lack of other options (36:12).

To an extent, what the Assyrian field commander says is the truth. But as he continues, he adds some lies as he tries to dissuade the people from counting on the faith of King Hezekiah (36:13–20). He says that trusting in their Lord will not work for the people of Judah, which is a wicked falsehood. To even attempt to compare Judah's God to the idols of other nations is a horrible deception. An earnest and humble request for God's help will not be wasted breath. God hears the pleas of His people, as will be clear in the chapters that follow.

The field commander finishes his speech, and the people remain silent as Hezekiah had instructed them—probably not the response the Assyrians had hoped for. The underlying theme of the message has been, "Fear Assyria and her king, and surrender now." And indeed, the people are shaken. Three palace officials with torn clothing (a sign of mourning) deliver the message to King Hezekiah (36:21–22).

Hezekiah shows great wisdom in responding to this crisis situation. He, too, tears his clothes and puts on sackcloth in a demonstration of repentance. He goes to the temple and sends for Isaiah, realizing that the words of the Assyrian messenger have been deeply offensive to God (37:1–4). When Isaiah receives God's reply for King Hezekiah, the first instruction is to not be afraid (37:5). Assyria will be soundly defeated, not due to any military competence on the part of Judah, but because God will intervene in those international affairs. God informs Isaiah that Sennacherib will return to Assyria, where he will be killed.

Just as God had promised, the King of Assyria makes a hasty retreat. Before he leaves, however, he receives word that Egypt is sending troops to help Judah, and he sends another threatening message to Hezekiah. Sennacherib is quite confident that Judah's God poses no more threat to him than all the other gods he had confronted in other nations. Sennacherib's plan is to deal with his immediate problem and then return to lay waste to Jerusalem (37:8–13).

Hezekiah reads the second letter, returns to the temple to lay his problem (literally) before God, and then prays. He recognizes the great power of Assyria but also acknowledges that the power of his God is much greater still, and he asks for God's deliverance (37:14–20).

In response, God sends another message to Hezekiah through Isaiah. God is pleased with Hezekiah's prayer, and He despises those who mock His name and threaten Judah. He has allowed Assyria to have power over Judah for a while, but He will remove them before they cause any further trouble (37:21–29). The people of Judah will have additional years of peace (37:30–32).

Furthermore, as Isaiah affirms for Hezekiah, Sennacherib's threats will never be carried out. He will not so much as shoot the first arrow or build a siege ramp (37:33–35). In a single night, an angel of the Lord kills 185,000 Assyrian soldiers. With his army decimated, the next morning Sennacherib returns to Assyria the way he had come. Eventually he is assassinated by two of his own sons (37:36–38).

📖 38:1–22

HEZEKIAH'S ILLNESS AND PRAYER

On another occasion, Hezekiah receives a message from Isaiah that he will not recover from a life-threatening boil (38:1, 21). God is giving Hezekiah advance notice of his death so he can put his house in order (38:1).

Demystifying Isaiah

Evidently, Isaiah's historical accounts concerning Hezekiah are not in chronological order. Hezekiah's near-death illness (38:1–22) must have occurred prior to his encounter with Sennacherib (36–37). For one thing, God's decision to extend Hezekiah's life is accompanied by His promise to deliver Hezekiah and Jerusalem from the Assyrians (38:6), so they must have still been a threat to Judah. Also, history tells us that Merodach-baladan, the Babylonian leader mentioned in connection with Hezekiah's illness (39:1), ruled *prior to* Sennacherib's invasion of Judah. It seems likely that Isaiah positioned the accounts as he did because Hezekiah's encounter with the Babylonian leaders segues into the prophet's next chapters foretelling a Babylonian captivity to follow.

Hezekiah turns to God with a plea for deliverance from this trouble. He attests to his own faithfulness as he weeps bitterly (38:2–3). The fact that Hezekiah can stand before God and point to his devotion is a good indication that he is indeed attempting to live a righteous life. Many kings of Judah are remembered primarily for doing evil in the sight of the Lord, but Hezekiah is a positive exception (although he is far from perfect, as Isaiah will record in chapter 39).

In answer to Hezekiah's heartfelt prayer, God sends Isaiah back to the king to tell him he will have another fifteen years of life. A poultice of figs applied to the boil will clear it up (38:21). The reversal of the prophet's message is so rapid (see 2 Kings 20:1–11) that perhaps Hezekiah is a bit reluctant to accept the good news at face value, so Isaiah gives him a sign from God. The sign is fascinating: A shadow that has just come down the steps of a stairway is reversed and goes back *up* (38:7–8).

Critical Observation

When Isaiah leaves Hezekiah after delivering his first message, he hasn't even gotten out of the palace before God turns him around to tell Hezekiah that he has fifteen more years to live (2 Kings 20:1–11).

Anyone who has been unexpectedly freed from an immediate death sentence is likely to be dumbfounded. Hezekiah expresses his emotions in a psalm-like work with the first stanza (38:10–14) describing his initial feelings of despair and the second stanza (38:15–20) focusing on praise and elation.

📖 **39:1–8**

VISITORS FROM BABYLON

Had Hezekiah's story ended with the account of his healing, he would be remembered more fondly. But Isaiah's final story provides a different tone. After hearing of Hezekiah's illness and recovery, a group of officials from Babylon visit him (39:1).

Critical Observation

At this time, Assyria is definitely the dominant nation in their part of the world. Babylon is not yet a great world power, but not for lack of trying. Merodach-baladan (39:1) has already led a few attempts to break free of Assyria and has actively sought to ally with other nations. So the appearance of his envoys in Judah merely to visit a sick king might be perceived as suspicious.

Hezekiah welcomes his visitors and hides nothing from them. He naively shows them everything about Jerusalem that might make it attractive to the invading force of a foreign power (39:2). After the Babylonians leave, Isaiah asks Hezekiah what they had said and where they were from. Hezekiah explains that they were from Babylon and that he had shown them all the treasures of Judah (39:3–4).

Speaking through Isaiah, God declares that the time will come when everything of worth in Jerusalem will be taken by Babylon. Even descendants of the king will be carried off, and nothing will be left (39:5–7). This was likely a surprising prophecy to Hezekiah. The predominance of Assyria made them the likely candidate to conquer smaller nations. But from this point onward through the writing of Isaiah, the Babylonian captivity is in view.

Hezekiah's response to Isaiah's prophecy is most troubling (39:8). Instead of repentance or regret, the king seems genuinely happy. His reasoning is that there will at least be peace and security in *his* day. Perhaps Hezekiah takes it as a foregone conclusion that the Lord will eventually fulfill His word and send His people into exile. He may have presumed that no amount of tears will change the situation. So, in a sense, it would have been good news that the day of reckoning for Jerusalem would not come during his lifetime. Still, his response to the foreboding warning concerning his nation appears insensitive and inappropriate, marring what is otherwise a respectable report by Isaiah.

Take It Home

The various accounts of Hezekiah may raise questions about prayer. It is amazing to read of Isaiah's declaration that Hezekiah will not recover from his illness (38:1) and then see that Hezekiah's prayer appears to change God's mind. Yet upon hearing the shocking news that his nation is destined to be conquered and destroyed by the Babylonians, Hezekiah hardly flinches (39:5–8). Which response is most like your own approach to prayer? Do you attempt to stoically accept the situations of life as they occur, or do you plead with God to change things for the better? Or does it depend on the situation?

ISAIAH 40:1–44:23

GOOD NEWS IN BAD TIMES

Setting Up the Section

This section begins a shift in tone and focus in the book of Isaiah, so much so that many believe it must have been written by someone other than the author of Isaiah 1–39. The regularity of judgmental pronouncements diminishes, as much more is written about salvation and restoration. The previous chapters present Assyria as the dominant threat; the following ones jump ahead to anticipate the end of the *Babylonian* captivity. (After the fall of Israel to Assyria, Judah remains as a nation for more than a century, and their exile in Babylon lasts another seventy years before they are able to return to their homeland.) But regardless of one's opinion of whether or not a second "Isaiah" takes up the writing of the original prophet at this point, this section contains some of the more optimistic looks toward the future in all the Old Testament.

📖 40:1–31

ANTICIPATION OF COMFORT

The fortieth chapter begins a new section of Isaiah. While God will continue to correct His people, His word from this point forward is filled with much comfort. Yet this is not a comfort defined by the spiritual equivalent of a plush sofa, but rather a deeper sensation that demands careful attention because it comes at a great cost.

In the opening verses it is interesting to note that God provides His prophet with not only a *message* to deliver to the people but also clear instructions as to the *emotions* to accompany the message. Isaiah is to speak tenderly to the people as he brings them an uplifting prophecy of comfort (40:1–2).

Yet despite the optimism of the message, Jerusalem will continue to face great difficulties for decades to come after Isaiah. When will this good news arrive for the people of God? It will first be announced by a special prophet who will be a voice crying out for the people to prepare the way of the Lord. In the style of many Old Testament prophecies, this voice is probably that of Isaiah for a short-term fulfillment of prophecy. But centuries later, this figure will be identified as John the Baptist for an entirely different generation of God's people (40:3–5; Matthew 3:1–3).

God is eternal and everlasting, as opposed to humanity that is like grass in its fleeting existence. This is a world of the perishing. People come and go in the blinking of an eye. But God provides permanence through His Word, which stands forever (Isaiah 40:6-8). The omnipotent God creates worlds and fashions mountains, islands, and waters. Compared to Him, the most powerful nations of the earth are but dust on the scales (40:12-17). And yet that Almighty God gently leads those who are His and gathers them in His arms like a shepherd (40:9-11).

When people begin to comprehend the reality of God, all idolatry seems foolish. God is the eternal Creator, Savior, and Deliverer. Idols, in contrast, must be man made. Care must be taken that they don't too quickly rot or fall over. Any glory of the idol comes from gold overlay and silver adornment (40:18-20). Yet God's people have repeatedly forsaken His leading and turned to such idols.

Isaiah attempts to renew the people's understanding of God. The Lord made all things, visible and invisible. The most impressive rulers do not faze Him. He can bring the high and mighty to nothing, and He can raise up the poorest slave to sit among princes. He is familiar with each individual star throughout the universe, so it should be no surprise that He is just as knowledgeable of each human being He has created (40:21-27).

God is not only *aware* of the struggles of His people but He also is actively *involved*. The affairs of life are demanding and tiring. But God is consistently present to provide strength to the weary and power to the weak. With the renewed energy He provides, God's people can soar on wings like eagles and run without wearing down. They can rest in the assurance that He has not forgotten them (40:28-31).

📖 **41:1–29**

ISRAEL AMID THE NATIONS

As Isaiah continues, he affirms that God is the one who was at work behind all of the power struggles and international events in the Near East in the eighth century BC. The people of Judah may have seen only a powerful king with an unstoppable army bearing down on them from the East, but Isaiah is trying to make them aware that God was behind the situation. The Lord takes no pleasure in disaster, but He works all things according to the perfection of His holy will.

Demystifying Isaiah

The observation that the threat from the East moved on unfamiliar ground (41:3) suggests that Isaiah is no longer talking about Assyria. The new power in the East is most likely Cyrus, the Persian leader whom the prophet will soon identify by name (44:28–45:1). In addition, Isaiah has already said that the Medes will conquer Babylon (13:17–19). A later reference to Cyrus speaks of him coming from the north (41:25) because that is the site of his Babylonian conquests. Worldly powers will continue to shift, but God remains in control of them all.

As trouble approaches, people will respond in different ways to the power of God. Those who don't know Him will be fearful, forming alliances and turning to the worship of other gods (41:5-7). But God's people can respond differently. God tells them not to panic. He will not only be with them but He will also strengthen and help them (41:10).

God's plan for His nation Israel is no insignificant part of His overall design for the glory of His name and the redemption of the elect. It will be from Israel that one special servant will come as the only Redeemer of His people. God had called Israel into being for a purpose, and He had never abandoned that purpose for His chosen ones. He was always with them and will continue to help them (41:8–16).

Strong enemies will continue to try to destroy God's people and undermine His plan. But God is able to defeat all such enemies, seen and unseen, and even demonstrate His strength through the weakness of His people. Through Isaiah, God foretells all that will happen. Then He challenges the nations and their idols to do the same, proving that their gods are worth nothing (41:17–24).

God will allow the Babylonians to conquer His people and carry them from Judah into exile, but God's people will then see Babylon defeated by Cyrus and the Medes (41:25–29). And one day the Lord will send a herald of good news—a servant who will bring good news of redemptive love to God's people.

📖 42:1–25

GOD'S SERVANT

As Isaiah continues, he begins to describe the character and responsibilities of God's servant. He describes a specially designated representative of God on whom God will bestow His Spirit. God's servant will faithfully promote justice until it is achieved throughout the earth. In the meantime, he will not add to the burdens of the weak, who are described as weak reeds and flickering candles. God will delight in this figure (42:1–4).

Demystifying Isaiah

Isaiah provides four servant songs: the first being found in 42:1–17, with three others to follow. Sometimes, as in this case, the servant he refers to will be the coming Messiah. On other occasions, he writes of Israel as the servant of God. His intended meaning is usually clear based on the descriptions he provides and the context of what he is saying.

This is definitely good news that should result in praise among all the nations. Kedar (42:11) was an Arabian area noted for its nomadic peoples and their flocks. Sela was an Edomite capital south of the Dead Sea. Edom, like Judah, had previously received Isaiah's words of warning (34:5–17), yet here they are invited to sing a new song to the Lord (42:10–12). God will take action to turn darkness into light, make rough places smooth, and guide the blind through unfamiliar territory (42:13–17).

Israel and Judah *should* have been a light for the Gentiles (42:5–9), but as it turned out, they were the ones who were actually blind and in desperate need of a savior. They had seen and heard God working among them, yet they paid no attention. As a result, God responded in anger (42:18–25).

GOD'S GREAT PROMISE

In their condition, the only effective savior for Judah will be the Lord Himself (43:3, 11), and in this section God promises them the best thing He can—that He will be with them as they go through the challenges they face. Yes, they will still have to deal with deep waters and flames, but the floods will not overwhelm them and the fires will not consume them. Even when Egypt and Cush fall, God will save Israel. With words filled with love and commitment, God tells His people not to be afraid (43:1–5).

God's people will be carried away to faraway nations, but God will gather them when their exile is over. It will be an act of redemption, salvation, and love. It will also be a demonstration of God's great power (43:6–13).

Critical Observation

This great promise of God to summon His people (43:1) will be fulfilled at several levels. First, Isaiah is prophesying an exile to Babylon, after which many of God's people will eventually be restored to the land under the leadership of Ezra, Nehemiah, and others. Second, after the coming of Jesus Christ and the outpouring of the Holy Spirit upon the church, people of faith will be gathered to the Lord in an amazing way. Finally, at the second return of Christ, the Lord will gather His people and take them home for good in His eternal kingdom.

Even before the people go into Babylonian captivity, God assures them of their release. The Israelites have always seen their exodus from Egypt as a historical high point, but God tells them to stop focusing on the past so they can see the new thing He is doing that will be even better (43:14–19).

Some people are likely to ask the question, if God is going to gather His people eventually, why would He go to the trouble of having them experience the pain of being conquered and forcibly leaving their land? Isaiah has already pointed out several times that the people are stubborn and unrepentant. Here God compares them (unfavorably) to wild animals. God is receiving more acknowledgment from jackals and owls than from the people who supposedly worship Him (43:20–28). After their exile, they will be much more receptive to the love and commitment He continually shows them.

LIFE-GIVING WATER AND LIFELESS IDOLS

It is common knowledge that people need water to live, but those dwelling in the ancient Near East were more regularly reminded of that fact than modern people who take water for granted. Without water, there is no life. And God uses this fact to teach that without His Spirit, there can be no spiritual life (44:1–5). Without the Spirit of God, people are first bone dry in a spiritual sense, and eventually dead in their sins.

The Lord is the provider of both needs: the water that sustains physical life and the Holy Spirit who bestows blessings to those who know God. Isaiah foretells the day when large numbers of people (springing up like grass and poplar trees) will turn to God. Not only that, but their reluctance will disappear and they will again *desire* to be known as believers in the Lord (44:4–5).

There is only one God, but the world has never had a shortage of false gods. Isaiah has already noted the futility of idol worship in a number of places (see 40:18–20; 41:7, 21–24), but this section (44:6–20) is one of the longer and more explicit descriptions. The images are truly ridiculous and pitiable.

The book of Genesis describes the wonder of God creating people, but Isaiah writes of people creating their gods. As they do so, the people get hungry, thirsty, and faint. Or someone gathers wood to cook a meal (food and fuel being two blessings of God), but the person sets aside part of a log with which he makes an idol, and then he prays to that god for salvation. People's minds were so spiritually cloudy that no one questioned the logic of praying to a block of wood (44:12–20).

Rather than being deluded by the practices of idolatrous nations, God challenges His people to return to Him for forgiveness, redemption, and renewed joy (44:21–23).

Take It Home

Isaiah has begun an emphasis on the comfort available for God's people, although there are going to be challenging situations they must face before experiencing such a degree of comfort. What are some situations you face that tend to prevent you from feeling the comfort you might like to sense in your life? What criteria do you use to determine whether or not you are at an appropriate spiritual comfort level?

ISAIAH 44:24–48:22

ISRAEL, BABYLON, AND CYRUS

Setting Up the Section

Isaiah has been attempting to help his people understand that they will certainly be conquered by Babylon and taken into exile. Here, however, he moves ahead to write of the fall of Babylon and the end of their captivity, predicting a benefactor that Israel might not have counted on: a foreign leader named Cyrus.

📖 **44:24–45:25**

HELP FROM AN UNEXPECTED SOURCE

In previous chapters, Isaiah has written that the Medes will bring the rule of the Babylonians to an end (13:17–22). More details are provided in 41:2–4, 25. But here Isaiah provides the name of the Persian leader: Cyrus (44:28; 45:1). Not only is Cyrus specifically named but he is also identified as the Lord's anointed—the same title used for Israel's kings and that will be given to the Messiah.

Critical Observation

Isaiah ministered during the eighth century BC, long before the birth of Cyrus, which leads some people to question this particular account. Those who aren't convinced of the reliability of predictive prophecy believe that the specific mentions of Cyrus must have been added to the narrative at a later date—perhaps even after the release of the exiled people of Israel. Some believe the omniscience of God was at work in Isaiah's writing and that the prophet's ability to be so exact only proves that he spoke for the Lord. Others have varying opinions (a second Isaiah, etc.).

An *anointed one* is someone chosen by God for a special task of deliverance and salvation for God's people. It is highly unusual to see the title applied to a non-Israelite emperor, yet God is able to use a wide variety of resources to accomplish His will. He will bring Cyrus to power by removing the obstacles that stand in his way (including the Babylonian Empire). God is more than capable of calling such a person for the benefit of His people Israel, even though the individual may not personally acknowledge God.

After defeating the Medes in 549 BC and Babylon in 539 BC, Cyrus is well-established as the leader of the Persian Empire. History may give Cyrus the credit for his accomplishments, but Isaiah declares that it was God who went before Cyrus to level mountains, break down strong gates, and accumulate wealth (45:1–3).

What wasn't evident at first was that whatever benefited Cyrus in his rise to power would eventually benefit Israel. To question God's methods was as useless as a lump of clay challenging the skill of the potter. As Creator of heaven and earth, surely God was a more than competent architect of plans to deliver His people (45:4–13).

God remains unseen (hidden), yet His will is accomplished among the nations, and He puts to shame those who seek the wisdom and help of idols (45:14–20). One of the end results of God's will is the deliverance of His people. But in addition, the population reaching to the ends of the earth can also turn to Him to be saved (45:21–22). Every knee will bow and every tongue will attest to the strength and righteousness of Israel's God (45:23–25).

📖 46:1–47:15

THE DEMISE OF BABYLON

Idol worship is a lot of work for the participants. People have to provide the gold and silver for the image, as well as pay a craftsman to create it. Then they have to transport the finished product with some difficulty, either carrying it on their shoulders or transferring it to a beast of burden. When they get it to the desired location, they then have to be sure to anchor it. Finally, they pray to it—all to no avail. It is just a hunk of metal that cannot answer (46:1–2, 6–7).

Demystifying Isaiah

The gods mentioned in Isaiah 46:1 were Babylonian. *Bel* is not synonymous with *Baal* of the Canaanites, although the two were similar in influence in their respective cultures because they were the prominent deities. Bel is also known as Marduk. Nebo was the son of Bel and the god of wisdom.

Idols had to be carried from one place to another—a difficult job left to people because the gods themselves were unable to help in any way (46:2). But Israel's God had carried His people from cradle to grave. He is always available to sustain and rescue them. There is no comparison between God and other gods (46:3–5).

The Babylonian leaders will fare no better than their gods. God's purpose will soon be revealed and accomplished. He will summon a bird of prey from the east (Cyrus). As a result, the Babylonian rebels will be defeated and salvation will come to the people of God (46:8–15).

God portrays the nation of Babylon as a young virgin girl. Things appear to be good. Babylon is recognized as a queen of the kingdoms (47:5) and has no inkling that anything will change their privileged status (47:7). Babylon will take God's people captive for a while, but the day will arrive when Babylon will be on the other end of the power scale.

The virgin daughter will find herself sitting in the dust, having lost not only her throne but also everything that had made her attractive. Forced to work and to roam, she will be subject to nakedness and shame (47:1–3). Sitting in darkness and silence, Babylon will have time to contemplate how it had arrived at such a state. God makes that point clear: He has allowed His people to be overpowered by Babylon, but the Babylonians had shown them no mercy. Soon it will be Babylon who will seek the mercy of other stronger powers (47:5–6).

Babylon is a proud nation, thinking itself invincible. The people practice magic and sorcery, and they feel their secret knowledge gives them an advantage. They are wicked at heart, even though they think no one is aware of their evil actions (47:8–10). The arrogance of Babylon is undercut as the taunts of God through the prophet Isaiah tell them to continue with their dark magic (to prevent their demise). Maybe they will scare someone. Maybe their famed astrologers and stargazers can come up with a plan (47:11–13).

Demystifying Isaiah

It can be a bit disappointing, if not downright frustrating, that Isaiah provides so few details regarding the transition between Babylonian rule and the conquest of Cyrus of Persia. The same event is noted in Daniel 5, with little more said between the feast of Babylonian leader Belshazzar with the writing on the wall one night and his replacement by Darius the Mede the next day. (Darius may be another name for Cyrus, or perhaps a different leader appointed by Cyrus.) Bible scholars who believe Isaiah was written by a single person point to the absence of details as evidence, suggesting that a second Isaiah, who would have written after the events, would not have omitted so much.

But no, God is going to bring certain disaster on Babylon, and when He does, their people will find themselves helpless (47:11). Those they had always counted on will not even be able to save themselves, much less the nation (47:14–15).

📖 48:1–22

ISRAEL'S OBSTINACY

When it comes to arrogance and stubbornness, Babylon is no worse than God's people. God observes that the muscles in His people's necks are iron, and their foreheads are bronze (48:4). They pride themselves in being associated with God and having a long, magnificent spiritual history. But in reality, they have strayed from God's truth and righteousness (48:1–2).

Of course, God sees through their pretense. His understanding of Israel's sin influences His revelation (or withholding of it). Recognizing their sinful tendencies, He had revealed certain things long ago so this generation of people cannot claim that their idols brought about those events. At other times He withholds sharing His plans so that His people cannot claim to know the hidden things of God (48:5–7).

Despite repeated rebellion among His people, God remains committed to them, ultimately for the glory of His own name. In the meantime, He continues to love them as He attempts to test and refine them through their struggles (48:8–11). Much of that refining process will be accomplished through the approaching Babylonian captivity, but Israel's testing will have limits. They can count on being released from their future captivity, although it is still tragic that such an action is necessary. If Israel had been obedient, they could have had peace, righteousness, fertility, prosperity, and more. Because of their lack of faithfulness, however, they will suffer much. Yet they will ultimately experience the great joy of freedom (48:12–22).

Take It Home

The sovereignty of God keeps coming through in Isaiah's writing. How do you feel when you read that God allows His people to be tested through captivity/suffering before returning to Him in joy? How about the fact that God uses a cruel enemy to dominate His people as part of their restoration? How about the haste of God's people to turn to idols rather than submitting to God in obedience? Do you see such things as exclusively historic events, or do you detect any similarities with how God and His people relate to one another in modern times?

ISAIAH 49:1–55:13

THE WORK OF GOD'S SERVANT

Setting Up the Section

The first of four songs for God's servant is found in Isaiah 42:1–4 (or possibly 42:1–7 or 42:1–9). The other three songs are found in this section: 49:1–6 (possibly 49:1–7 or 49:1–13); 50:4–9 (possibly 50:4–11); and 52:13–53:12. These songs and the surrounding material foretell a servant of God who will be a deliverer not just of Israel but of all the nations as well. In fact, the emphasis of Isaiah's writing shifts to the point that neither Babylon nor Cyrus is mentioned again. The people of God are still in a captivity of sorts, but it is less the harsh physical captivity of specific nations and more of a spiritual bondage that only a special agent of God can remedy.

📖 **49:1–26**

AN INTRODUCTION TO THE SERVANT

The servant songs of Isaiah are among the most exciting features of this impressive book of prophecy. The second of the four songs begins in chapter 49 and, depending on which scholars one consults, comprises the first six, seven, or thirteen verses of the chapter.

The figure at the center of these songs is the personification of the faithful Israel. As the songs progress from first to fourth, it becomes clearer that this perfection of Israel will actually come as a person with an appeal that extends far beyond the nation of Israel. His initial address is to the distant nations (49:1)—Gentile territory. He was born for the role he is to play. His words are powerful, like a sharp sword. God will use him and protect him from danger (49:1–4).

At first it will appear that his mission has yielded nothing. However, the Lord will reassure His servant, who will not only restore the Jews to God but also become a light to the Gentiles. The work of the servant will result in salvation reaching the ends of the earth. Nevertheless, he will first be deeply despised—a theme that will be further developed in the remaining songs. Despite the fact that some people will hate the servant, God will encourage him until someday many powerful rulers will bow before him. He will serve others in suffering and humility, but they will eventually prostrate themselves before him (49:5–7).

Additionally, the land will be restored and firmly established. Prisoners of sin and death will receive their liberty. The hungry will be fed and satisfied. Streams of living water will be available for those who thirst. Those brought to God's city from afar can expect protection and provision (49:8–13).

Critical Observation

In retrospect, it is easy for modern believers to see that many of Isaiah's prophecies describe the life and ministry of Jesus Christ. For the original hearers, however, those promises must have seemed wonderful, yet also mysterious and possibly confusing.

Such promises may have been hard to believe. When times get difficult, it is more challenging to see with eyes of faith. People might think that God has turned away from them and ceased to love them, but the Lord is like a tender parent. He might discipline His children, but He will never forget or fail them. Indeed, it is as if their names are engraved on His palms (49:14–16).

Israel will undergo a period of bereavement, yet when times improve she will discover great numbers of descendants she was not aware of prior. She will even be a strong and positive influence on Gentile nations. Normally captives are not expected to ever be rescued, but God will certainly deliver His people from the hands of their captors (49:17–26).

Demystifying Isaiah

This section may be an instance where both short-term and long-term fulfillments occur in regard to the same prophecy. When Israel was released from Babylonian captivity and returned to their homeland, it might have seemed that Isaiah's prophecy was coming true. Yet at that time they were weak and disorganized, and they demonstrated no influence on other nations. It would seem that Isaiah, then, was also referring to a future event.

📖 50:1–11

A SUBMISSIVE SERVANT

A shift of address is made between Isaiah 49 and 50. In Isaiah 49, Israel is addressed as a mother. But as chapter 50 begins, God is addressing children—perhaps the faithful remnant among His people—and explaining that He has allowed their mother to be sent away for a while because of her sins. It is not unlike a husband declaring a divorce, which was accepted at this time of Israel's history (Deuteronomy 24:1-4). But in the case of God and His people, the divorce is only temporary (see Isaiah 54:5-7; Jeremiah 3:6-13). God could easily have protected His people, but they had repeatedly refused to call on Him (Isaiah 50:1-3).

The narrative now shifts to the perspective of God's servant once again in the third of the four servant songs (50:4-9 or possibly 50:4-11). Israel is in a desperate state, yet they are not helpless. The wonder of the gospel is that God, in His justice, comes again as God in His mercy. Unlike the other people of Israel, the servant of God welcomes instruction and is never rebellious. His words bring life. His ear listens to the voice of the Lord morning by morning. He stands on the side of the covenant people and never turns back from his mission to love God.

Consequently, he must be willing to suffer according to the need. He will give his back to those who strike him. He will turn his face toward those who spit on him. He is the only hope for the people, yet he receives their hatred (50:4-6).

What will be different about the servant to enable him to remain strong while others falter? He knows where to turn for strength. His help will come from God. As long as God is his vindication, he will never be overcome or put to shame (50:7-9).

The Lord and His servant provide the people an option that is otherwise unavailable. Some are likely to insist on providing their own sources of "light," but God declares that such people will lie down in torment. Everyone will fare far better if they will willingly fear the Lord and obey the word of His servant (50:10-11).

📖 51:1–16

A HISTORIC REMINDER

God has a long, reliable record of proving that He can deliver His people even when things seem hopeless. Citing one such instance, He tells the people to recall the story of Abraham. Sarah and Abraham had wanted a child throughout their entire lifetimes, but Sarah had been unable to conceive. God waited until Sarah was well past childbearing age, so that when she got pregnant there could be no doubt that God was the one responsible for the miraculous event. Through Isaac, and then Jacob (Israel), comes a nation that inherited the promises God had initially made to the faithful Abraham.

In time that nation turns away from the Lord. But God's point is that just as He had been able to create a great number of people from the aged Abraham and barren Sarah, so, too, can He restore them even when all they see are ruins and wastelands (51:1-3).

The world and all it contains will pass away, but the salvation that God makes available to humanity—not just to Israel, but to all the nations—will be eternal. They who insult and persecute God's people have no future, but God will be available to His people forever (51:4–8).

Without the love and power of God, humanity has no chance of life, even for a moment. But by the strength of the Lord, His redeemed will be forever kept alive. They will come to Zion with joyful singing. The return under Cyrus will be only temporary, but one day a heavenly Zion will be made available to them forever (51:9–11).

Demystifying Isaiah

Rahab (51:9) is a reference to Egypt, and other references to Israel's exodus from Egypt are found in the passage: "days of old" (51:9 NLT), "dried up the sea" (51:10 NLT), and "making a path of escape through the depths so that your people could cross over" (51:10 NLT). Egypt's association with the monster (51:9) is similar to the link between Leviathan (27:1) and some of the Canaanite nations.

God is the only guarantee for the people to gain for themselves what they cannot acquire by their own strength. He is the Creator who set the heavens in place, laid the foundations of the earth, and controls the raging sea. He can surely remake His people and secure for them blessings that will never be taken away (51:12–16).

51:17–52:12

WRATH, THEN ASSURANCE

The people of Judah are hearing both good news and bad news from God through the lips of Isaiah. They will certainly experience the wrath of God, symbolized by potent wine that causes them to stagger. Alcoholic intoxication can be a deadly thing, but even more devastating is to be drunk on one's pride and false delusions of safety. For a while the people of Judah will be inconsolable as they undergo famine, violence, and ruin. They have sinned, and they will suffer the consequences (51:17–20).

But God's wrath will not last. After a time, He will deliver Israel as He passes the cup of wrath to her enemies (51:21–23). For God's people it will be like waking from a fitful sleep to greet the day with a message of truly wonderful news. Their enemies will threaten them no more. The people can dress in beautiful garments again, feeling anew the thrill of freedom and redemption. Shaking off the dust of the past, they will arise as a glorified city of God. They had previously been at the mercy of Egypt, and more recently Assyria had been a major threat. But God has demonstrated His sovereignty by delivering them from both worldly superpowers. Babylon will be next, but the Babylonian Empire will be no more a problem for God than any previous threat (52:1–6).

Not surprisingly, messengers bearing good news from far away were well received in ancient times. Watchmen were stationed to hear and report updates. But the best news that Judah could hear is a simple message: The God of Israel reigns (52:7–8).

Critical Observation

Naturally, any good news is reason for celebrating. Judah's release from Babylon is one such example. But the emphasis on peace and salvation (52:7) suggests that here, too, Isaiah is looking beyond his own times to the coming of the Messiah and His kingdom. At that time people can see the Lord return to Zion with their own eyes (52:8).

God's deliverance of Judah will get the attention of all nations (52:9–10). His people will burst into song in response to God's comfort, redemption, and salvation. He will call them out of unclean places, personally escorting them both before and behind (52:11–12).

📖 52:13–53:12

THE FOURTH AND FINAL SERVANT SONG

Any lasting positive change among God's people must come about through the work of God's servant. This section is the last (and longest) of the four servant songs in Isaiah. It is also probably the best known because various portions of it are frequently cited throughout the New Testament.

God's servant will not look like a specially designated leader of humanity. In fact, his appearance will be appalling and disfigured (52:14). Perhaps this is a reference to Jesus' disfigurement on the cross. Or the point might be simply that the Messiah will not be a physically striking figure. Still, the servant's ministry will be effective. World leaders will acknowledge the truth of his message, and ultimately he will be raised up and highly exalted (52:13, 15).

The news Isaiah is revealing is almost too good to be believed (53:1), although it may not appear that way at first. The servant is nothing to look at. He is despised. He is a man of sorrows. People do not esteem him. He will suffer to the point that people have to look away (53:2–3). Yet the actions of the servant are for the benefit of humanity. He is standing in the place of weak and sinful people. He carries the grief they should feel. He receives the wounds they should receive as a result of their transgressions. He takes the weight of the Lord's crushing justice in response to human iniquity. He endures the punishment so people can have peace. People have wandered away from God, but the servant pays the penalty for their iniquity (53:4–6).

Critical Observation

It is evident in Isaiah's writing, and becomes even clearer in the New Testament, that humanity's penalty is not owed to any person or spiritual force other than God the Father. From the beginning, God made it clear that justice demanded consequences for sin. But through a plan between the heavenly Father and His Son (the servant in Isaiah), the death penalty fully deserved by sinful humanity was paid by Jesus Christ. Because of the great mercy of God, believers have the gift of freedom and eternal life.

Amazingly, the servant will face God's terrible wrath in silence. He will go to his death with complete awareness of what will happen to him. But he also knows what his action will accomplish, so he approaches death like a lamb about to be slaughtered. It will not be his own will to do so, but the servant submits to the Father's will in silent willingness (53:7–8).

He has done nothing wrong, yet he will face oppression, the corrupt judgment of his human peers, physical death, and finally, the grave. If this all seems unjust for the servant, it must be emphasized that he is acting to ensure God's justice. Isaiah makes it clear: It is the Lord's will for him to suffer (53:9–10).

But God's plan does not end there. Beyond the grave awaits the greatest exaltation for the righteous servant. God's plan involves the suffering of His Son, but also great honor to follow. The servant's selfless act of obedience will yield blessing upon blessing and grace upon grace as the centuries move forward (53:11–12).

Demystifying Isaiah

Isaiah's final song about God's servant speaks with precision about the final days and moments of the life of Jesus Christ. Among other things, Jesus was:

- Pierced (Isaiah 53:5; John 19:33–34)
- Wounded (Isaiah 53:5; Matthew 26:67–68; 27:26–31)
- Silent (Isaiah 53:7; Matthew 27:12–14)
- With the rich in His death (Isaiah 53:9; Matthew 27:57–60)
- Numbered among transgressors (Isaiah 53:12; Luke 23:32–43)

📖 **54:1–55:13**

A NEW OPPORTUNITY

The willing submission of God's servant will yield a number of lasting results, beginning in Israel but soon spreading to affect the entire world. God's elect has become like a barren woman longing to be a mother. Indeed, the situation is familiar to those who know the stories of Sarah (Genesis 18:9–15; 21:1–7) and Hannah (1 Samuel 1). Few things are more disheartening than infertile women who long to have children, and a similar feeling will permeate the nation during their time of exile. But just as God eventually rewarded Sarah and Hannah with a cherished child, so too will He end the barrenness of His people.

Indeed, the barren woman is commanded to shout for joy because she will bear children in abundance (Isaiah 54:1). In fact, God tells His people to prepare to expand. As a fertile mother, they will produce descendants that will not be restricted to the promised land in Palestine. They will spread out to many nations and provide an international scope from that point onward. Israel will no longer suffer the shame of its youthful sins or the temporary widowhood of exile and captivity (54:2–4).

In addition to being a fruitful mother, the nation will also become a beloved bride with God as her Husband, Creator, and Redeemer. The international aspect is again seen in this promise because the Lord is the God of all the earth (54:5).

God seems to have abandoned His people for a short time, but after hiding His face for a moment, He extends His great compassion and kindness as He renews His relationship with them (54:5–8). God has been angry with His sinful and unrepentant people, but He recalls His previous promise to Noah (Genesis 9:12–17) and determines not to take action that will destroy them (Isaiah 54:9–10).

God's people will be like a fruitful mother. They will be like a beloved bride. They will also be like a beautiful building, adorned with precious gems (54:11–12). The turbulence of the past will be forgotten as the future looms bright. Clearly, the riches of the city refer to people rather than literal precious stones. As the passage continues, the promise is made that God will teach the children, providing peace and righteousness. What other treasure can approach the value of being continually in the presence of God?

Finally, God promises that His people will be safe from all enemies. Tyranny and terror will be far removed (54:13–14). This promise has never been perfectly fulfilled because God's people throughout the ages have had to contend against ungodly people and forces. Yet no weapon directed against the church can ultimately prosper. One day the perfect peace of God will be realized (54:15–17).

Until then, people will struggle with temptations to pursue things other than the Lord, but God extends an open invitation for all to come to Him (54:1). This invitation begins, in a very literal sense, with a call extended to the people of Judah after their captivity in Babylon. On a broader level, however, it is an appeal for them to return to God. Those who come to the Lord need no money because the servant of God has paid the price necessary for sinful people to approach a holy Lord (53:4–6).

Still, people tend to invest in other things that are far less rewarding. Idolatry is like a spiritual diet of junk food when God is offering fresh bread. No matter how hard people may work, they are not likely to be satisfied if their efforts have no lasting purpose (55:2). God's spiritual food and drink is His Word. It costs nothing, but it does require a listening ear (55:3).

God reminds His people of the covenant He had made with David (55:3). God had promised David that one of his descendants would be on the throne of an everlasting kingdom (2 Samuel 7:8–9, 16). It appears for a while that the dynasty of David had come to an end when Judah falls to Babylon and the people are carried away as captives. But Paul will later quote this verse from Isaiah as proof that Jesus is the one from the line of David who will fulfill God's former promise (Acts 13:34).

In light of this leader who will eventually arrive, the previous invitation to come is extended to everyone. God's people will become a beacon that will attract other nations (Isaiah 55:4–5). So it is especially important for Israel to turn to God while they have the opportunity. He will show mercy and pardon them freely (55:6).

People don't have to understand the mind of God. In fact, it is impossible to do so. God's thoughts and ways are far beyond human capacity to comprehend. Yet God's Word and works never fail. Isaiah compares them to rain. Water falls from the sky as rain and snow and evaporates back into the atmosphere. Yet as it follows that simple cycle, it waters the earth, causes seed to sprout in the soil, and provides food for everyone on earth. Similarly, God's Word falls on people and returns, and as it does, it accomplishes all that God intends it to do (55:10–11).

These are indeed assuring words for people coming out of exile. After decades of captivity and dejection, they can expect joy and peace, with even nature seeming to burst into song around them. It will be a historic event that will stand as an everlasting sign of God's power and love for His people (55:12–13).

Take It Home

The people who first heard the prophecies in this section were most likely confused. God is promising to send a servant who will make life much more rewarding. Yet the people are also being told to expect Babylonian conquest and captivity. Similarly, modern believers have many promises of God, the assurance of Jesus Christ, and the empowering of the Holy Spirit. Still, most of them face times when they cannot see beyond the harsh realities of daily life. To what extent do the promises of God lift you above undesirable circumstances and mundane responsibilities?

ISAIAH 56:1–59:21

PROMISE FOR (AND PREVIOUS FAILURES OF) GOD'S PEOPLE

Setting Up the Section

Isaiah has been writing about a rather optimistic future for the people of God. But the spiritual strength of their future will be largely dependent on their willingness to take action in the present and correct the things they are doing wrong. The invitation of salvation is being extended to those outside of Israel, and God's people need to start taking an honest look at their own spiritual actions and attitudes.

📖 56:1–8

BROADENING THE INVITATION

The Lord's instructions to His people through Isaiah are nothing new. He isn't asking great things of them. He simply expects them to maintain a sense of justice in the land, to do what is right—keep the Sabbath, stay away from evil. Those who do such things will see God's righteousness revealed (56:1–2).

The people of Israel and Judah have developed a sense of special status in their relationship with the Lord. God's intentions to rescue His elect will broaden to include foreigners and eunuchs, two groups that have never before had full privileges in Israel. Among other restrictions, foreigners and eunuchs have not automatically been allowed to worship with the Israelites (Deuteronomy 23:1–3), but that is about to change.

God is appealing to His covenant people for a greater level of obedience. At the same time, others outside the nation are invited to demonstrate the same spiritual commitment and receive the blessings of God. Eunuchs can never bear children, but God promises them something even better. Foreigners who choose to worship God will find great joy and satisfaction and will no longer be treated as aliens (Isaiah 56:3–7).

Sincere worshipers from all nations will be welcomed at the altar of God. All will be encouraged to pray there. Israelites returning from exile will be joined by many others in a renewed devotion to the Lord (56:7–8).

📖 56:9–57:21

ISRAEL'S INGLORIOUS HISTORY

God's plan reflects His love and mercy toward all people. Unfortunately, Israel's leaders have not yet developed the same attitude toward others. Like the prophet Jonah, they do not want to witness the fullness of God's mercy if it means that people who have long been their enemies will also be able to find peace with God and receive His greatest blessings. The leaders have drifted away from a real understanding of the plan of God and have turned instead to furthering their own private interests. They make no effort to help the weak and confused but rather plan great things for themselves while focusing on sleeping and drinking. The result will be an invasion of beasts that, here again, symbolize foreign nations (56:9–12).

Critical Observation

In Isaiah's day, as in every generation, there are those who desire the outward label of covenant-keeper, yet they actually prefer false gods. But in this case, the corruption will be so pervasive that righteous people will feel completely out of place. It will get to a point where upright people will be taken away by God through death, not as a punishment but as a reward (57:1).

Only in death can peace be found (57:1–2). Even so, God is not willing to ignore the widespread sin and idolatry among those who claim to be His people. In a culture that should have known purity and faithfulness to the Lord, the people are linked to sorceresses, adulterers, and prostitutes (57:3). Their pursuit of idolatrous practices has exposed them to numerous habits that God had prohibited in their law. While they mock other people, they participate in magic, rebellion, lying, lust, and even child sacrifice (57:4–5).

The irony is that the people are faithful to their false gods while ignoring the living Lord. The imagery is graphic. The people of Israel are depicted as shamefully leaving a marriage bed to partake of affairs with various other lovers, among them the Ammonite god Molech, to whom parents sometimes offer their own children. Even though such a lifestyle becomes quite wearisome after a while, the people will not give it up (57:6–10).

God's promises are still sound. Those who turn to Him for strength and deliverance will inherit the land and find refuge (57:13). Those who don't, however, will be left on their own. Since the people insist on worshiping false gods, the Lord will direct them back to those useless forms of wood and stone when trouble comes. They will discover too late that the power of idols disappears with a mere wisp of wind (57:11–13).

God's plan for people is always substantially better than what they tend to choose for themselves. Those who choose to pursue idolatry have to remain in good standing with those gods by providing regular gifts and offerings. God is in need of nothing, yet rather than remaining in His holy place, He willingly reaches out to provide help, strength, and fellowship for those who are contrite and lowly in spirit (57:14–15).

God holds His people accountable and is displeased with sin, but He never loses control. He has seen His people's sinful greed, and He has punished those who are guilty. Yet His accusations and anger are short-lived. Rather than enforcing lingering and lasting punishment, God instead offers healing, guidance, and comfort. Those who respond to Him discover peace and restoration. But those who remain unrelenting in their wickedness are unable to find peace and will continue to suffer (57:16–21).

📖 58:1–14

A CALL FOR GENUINE WORSHIP

People can be far away from God yet still consider themselves to be in His good favor. While maintaining a form of godliness, they lack the power to break free from the prisons of laziness, self-centeredness, and addiction. Such is the case with Israel.

Isaiah is being told to shout out the truth of the people's rebellion, to broadcast it with the volume and intensity of a trumpet fanfare. The people are apparently oblivious to the extent of their spiritual lethargy. They claim to seek God's will, proclaiming eagerness to hear what He has to say. They even go to the point of blaming God for not noticing their faithfulness, their fasting, and their humility (58:1–3).

But God has indeed noticed. The purpose of fasting is to focus on the things of God rather than the usual comforts of life. Yet on days of fasting, the Israelites ended up quarreling with one another and fighting. They are self-centered and violent, with their minds remaining far from disciplines such as humility and repentance. Yet they still expect God to respond to their requests (58:3–5).

Had they truly been listening for God's voice, they would have known what they should be doing: fighting injustice (rather than each other), freeing the oppressed, feeding the hungry, sheltering the homeless, clothing those in need, and taking care of their own family members (58:6–7). God cares about how people deal with those created in His image.

Critical Observation

True humility before God must involve more than tears and sadness over the misery of one's life and disappointment in what may appear to be unanswered prayer. Genuine submission allows humble people to see the beauty of God's perfect law and, in response, creates a sense of abhorrence when confronted with their sin.

If the people had offered heartfelt worship to God, it would have included ministry to those around them, and they would have noticed an immediate difference: light in their darkness, healing, righteousness, and clear responses from God to their cries for help (58:8–10).

With a genuine concern for worship and the welfare of others, God's people will discover the ongoing strength and guidance of the Lord. Even in a desert setting, they will be like lush gardens. The ruins of their city will be rebuilt. Rather than having a reputation for quarreling and exploitation (58:3–4), they will be known as rebuilding and restoring their city. Keeping the Sabbath will not be a joyless obligation but a time of true delight. Instead of dry and tasteless religion, the people will be blessed with joy and feasting. All their holiest desires will be satisfied, and a new day will come for following generations (58:8–14).

📖 **59:1–21**

ACCUSATIONS AND CONFESSION

Many people acknowledge the problems created by sin, but few describe it as precisely as God does in this section of Isaiah. Sin is sometimes defined as "separation from God," which is an accurate description according to 59:2. But that is just the starting point of this depiction.

When the Lord speaks about the sin of His beloved people, He does not ignore the depth and ugliness of it. Here He speaks of bloodstained hands, lying lips, and discomfiting involvement with spiders and snakes (59:3–5). Sin results in an empty and meaningless life, and attempting to hide behind one's sinful lifestyle without being exposed is no more successful than attempting to make clothing from cobwebs (59:6). Actions, thoughts, and direction in life are all affected by sin. Whatever the person seeks remains hidden. Those who wallow in their sin find neither contentment nor peace (59:6–8).

Demystifying Isaiah

At this point in Isaiah's narrative (59:9), he shifts from God's observations to the people's response. The prophet joins his people in confession and repentance.

The spiritual state of God's people is not good, and they begin to admit the truth. They describe seeking light but not finding it. As a result, they are attempting to feel their way in the dark, stumbling like blind people as they do. Justice and deliverance seem unattainable.

They are both angry and mournful, yet for all they are able to accomplish on their own, they may as well have been dead (59:9–11).

To their credit, the people acknowledge that their sin is against God. Their offenses are numerous and include rebellion, treachery, rejection of the Lord, instilling oppression, and lying. The standards by which their society had been founded—justice, righteousness, and truth—are now nowhere to be found (59:12–15).

It is a distressing situation, but not a hopeless one. The people may not realize it, but the Lord knows that they lack the power to solve their problems. Because no one else is capable of intervening and dealing with the lack of righteousness, God will solve the problem Himself (59:15–16). In fact, righteousness and salvation are so integral to the Lord that they are described as His breastplate and helmet. For those who repent of their sin, God will be a certain redeemer (59:17, 20). But those who continue to resist Him will discover that the Lord's garments also include vengeance and zeal. They will face His wrath and retribution (59:17–19).

Eventually the relationship between the Lord and His redeemed people will become permanent, thanks to the power of God's Word and His Spirit (59:21).

Take It Home

In this section of Isaiah, God reveals a direct connection between the sincerity of one's worship and the response the worshiper can expect. God wants His people to notice the needs of the people around them and, where possible, attempt to make a positive difference among those who are prisoners, homeless, hungry, family members, and so forth. As you think of these categories, do any ministry opportunities spring to mind? If so, what can you do this week to help in one or more of those situations? If nothing immediately comes to mind, spend time during the next few weeks asking God to provide opportunities for you to supplement your worship by helping others.

ISAIAH 60:1–62:12

THE GLORY OF THE LORD

The City of the Lord	60:1–22
The Favor of the Lord	61:1–11
The Lord's New Relationship with Zion	62:1–12

Setting Up the Section

This section is a bright respite coming after a number of dark and sometimes even disturbing passages. Israel's recent past has been one of drifting away from God. Their immediate future will involve God's judgment on them as well as on numerous other nations. But their long-range future is something to look forward to. Isaiah has already written of God's servant who will make possible such a future. In this section he describes a number of wonderful outcomes that result from the work of the servant.

60:1–22

THE CITY OF THE LORD

The Old Testament describes a clear distinction between the Israelite people and everyone else. The Israelites are God's chosen people; the other nations are without God and in spiritual darkness. However, Isaiah has already explained that God will be close to His people so that they will be a light to the Gentiles (42:6–7).

Just as the Israelites are special to God, so is the area of Zion, near Jerusalem and the temple. In this section, Israel is instructed to prepare for a great influx of people from other nations to stream into Zion (60:1–3). The hostility between Israelite and Gentile will come to an end, and the grace of God can be embraced by those who had once been strangers to Zion. They, too, can count God's city as their city.

This must have been a difficult concept for the Israelite people to comprehend. Never before had Gentiles been considered to be in right relation with God without first becoming circumcised Israelites. But the image portrayed by the prophet is by no means threatening. God's fulfillment of His promises will somehow bring something much bigger than His people had previously known.

Not only are people coming to *visit* Zion; they are coming to contribute and to get involved with the good of the area. The wealth of other countries will flow into Zion. The mighty ships of Tarshish will bring back people and riches. Herds and flocks will be commonplace. Foreigners will willingly rebuild walls and make repairs. The anger that God felt toward His people at one time will be gone, replaced by His great compassion (60:4–10).

Critical Observation

In Isaiah's time, seeing camel caravans in the area (60:6) was the equivalent of someone today seeing a UPS truck in the neighborhood. It was a sign that something good was being delivered from a great distance.

It is likely that Isaiah is describing the church age or beyond, using the knowledge and worship idiom of his day. If so, think how challenging it would have been for a prophet from the eighth century BC to adequately describe a worship experience where Christ is head of a body of believers and the Holy Spirit is active in involving and empowering all believers, whether Israelite or Gentile.

Other indications suggest this scene comes from beyond the church age, after Christ has returned again. All the kings will either be supportive of Zion or destroyed (60:11–14). It will be a time of pride, joy, and great prosperity (60:15–17). Violence will be ended and peace will rule (60:17–18). In addition, there will be no more need of sun or moon because God Himself will provide everlasting light and glory (60:18–20).

This time, the people of God will never again lose the land. It might take centuries for this change to take place, but when the time comes, God will see it done quickly (60:21–22).

📖 61:1–11

THE FAVOR OF THE LORD

Some of the prophecies in these chapters seem to apply to a still-future time, but others are fulfilled with the first advent of Jesus. The opening verse of Isaiah 61 would have been good news at any time, of course. Most likely the *me* was first thought to be Isaiah, or it might have been believed to be the servant of the Lord that Isaiah had foretold. But centuries later all doubt is removed. This is the passage that Jesus reads in a Nazareth synagogue very early in His ministry. After reading the passage, He sits down and tells those in attendance: "Today this scripture is fulfilled in your hearing" (Luke 4:16–21 NIV).

Demystifying Isaiah

Isaiah's readers were probably a bit in the dark, being unable to fully understand his promises involving the coming of the Messiah. Similarly, when Jesus arrived on earth, He promised to return. Consequently, today's believers still remain a bit in the dark as to their expectations involving His second coming. In retrospect it appears that Isaiah addresses both events: the initial incarnation of Jesus and His subsequent return to earth. In places it is debatable as to which occasion the prophet is referring to.

As the kingdom of God is coming near, it will be Jesus who is appointed to preach good news to the poor, to nurture the brokenhearted, and to free those who are captive to darkness and sin. It will be a time of the Lord's favor, when the garments of mourning and the ashes of grief will be exchanged for a beautiful wardrobe of celebration to the praise of the great God.

This is the announcement of something solid—something strong, like a mighty oak of righteousness. Ancient ruins will have new life. Strangers and foreigners will find their place in the drama of bountiful blessing. Faithful people will serve as priests of the true and living God, supported by the wealth of many nations. Shame and dishonor will be replaced by sounds of everlasting joy that cannot be contained (61:2–7).

This period of rejoicing will not come about due to God's mere excusing of human wrongdoing. Human sin cannot be overlooked. God's day of vengeance, as Isaiah had previously noted, will still be very real (61:2). God's justice will not be preempted. The demands of God's law must be satisfied; to do less is unjust. The penalty for disobedience requires a just and holy atoning sacrifice. Jesus will be not only the prophet who announces the coming good news but also the sacrifice that satisfies divine justice and reconciles people to God.

God is clear that He not only loves justice but also hates iniquity. Yet after sin is atoned for, God will reward faithfulness and bless the people and their descendants (61:8–9). Those who respond to His forgiveness will experience great delight at a level best compared to a bride or groom preparing for a formal wedding ceremony. The Lord will continue to cause praise and righteousness to spring up like shoots in a fertile garden (61:10–11).

📖 **62:1–12**

THE LORD'S NEW RELATIONSHIP WITH ZION

God will not keep silent. Jerusalem and Zion had once displayed His glory but in time had fallen away and earned the nicknames such as "The Forsaken City" and "The Desolate Land" (62:4 NLT). God is not content for His cherished land to bear that reputation, so He will act to restore and rename Zion. The new names associated with the area will be *Hephzibah* ("My delight is in her") and *Beulah* ("Married"). The surrounding nations will no longer see Jerusalem as a wasteland but as a crown of splendor and a royal diadem. The land is portrayed as a bride, thrilled to approach her wedding, with God as the bridegroom (62:1–5).

In an interesting challenge, God exhorts the people not to rest until Jerusalem is again recognized as the pride of the earth. But more than that, God urges them to give *Him* no rest until that day. They are supposed to keep praying until He establishes Jerusalem in full. Like watchmen, they are supposed to be ever vigilant in their watchfulness and expectation (62:6–7).

Critical Observation

The prophets serve as a type of spiritual watchmen (see, for instance, Ezekiel 3:16–21; 33:1–9). They receive messages from the Lord and try to move the people in the actions of faith. But whether or not the people respond, the prophets are expected to proclaim the truth revealed by God.

Israel's history has involved many cycles of oppression by their enemies with periods of freedom interspersed. Foreigners had eaten their grain, drunk their wine, and killed their loved ones. But here is the promise that the day will come when the enemies of Jerusalem will never again take control of the city (62:8–9).

The people are to anticipate the arrival of their Savior. Their preparation will involve both work (clearing a pathway and building the road) and celebration (raising a banner). The nations (Gentiles) will be involved, too—not just the Jewish people. *All* believers will be deemed holy people and redeemed ones. Together they will give Zion new names (62:10–12).

Take It Home

It will be centuries before many of the prophecies of Isaiah are fully realized with the coming of Jesus Christ. And it has been additional centuries of waiting for Jesus' return for the fulfillment of even more of the promises in Isaiah. But it is as important as ever for God's people to act as watchmen, looking in anticipation for good news of sure deliverance. In the meantime, the evil one continues to prowl like a roaring lion, seeking someone to devour (1 Peter 5:8). On a scale of one (least) to ten (most), how good are you at patiently waiting for something to happen? How can you be more faithful in your watchful waiting, as you continue to anticipate the eventual return of the Savior?

ISAIAH 63:1–66:24
LOOKING AHEAD WITH HOPE

God Is Mighty to Save   63:1–64:12

The Futures of the Righteous and the Wicked   65:1–66:24

Setting Up the Section

As the book of Isaiah concludes with this section, the prophet reviews several of his ongoing themes, including God's vengeance, judgment, salvation, and redemption. But throughout it all is the assurance that Israel's future will be much better than its recent past, or even its present state. The Lord is in control of everything that is taking place, and His ultimate plan is to restore His people and renew close fellowship with them.

📖 63:1–64:12

GOD IS MIGHTY TO SAVE

The final section of Isaiah (60–66) is largely positive and optimistic as the prophet describes God's glory and the future redemption and restoration of Israel. But throughout his writing, he has included occasional references to God's vengeance (see 61:2), and this section opens with yet another such passage.

A figure is described coming from Edom, one of Israel's regular enemies to the south. (Bozrah [63:1] was one of Edom's key cities.) The figure identifies himself as the Lord. He is a solo warrior, stained with the blood of His vanquished enemies. His blood-spattered clothing is reminiscent of those who trod on grapes in a winepress. The Lord goes into battle alone because no one else can accomplish the victory. When no one else is capable, God is mighty to save (63:1–3). And the result of the battle is significant: It prepares the arrival of the year of God's redemption (63:4–6).

Critical Observation

The Lord's solo battle against Israel's enemies is symbolic of what His servant (the Messiah, Jesus Christ) will do later on the cross. One of the consequences of Jesus' atoning for the sins of humanity is the ultimate defeat of their spiritual enemies. It is a painful but victorious battle He endures alone.

Although the imagery is violent, the response is one of prayer and praise. It is the power of God that effects salvation and deliverance, as Isaiah (speaking for the nation) recalls in 63:7–64:12. God had repeatedly proven His faithfulness to Israel in the past. Their distress is His distress, so He had lifted them up and carried them for many centuries. Though they had rebelled against Him, He remains committed to them. His people had always needed Him, although sometimes they realized it more than others, as in the days of Moses when mighty waters parted before them and each day's food fell from heaven. On later occasions, they would remember such times and realize how far away they had drifted from God, causing them to cry out for Him (63:7–14).

This is another such occasion. The prophet asks God to look down from heaven and renew His zeal, power, tenderness, and compassion among His people. He also confesses the problem is that the people's hearts have become hardened. Those who had once lived in peace and joy will see their enemies trample down the temple. The appeal is to God's reputation: If the people who were called by His name are permanently overthrown by other powers, it will seem that God is helpless (63:15–19).

So as the praise/prayer continues, Isaiah asks God to deal with their enemies. God had always been in control, of course (64:4–5), but many times His government of all things had appeared to be subtler than His people would have preferred. By His continual providence, He works through countless ways to achieve His holy will, rarely drawing enough attention to Himself to be noticed. Isaiah prays for a clearer manifestation of God's presence. He wants God to come down from the heavens—much like a football team bursting through a paper banner to take the field. He wants mountains to tremble and nations to quiver (64:1–3).

Isaiah makes no attempt to downplay the sin of the people (64:5–7), yet he boldly continues and asks for God's forgiveness. Only God is the Father. Only God is the Potter who can make things right amid the broken lives of His clay vessels. Only God can change the land that has become a desert back into the flourishing garden it had been before. Only God can rebuild a city that has been left in ruins (64:8–12).

Although the people had sinned, they had not been utterly consumed. They have faith that God will still act. Although God may usually appear silent to human senses, the fact remains that He is still almighty and will speak clearly to those with ears to hear.

📖 65:1–66:24

THE FUTURES OF THE RIGHTEOUS AND THE WICKED

When God responds to Isaiah's prayer, He explains that He has not been as silent as the people think. He has revealed Himself, but the people weren't seeking Him. He had said, "Here I am," but the people had made no attempt to listen. He had extended His hands many times, but the people remained obstinate (65:1–2).

God knows why they had not heard Him. They had been too busily involved with pagan practices while defiantly disregarding their own laws. And while doing so, they had developed a smugly superior attitude. They were certainly religious, but they had completely lost touch with the one true God (65:3–5).

Demystifying Isaiah

Sitting among the graves (65:4) was often connected with practices of ancestor worship. People who tried to contact the dead would frequently spend time where the person was buried in the belief that the message would be clearer.

Theirs was not a spiritual slipup from giving in to temptation or being cleverly misled. No, they were provoking God to His face continually (65:3). So God will no longer be silent. However, when He breaks His silence, it will be in judgment (65:6–7).

But not everyone had defied God. A remnant of people continued to seek Him, so He will show mercy to them. Israel is compared to a cluster of grapes that is going bad. But before tossing out the entire bunch, the good ones will be picked and kept. The people had not valued God's prior promises to Abraham (63:16), but those assurances are still in effect. The line of Abraham's descendants through Jacob (Israel) will continue. Those who seek the Lord will continue to be blessed (65:8–11). The locations mentioned in 65:10 (Sharon and Achor) were both fertile and geographically pleasing areas. But the unrepentant people who had forsaken God will not share in the blessing. Because they followed pagan gods (Fortune and Destiny), they will be destined for destruction (65:11–12).

So one group of people will eat, drink, rejoice, and sing. Another group will go hungry and thirsty, experience shame, and wail in anguish (65:13–14). But after that separation is made, God's people begin to experience entirely new things. They get a new name, with their previous sins forgiven and forgotten (65:15–16). God will even create new heavens and a new earth. Jerusalem will be renewed, with no more weeping or early death (65:17–20).

Homes will be established with fruitful vineyards. The blessings of God will be so effective that work and child rearing are completely fulfilling pursuits. Even before a prayer leaves the people's lips, God will answer it. The dangers of nature are suspended as wolves and lambs, lions and oxen mingle together. The protection of the Lord will ensure complete security and satisfaction (65:21–25).

Throughout his entire writing, Isaiah has been faithfully relating what God has told and shown him, and he makes that point clear again as he closes. A prophet is nothing at all unless he is an authoritative spokesperson for God. So the Lord—the speaker in this section—has heaven for a throne and earth as a footstool. He has no need for people to build Him a house (temple). He does not go hungry, whether or not animals are burned on altars (66:1–3).

Worship ceremonies should have inspired the people to keep their hearts and minds focused on the Lord, but the Israelites had gradually lost their love for God. Yet they had continued to pray and sacrifice as mere rituals, and their actions became blatantly offensive to the Lord. What God desires from His people is not a thoughtless sacrifice but rather a contrite spirit and a sense of humility (66:2–3).

Demystifying Isaiah

In graphic terms, God points out that the people have lost any sense of distinguishing the holy from the unholy (66:3). Dogs and pigs are unclean animals, and the very thought of using them in a sacrifice should have been horrific. The people's sacrifices have become little more than animal abuse, and God deems their so-called devotion to Him the equivalent of idol worship.

Throughout Isaiah, God has made clear distinctions between the righteous and the wicked, and the prophet's writing concludes with yet another instance. Those who choose their own ways and delight in abominations will experience great dread as the judgment of God comes upon them. He has spoken, but they neither listen nor respond (66:3–4).

The Lord will be coming with fire and sword in His judgment. His fury and judgment will be widespread (66:15–16). Isaiah never attempts to downplay the severity of this horrible news. Yet the reality of God's furious judgment is offset by another reality.

Judgment is for those who reject God. But others will hear His Word and respond in fearful reverence. The obedient have been hated, mocked, and scorned by the wicked. Yet God has seen and heard it all, and He will mete out terrible punishment for the evil that has been done (66:5–6).

As for the faithful, they are in for a surprise. God will renew His land and His people, and it will be both sudden and delightful. It will be like the joy of having a child, but without the discomfort of labor pains. Zion will give birth to her children, and a new nation will be born in a day. The people will have Jerusalem as a mother (66:11–12). In addition, God Himself will provide the comfort that a mother offers her child (66:13). The righteous will be rewarded with new life and joyful hearts (66:14). The previous injustices of life are brought to an end with God's just and fair judgments.

When Jerusalem is reestablished, God's grace and mercy will extend to all nations (66:18). The righteous will be sent out to faraway lands, where people will hear of God's love and travel to Jerusalem to worship Him, bringing back with them others from Israel who have been relocated. Some of those from other nations will even become priests and temple workers (66:18–21).

Critical Observation

In His original call for Abraham to leave Ur and go to an as-yet-unrevealed land, God had promised that all peoples on earth will be blessed through the great nation that Abraham would become (Genesis 12:1–3). This final image in Isaiah describes the fulfillment of that promise.

God will establish new heavens, a new earth, and an enduring kingdom. With the unrighteous removed in the judgment of God, the righteous remnant of all humankind will bow down to worship the Lord in joy and peace (66:22–24).

Take It Home

The problem described in this section of Isaiah is one that has continued for centuries: Righteous people are mocked, manipulated, and abused by wicked people who wield power. Can you think of any similar examples in your own life and your associations with others? How can the words of Isaiah help inspire faith and perseverance (and maybe even peace) the next time you personally encounter such a problem?

JEREMIAH

INTRODUCTION TO JEREMIAH

The Old Testament book of Jeremiah is considered one of the canon's major prophets and is named after the book's author, the prophet Jeremiah. By word count, Jeremiah is actually the longest book of the Bible, with even more words than Psalms, making it the lengthiest prophetic work in the canon. It follows the work of another major prophet, the book of Isaiah, and precedes the short poetic work Lamentations.

AUTHOR

The book of Jeremiah is highly autobiographical, and more can be learned about the prophet from his work than from any other historical source. Jeremiah was a Judean, from the town of Anathoth, located about three miles outside of Judah's capital city, Jerusalem. We don't know when he was born, but he probably died in Egypt after the exile of 586 BC. His call to prophecy came around 627 BC. Jeremiah was assisted in compiling the book of Jeremiah by his scribe, Baruch, who is referenced several times in the work and accompanies Jeremiah on many of his journeys.

Jeremiah's writing is permeated with his personal feelings and the emotional turmoil he experiences as he ministers to the people of Judah. These are his fellow countrymen, and he is deeply burdened for their spiritual state. It is from the emotional overtones and many recorded laments that Jeremiah receives the nickname "the weeping prophet." The prophet is chosen by God to speak judgment to a people who have turned their backs on Him. For his troubles, Jeremiah is beaten, thrown in pits, placed in stocks, and publicly ridiculed. His own townspeople put out a contract on his life. Even his family members become his enemies. God had instructed Jeremiah to not take a wife—his ministry was to be too difficult to sustain a marriage and the coming judgment so severe as to preclude having a family. Jeremiah lives a life of loneliness and depression, and he certainly earns his nickname of "weeping prophet."

PURPOSE

As a prophet of God, Jeremiah is tasked with communicating God's message of coming judgment to the people of Judah, the southern kingdom, and more specifically the city of Jerusalem. The people had fallen into a pattern of idolatry, and it was going to destroy the nation if they did not soon repent of their sins and turn back to God. Jeremiah preaches a message of hope and repentance until it becomes evident that the people have no intention of repenting. Then his message becomes one of warning about God's coming judgment as he prophesies the invasion by a nation from the north that will destroy Jerusalem. Jeremiah's prophecies target all people groups in Judah: kings, priests, prophets, and ordinary townspeople. The book also includes a series of oracles to foreign nations, in which God voices judgment on them for their sins as well. It should be noted, however, that Jeremiah saw beyond the judgment to the restoration after the judgment. Chapters 30–33, in particular, reveal this restoration as a part of Jeremiah's task.

OCCASION

The book of Jeremiah is composed of writings and preachings throughout Jeremiah's ministry, which began in approximately 627 BC. The precise date the final work was compiled is unknown, but it can be estimated to be sometime after the last historical reference in the book, which extends beyond the release of King Jehoiachin from Babylonian captivity in 561 BC (52:31–34) and into the return of the Jewish exiles to Jerusalem after 586 BC in chapters 40–44. It is important to note that the events recorded in the book of Jeremiah do not unfold in chronological order. Jeremiah's prophecy takes place during the reigns of Judah's last five kings: Josiah, Jehoahaz, Jehoiakim, Jehoiachin, and Zedekiah. This is the time leading up to the Babylonian invasion of 586 BC, when Jerusalem falls. The historical events surrounding Jeremiah's prophecies are recorded in 2 Kings 21–25 and 2 Chronicles 33–36.

THEMES

A few main themes make up the bulk of Jeremiah's prophetic work. Chief among these is God's personal involvement with His people. Jeremiah's role as prophet is to communicate God's words to His people on His behalf. The reason such communication was necessary was because of the sin of idolatry the people had made a habit in their lives, the second main theme of the book. By sinning in such a manner, the people are guilty of breaking their covenant with God, established just after the Exodus. Another theme in Jeremiah's prophecies is the nation's repentance, or turning from idolatry back to God. Many of Jeremiah's prophecies also cover the theme of God's judgment, which was what the people could expect if they failed to repent and continued down the path of idolatry away from God. Ultimately, Jeremiah includes the theme of God's restoration of His people.

HISTORICAL CONTEXT

The superscription to the book of Jeremiah dates his prophecies from 627 BC (the thirteenth year of Josiah's reign) to 586 BC (the eleventh year of Zedekiah's reign), with chapters 39–44 extending beyond this time frame into the exilic period. Jeremiah's contemporary prophets were Ezekiel, Daniel, Zephaniah, and Habakkuk. The two national superpowers at that time were Egypt to the south and Assyria to the north. The northern kingdom, Israel, had been infiltrated and dispersed about one hundred years earlier, but Judah had survived through the faith of Hezekiah and Isaiah.

In 640 BC, Josiah becomes king of Judah at the age of eight and eventually begins to purge his country of idolatry, about the time that Jeremiah begins his ministry. In 622 BC, Josiah finds part of the Mosaic Law in the temple. These writings had not been seen or read for many years. Assyria was too distracted with her enemies, the Babylonians and the Medes, to control Josiah's reform. Later, in 609 BC, Josiah is defeated and killed when he tries to stop the Egyptians at Megiddo. He is succeeded by Jehoiakim and Zedekiah, his sons, and Zedekiah rules until the fall of Jerusalem in 586 BC.

Much of the prophecy of Jeremiah has to do with this political and spiritual climate. Judah was like a pawn in this major political upheaval, a mere buffer between Egypt and Assyria, and later between Egypt and Babylon. A major part of this book deals with Judah making unwise treaties with these nations to gain protection and deliverance. In the midst of this tumultuous time, God announces judgment, but He is still reaching out to save His people. During the ministry of Jeremiah, Babylon to the east begins its ascent and is on its way to becoming the next world power, replacing Assyria. Babylon becomes the invader from the north, mentioned several times in Jeremiah's prophecy. In 586 BC, Jeremiah's prophecy of Judah's downfall and the people's exile comes true when Babylon, under the reign of King Nebuchadnezzar, destroys Jerusalem.

CONTRIBUTION TO THE BIBLE

As part of the biblical canon, Jeremiah is considered one of the three major prophetic books. Although it is largely a prophetic work, the book of Jeremiah contains a wide variety of literary elements in addition to prophecy, including history, poetry, and narrative. The presence of all of these elements makes Jeremiah's work arguably one of the most compelling books of the canon. The book of Jeremiah has also been referred to as an anthology of Jeremiah's prophecies and an autobiographical account of the prophet's life.

OUTLINE

JEREMIAH 1:1–6:30

JEREMIAH'S CALL AND PURPOSE

Setting Up the Section

The book of Jeremiah begins with an introduction of the prophet and his call to prophesy to his own people as well as all nations. In the first section, which includes chapters 1–6, God sends His prophet to the people with a warning of impending judgment and punishment because of their lifestyle of sin. This judgment is based on the covenant God made with this nation and the consequences that would come to them if they failed to follow God's laws.

📖 1:1–19

JEREMIAH'S CALL AND CONFIRMATION

As is customary for the prophetic books of the Bible, the book of Jeremiah begins with a brief biographical introduction to the prophet (1:1–3). Jeremiah, for whom the book is named, was called to be a prophet of the Lord as a teenager in 627 BC, and ministered in that capacity for forty years. He grew up in Anathoth, a city about three miles northeast of Jerusalem. Anathoth was one of the Levitical cities, but there is no evidence that Jeremiah functioned as a priest. His name means "Yahweh loosens" (referring to the womb), or "Yahweh exalts."

Verses 4–19 detail Jeremiah's call to prophecy and the two initial visions he receives from the Lord, the first being evidence of his calling and the second a preview of the message the Lord will deliver to the Israelites through him. Verse 5 specifies God's personal involvement in Jeremiah's life. The verb *formed* means "to create or craft," like a potter (see chapter 18). God carefully designed and crafted Jeremiah in the belly of his mother. *Consecrated* means "to make holy, sanctify, set apart." Before Jeremiah came out of the womb, he was chosen to be on God's side, but he still has to be obedient. *Appoint* here is actually the word meaning "gave." Jeremiah was designed and set apart by God so that God could give his life away.

Jeremiah responds to God's call with reluctance in the same way that Moses answers God's call in Exodus 4 (1:6). Jeremiah feels inadequate because of his young age. He claims he doesn't know how to speak. But God encourages him with a series of promises, instructions, and signs (1:7–10).

Critical Observation

Deliver means to rescue, save, snatch away, or free from the firm grip of distress. God's promise of deliverance in verse 8 is one that is tested repeatedly throughout the book of Jeremiah. However, God never removes Jeremiah from the tough situations he finds himself in; rather God meets him in these situations and delivers him by bringing him into His company and under His hedge of protection.

Touch is important to God; He is not a distant being. God touches Jeremiah in order to put His words on his lips (1:9). He is very specific with Jeremiah about this message that he is to speak to Judah, Egypt, Assyria, and Babylon. God uses six verbs related to agricultural and architectural processes as images (1:10). Four of the verbs speak of demolition: to pluck up, to break down, to destroy, to overthrow. Two speak of renewal: to build and to plant (see Jeremiah 31:28). These images sum up the message Jeremiah is to deliver to the people of Israel—a message of great judgment, followed by renewal.

To confirm his calling, God reveals two visions to Jeremiah. The first sign is an almond branch (1:11). In the original language, the word *almond* sounds like the word that means *watch* in verse 12. The almond is the first tree to greet the spring. Everything seems dormant, but God is watching, waiting to open. When Jeremiah sees the blossom, he will anticipate the fulfillment of God's Word.

The second vision, a boiling, seething pot, is a sign that judgment will come from the north, from Babylon (1:13–15). A flash flood will engulf the land and burn everything it touches, and the armies of Babylon will use the old invasion route of the Assyrians to invade Judah. Although this vision is tied to Israel's political future, God's judgment is deeply theological. Judah commits the gravest of sins by burning sacrifices to other gods and bowing down to them (1:16).

God warns Jeremiah that because of his prophecies, all of Judah will fight him. But God also promises that he will prevail as long as he stands firm in God's message (1:17–19). God contrasts the fate of Jeremiah with the future of Jerusalem. The people will not be able to save Jerusalem, but Jeremiah will be as strong as a fortified city (see 1:8). God calls Jeremiah to ministry, but with it comes the reality that his life will be largely filled with pain, doubt, anxiety, depression, fear, anger, and hopelessness. He will be rejected, persecuted, mistreated, and misunderstood.

📖 2:1–4:31

GOD'S MESSAGE TO ISRAEL

Jeremiah uses metaphors to remind Israel of their former relationship with God, a literary trend that will continue throughout his prophetic work. The first is marriage (2:2). From God's perspective, the honeymoon phase was during the wilderness wandering, a time when Israel depended heavily on God. Another of Jeremiah's metaphors is harvest (2:3). Israel is the firstfruit of God's labor. Other fruit will come as other nations become God's people, but Israel was the first.

God brings a series of charges against Israel as if in a courtroom (2:4–13). The word *contend* means to bring a case against someone (2:9). The defendants are the house of Jacob and all the families of the house of Israel (2:4). The witnesses are heaven and earth (2:12).

Among the charges, God names two crimes: forgetting the Lord and walking after idols (2:5). God specifically mentions land (2:6–7) because He brought Israel out of Egypt through a land of desolation into a land of promise, but Israel defiled that land through their worship of Baal. The leaders and priests are just as guilty (2:8), which causes a breakdown in public life and collapse in public institutions.

Israel follows after things from which they cannot profit: the idols of the Canaanites (2:8, 11). God expresses the absurdity of idolatry. He questions why Israel would leave her faithful husband (2:5), notes that never before has a nation traded gods (2:10–11), and asks even the heavens to be appalled and shocked (2:12). Israel's choosing idols over God is like working tirelessly for dirty water instead of letting fresh water flow to her (2:13).

In verses 14–28, Jeremiah uses more metaphors to describe Israel's behavior. Slavery is the first. God had freed Israel to never enter slavery again (2:14), but Israel became slaves again because they were continually drawn into compromising and dangerous alliances with Egypt and Assyria. Memphis and Tahpanhes were cities in Egypt (2:16). The reference to the Nile (also called Shihor in some translations) and the Euphrates in verse 18 connects back to verse 13. Israel left her true protector to trust in changeable political alliances (2:19).

The second metaphor of a harlot, an unfaithful wife (2:20, 23, 32–33), is familiar in the Old Testament. Israel was God's adored bride, but she was unfaithful. She was a Baal worshipper, a cult preoccupied with fertility whose worship practices included prostitution. Within these same verses, God also compares Israel to a choice vine that becomes degenerate and wild (2:21). Israel's salvation could not be done by her own means, and God claims she is even in denial of her sin (2:22–23).

The she-camel (2:23–24) was known to be unreliable and easily disturbed, and even violent when in heat. She sniffs out the scent of the male and chases him instead of vice versa. Likewise, Israel is so intent on pursuing her lusts that the idols do not have to seek her—she finds them. God portrays Israel as having given up on trying to resist such behavior (2:25).

The metaphor of the thief who is exposed (2:26) applies not just to the common people of Israel but also its leaders, the kings, princes, priests, and prophets who also worship Baal. Ironically Israel can't even get its idolatry right. Trees represent female Canaanite deities; stone pillars represent male Canaanite deities. Israel should be ashamed, humiliated, and embarrassed (2:27–28).

Despite God's efforts to discipline Israel, she continues to misbehave (2:30). God describes her as a bride who forgot her wedding attire—the jewelry and sash that marked her as being married (2:32–33). Israel has become so accomplished at her harlotry that she teaches the wicked women her ways. The people's sins even include taking the lives of innocent people who have done no wrong (2:34).

Because Israel will not accept guilt (2:35), even though God has tried repeatedly to restore her (2:30), God responds the only way His justice allows: by promising judgment. Israel will be put to shame by Egypt and Assyria (2:36–37).

In chapter 3, God continues to expose Judah's idolatry and sin (3:1–11) but invites both Israel and Judah to return to Him (3:12–25). God leads with a rhetorical question about the law of marriage and divorce to continue the imagery of unfaithful Judah (3:1–2). The law prohibits the return of the first husband to his wife because, socially, the woman is considered defiled and rendered unacceptable. According to the law, then, God does not have to accept Judah if she chooses to turn back from her unfaithful ways. In other words, there is no provision in the law for God and Judah to be reconciled. As a result of her harlotry, Judah defiles and pollutes the land (3:3). Ironically, the people of Judah join the fertility cult so as to invoke blessing on their crops, but God withholds the spring rain. Judah's harlotry is more brazen than the Israelites'; they speak admiringly of God and continue to turn to Him even in the midst of their idolatry (3:4–5).

Jeremiah recounts the history of faithless Israel, the northern kingdom, in contrast to Judah, the southern kingdom (3:6–25). God judges Israel, and Assyria takes the northern kingdom into exile; God sends Israel away with a writ of divorce (3:6–8). Not only does Judah follow Israel's example, but they also feign allegiance to Yahweh (3:8–11). In this way, Judah's treachery is worse than Israel's.

But God assures hope to unfaithful Israel through an extraordinary invitation that goes against the earthly law (3:12–14). Israel's opportunity to return to God is not based on their becoming acceptable, but on God accepting them. The one condition, however, is that Israel has to acknowledge their guilt and sin (3:13).

Critical Observation

Return is the word used most often in the Old Testament to picture repentance. God extends His invitation to return several times in the following verses. The first invitation is to Israel, the northern tribes that have already been scattered by Assyria (3:12). (The assumption is that both north and south will return from exile.) The words *return* and *faithless* come from the same root word. They speak of moving in opposing directions, either toward or away from something. Literally, the text is saying, "turn to me, turning-away Israel" (3:12, 14, 22).

The word *master* (3:14) is a wordplay with Judah's idol, Baal. It is actually the same word. God is saying that He is the true *Baal*. Among the things God promises the people if they will return to Him are that leaders and rulers will not be unjust but will feed the people knowledge and understanding (3:15); the people will be cleansed from all idolatry; God's throne will no longer be an ark but a city (3:16–17); He will bring a remnant of Israel and Judah home to Zion (3:18); the sons of Abraham will be joined by all the nations; and they will inherit the most beautiful of all the nations (3:19).

The weeping heard in verse 21 is characteristic of Baal worship. Perhaps the hills were bare because Josiah destroyed their idols as part of his reform. Perhaps the people are weeping because they are saddened by the consequences of their sin. The people have loved wrongly and badly, and have done so from their youth (3:23–25).

The next part of God's invitation through His prophet Jeremiah highlights three more characteristics of repentance: remove all idols and cast off all other loyalties (4:1); swear obedience to the true, living God (4:2); and make hearts receptive to God's Word (4:3–4). The images of breaking up fallow ground and circumcising hearts are akin to the idea of confession and exposing one's sins before God. Fallow ground is unplowed, hard land. The crusty earth has to be ploughed so that the seed will germinate. Breaking up the ground is equivalent to not planting among thorns, since one function of plowing is the removal of noxious weeds that inhibit a fruitful harvest. Jeremiah warns that if such repentance does not occur, God will judge.

The next section (4:5–18) describes an invader from the north (Babylon) coming to destroy Judah and bringing God's judgment (4:5–6). The prophecy includes metaphor sprinkled with an exhortation for the people to repent and reminders of the reasons for the situation (4:7–9). Verse 10 includes one of several pictures of Jeremiah's anguish at this message.

Another metaphor emerges in verse 11 of a scorching wind. This wind is not the gentle breeze that aids the winnower at harvest time; rather it is a blast that will strike down everything in its path. The next verse reminds listeners why the judgment is certain (4:12), and another metaphor of threatening clouds foretells impending darkness and devastation (4:13). This section closes with another exhortation to repent and a reminder that this invasion is God's justice (4:15–18).

The final verses of this chapter (4:19–31) reflect Jeremiah's anguish and include descriptions that convey the utter devastation of the Lord's coming judgment. Verses 19–21 are an intercession from Jeremiah as he reflects on the gravity of the message he is delivering and the details of God's pending judgment.

Demystifying Jeremiah

Jeremiah's prayer of lament in verses 19–21 gives evidence as to why Jeremiah received the nickname "the weeping prophet." Jeremiah is intensely troubled. He is anxious and convulsing over what will happen to Jerusalem. Jeremiah's agony reflects God's agony. God lives with great heartache and turmoil. He doesn't like the idea of judgment, but He is committed to making a holy people. He is anxious for His people to obey Him, and He can't overlook their sin.

God resumes speaking in verse 22, when He claims His people no longer know Him. The next verses remind listeners of the condition of the universe before God formed creation out of chaos (4:23–26). The connection between these verses and Genesis 1 is unavoidable. Four times in the text God looks and sees the conditions of the universe prior to creation—the earth is formless and void; there is no light in the heavens; there is neither man nor bird. All that exists is barrenness and wilderness—the murky conditions of the beginning. The destruction of Jerusalem is likened to the creation coming undone and returning to a state of chaos. That which was proclaimed good by God is now evil. All of creation will pay the price for Judah's sin. God's comments also remind listeners of His actions in Noah's time, when He took disciplinary action but chose not to completely destroy creation (4:27–28). Some people try like harlots to allure the invaders, but neither sweet-talking nor cries of agony will ward off the attackers or change God's mind (4:30–31).

GOD'S JUSTICE

As with Abraham at Sodom (Genesis 18), Jeremiah unsuccessfully tries to find one righteous person to persuade God to spare Judah (5:1–2). The prophet comments on the truth of God's only remaining option: judgment in the face of Judah's refusal to repent (5:3–6). But God continues to argue that His people are following false gods and committing adultery against Him (5:7), and He uses the stallion metaphor to illustrate His point (5:8). In the Old Testament, horses were often associated with the powerful that assert their might and seize the initiative. Here the metaphor illustrates shameless self-assertion. Then in verse 9, God restates His need for justice: "Should I not punish them for this?" (NIV).

In verse 10, God again applies the image of Judah as a good vine that turns bad (see 2:21) and has to be dealt with. Regardless of how God's justice will be enacted, however, God reminds again (see 4:27) that He will not destroy the nation completely (5:10). He also restates the reasons for the discipline: idolatry and refusal, even among the prophets, to recognize sinful actions (5:11–13).

Critical Observation

The people's sins against God aren't limited to Judah. Israel has been treating God with irreverence and apathy for some time. As verse 12 notes, one of the lies spread by people from both the northern and southern kingdoms is that God won't judge them, even though He has proven otherwise in the lives of their ancestors. And as if that isn't bad enough, some of God's own prophets had taken on the same complacent spirit and no longer feared Him (5:13). But Jeremiah, a prophet who continues to speak God's truth, is quick to remind them that no one can escape God's judgment.

God has chosen Jeremiah to speak this harsh truth to the people (5:14). His judgment will come in the form of an invasion from a foreign nation (see Deuteronomy 28:49) that will overpower Judah, bring unfamiliar language and customs, and take everything Judah has for their own (5:15–17). It will be the nation of Babylon that fulfills this prophecy. Again, though, God reiterates through His prophet that He will not completely destroy Judah, only discipline them for their sins (5:18–19).

The final verses of this section (5:20–31) restate God's case for His discipline and judgment. God reminds His people, who have stopped listening to Him, of His nature and power: He is the Creator (5:20–22). Unlike the sea, God's people have stopped responding to His law, yet they still continue to enjoy the fruits of creation until God chooses to withhold them (5:22–25). The nation's sin is so bad that it entraps others (5:26). It leads to corruption that causes the innocent and powerless to suffer, and God responds with punishment (5:27–29). Kings, princes, prophets, and priests—all of them are out for their own gain, proclaiming peace where none exists. The final verse of this chapter blames Judah's leaders for turning away from God, allowing sin to affect the entire community and nation, and doing nothing to repent and restore justice (5:30–31).

It is interesting to note in the first verse of chapter 6 that Jeremiah belongs to the tribe of Benjamin, so he sends this particular warning of God's approaching justice to his own tribe. Again the warning is that God's justice is coming from the north to God's people (6:2–3). This appears to be a well-planned, premeditated attack on a nation that continues to defy God (6:4–7). God likens His power and ability to completely destroy them to a good harvester who picks all the grapes off a vine (6:8–9).

Demystifying Jeremiah

Jeremiah's role as prophet to God's people looks a lot like God's vinedresser metaphor. God uses Jeremiah to examine the state of the vine—the people of Israel—and attempt to glean whatever vines he can by spreading God's message of approaching justice. Before God brings His judgment down on the people, He is certain to make sure everyone has been warned and given a chance to repent and escape judgment. The state of the Israelites' souls is placed in the hands of God's vinedresser, Jeremiah (6:9).

The next section (6:10–21) both condemns Judah for not heeding Jeremiah's warnings and extends the reasons for God's judgment. The people are accused of not hearing the word of their Creator, and the Lord has had enough (6:10–11). Jeremiah prophesies specific details of what can be expected from the Babylonian invasion, and again God blames each of the citizens of Judea for the nation's collective sin (6:12–13). His accusations toward the religious leaders are telling: They perform rituals and chant words, but their spirits are not pure (6:14–15).

The Judeans had the chance to listen to the priests and prophets who spoke truth and return to the true God, but they refused and chose to continue sacrificing to God while living in a way that did not bring Him glory (6:16–20). God doesn't tolerate their hypocrisy, and Jeremiah proclaims that God's correction will have devastating consequences (6:21). Again, in effective oration, the invaders from the north are predicted and their actions detailed (6:22–23). Peace and normal life for the nation is quickly coming to an end (6:24–26).

Jeremiah's final metaphor of this chapter likens his search for people who do not deserve God's judgment to a metalworker searching for good, strong metal among weaker metal. The process includes hot fires stoked with bellows, and yet the metalworker burns and burns without finding any good metal (6:27–30).

Take It Home

The first six chapters of Jeremiah are filled with warnings about coming judgment, but the warnings are laced with opportunities for repentance. Jeremiah's message to the people of Judah starts out hopeful, but as will be seen as the book progresses, this hope and the opportunities for repentance begin to dwindle.

JEREMIAH 7:1–10:25

HYPOCRISY AND WRONG RELIGION

| The People's Sins | 7:1–8:3 |
| Responses to the Message | 8:4–10:25 |

Setting Up the Section

This section of the book of Jeremiah continues with the prophet's warnings to the nation. In this portion of prophecies, the warnings are more specifically geared toward the sins of hypocrisy and practicing false religion, and the consequences of those sins.

📖 7:1–8:3

THE PEOPLE'S SINS

Chapter 7 is from a sermon God instructs Jeremiah to deliver at the gate of the temple in Jerusalem (7:1–2). Chapter 26 refers to the same occasion or a similar one. This event could have been at the beginning of Jehoiakim's reign, when, despite Josiah's restoration of the temple and true worship, cultic practice was again the norm. The temple gate was the most sacred and public place in Jerusalem. Jeremiah's message would have been very upsetting to the establishment, but the nation's leaders were clearly at fault for leading the people down a path of such disobedience.

The first two commands of this chapter are designed to get the attention of the people of Judah (7:3–4). They are repeated twice, the second repetition filling out the first. To amend one's ways means make good, do well, do right, do what is pleasing. It is concerned with practical elements of everyday life: practicing justice, loving one's neighbor, caring for orphans and widows, and not walking after false gods (7:5–7). The people of Judah are failing to do what is right, and they are worshiping the wrong god to their own ruin. They are being selfish, exploiting people for their own gain. *Deceptive* means to deal falsely, or to lie, which is the opposite of being faithful and true. This word is used 113 times in the scriptures, one-third of which are found in the prophecy of Jeremiah (7:8).

The deception that the people are trusting in is the notion that they can do anything they want and then find safety in God's temple (7:9–11). God uses Jeremiah to remind the people that the presence of the Lord's temple didn't save the people of Shiloh, so they shouldn't expect it to save them either (7:12–14). Just as God exiled the Israelites in the northern kingdom, the people of Judah can expect the same fate if they don't repent and turn back to Him (7:15).

In verse 16, God speaks directly to Jeremiah, telling the prophet not to waste his time praying for God to forgive the sinful people of Judah because it is too late. Their doom is certain, and they have definitively rejected the possibility of repentance. This can seem confusing, because in this part of Jeremiah the oracles are not in chronological order. Some are from the period when repentance was possible, but others are from the period when repentance was no longer an option.

Demystifying Jeremiah

The Queen of Heaven in verse 18 is a reference to the worship of any number of Babylonian goddesses (see 44:17; see also 2 Kings 21; 23:4–14; Amos 5:26). This worship of these goddesses often appealed more to women, and one of the customs involved making cakes in the goddess's image (Jeremiah 7:18). The fact that people are making cakes in the privacy of their homes as a form of worship to a false god and then showing up at the temple in public to worship Yahweh was the ultimate form of hypocrisy.

Because of the people's attempts at worshiping more than one God, Jeremiah includes a warning emphasizing the importance of obedience instead of empty sacrifices (7:21–29). God knows the offerings are futile if the people's hearts aren't engaged in worshiping Him (7:21–22). What He cares about is obedience, as He told their ancestors when He led them out of slavery in Egypt (7:23–24). A key word in the text is the Hebrew word *shema*. It appears eight times in chapter 7 and is translated as both "listen" and "obey." God desires a simple obedience from a heart devoted to Him. But no matter how often God sends this message to His people, they reject Him and His messenger (7:25–28). God urges Jeremiah to mourn (including the act of cutting off his hair) because of Judah's grave sins (7:29).

Among Judah's sins is the practice of child sacrifice (7:30–31). The valley of Topheth, or Hinnom, was just outside the city of Jerusalem to the south. This was a garden of the Canaanites and later a center of Baal worship. Jeremiah says that the valley of Topheth will become the valley of slaughter and will be a dumping ground for all the bodies of people who die in the coming invasion (7:32). The word *topheth* rhymes with the Hebrew word for shame. The valley of the son of Hinnom will become Jerusalem's garbage dump, and the ruined land will be devoid of all joy (7:33–34).

Verses 1–3 of chapter 8 close out the sermon at the temple gate. Jeremiah prophesies that when the city is invaded, the intruders will dig up the graves of everyone from kings to laypeople. Proper burial is highly valued in the Jewish culture, and this is a further example of the disgrace and ruin that will come upon the land. Their disgraced remains will be exposed to those aspects of creation (sun, moon, stars) they worshiped. The final word leaves no comfort—death will be better than life for those who survive the Babylonian invasion (8:3).

RESPONSES TO THE MESSAGE

True wisdom involves being aware of the health of one's spiritual life and, if necessary, course correcting immediately. Judah hasn't been doing that (8:4–6). The metaphor of the birds knowing their migratory patterns implies again that people—who have much more intimate relationships with God—should know their role with God but do not (8:7).

Not even the ability to literally write down the law of the Lord is immune from corruption (8:8–9). The scribes take out their red markers and trim God's Word to what is acceptable to them. Their pen has changed truth into lies. Others reject God's Word completely. The people are caught in their own trap.

The wives and fields being gone is a reference to the coming exile, when the invaders will take what matters most to the leaders of the nation (8:10). The spiritual leaders are guilty of lying to the people about the gravity of their sins, a lie that should have brought about feelings of guilt and shame (8:11–12). However, the priests and prophets feel no guilt about their misleadings, and it is because of this lack of a repentant heart that God will punish them (8:12).

No harvest is available for the people, which means there are no resources for them (8:13). Being inside a city means protection inside the city walls, but once resources run out or spoil, the people will suffer from starvation and likely die (8:14). Peace is no longer an option, and the invaders from the north are coming as Jeremiah prophesied (8:15–16). In verse 17, God compares the coming destruction to poisonous snakes that can't be charmed—there is no way to resist the fatal strike.

Critical Observation

Chapters 8–10 of Jeremiah include a miscellany of prophecies in no chronological sequence. The key word linking all of the prophecies is *hokma*, which is translated "wisdom." The word *wisdom*, or *wise*, appears nine times in this portion of the text. It refers to the idea of being skilled in an activity. In the context of the kingdom of God, wisdom is the skill of living life rightly and beautifully. The opposite of wisdom is *foolishness*. This word occurs three times in chapter 10. It means brutish, dull-hearted, and unreceptive. Sin and idolatry are the context for this study of wisdom in contrast to foolishness.

In the closing section of chapter 8, Jeremiah grieves over Jerusalem's fate (8:18). Jeremiah laments that his people question God's presence and recalls God's warning about worshiping other gods (8:19). Because of their failure to repent, the people now face inevitable judgment (8:20). Jeremiah believes the people's salvation is within reach, that all they have to do is repent, but they are acting like salvation isn't possible. The metaphor he uses is "balm in Gilead," a reference to medicine from a neighboring town that the people were unable to get (8:21–22). This section closes with a picture of how much pain Jeremiah is in for his people: The weeping prophet wants his eyes to become never-ending streams of tears for their suffering (9:1).

Chapter 9 begins with several verses describing just how depraved Judah has become. Disgusted at the spiritually adulterous people around him, Jeremiah wishes for reprieve from his situation and his people (9:2). God describes His people as so treacherous that no one can rely on anyone, making trust and true community impossible (9:3–6). The only recourse God has is to refine (see 6:27–30) the people because of their deceitfulness and their actions toward one another (9:7–9). The punishment will be so thorough that even nature will mourn, and only jackals—animals that thrive in the wasteland—will be left (9:10–11).

The people of Judah find themselves in this situation because they did not choose wisely. Verses 12–16 highlight characteristics of what would have been the wiser choice for them. The people should have chosen to keep to God's law and listen to His voice instead of worshiping the idols of other nations (9:13–14). Because they chose poorly, they are subjected to bad food and water (9:15; 23:15) and will be destroyed as a community (9:16).

God tells the people to prepare not only the current generation for mourning but also the following generation, because the losses will be so great and continuous (9:17–21). The massiveness of the destruction is seen in the prophecy that corpses will not even be buried, an indicator of how completely incapacitated and humiliated Judah will be—they won't even be able to bury their own dead (9:22).

The theme of wisdom appears again: True wisdom means not trusting in human and earthly resources (9:23). Evidence of following the true God will not be seen in earthly treasures but in loving-kindness, justice, and righteousness (9:24).

Verses 25–26 emphasize God's thoughts about religious actions versus true righteousness; even people who think they are of the true religion (the circumcised) are no better than those who are not, and all will be punished equally (9:25–26).

Critical Observation

The first sixteen verses of chapter 10 are a satirical contrast of God and idols. Such writing is not uncommon to the Old Testament, and the prophet Isaiah often employs similar rhetoric in his writing (Isaiah 44:9–20). Later in the book of Jeremiah, the prophet reiterates verses 12–16 (51:15–19).

True wisdom recognizes the difference between the impotence of idols and the majesty of God (10:1–16). The first part of this section emphasizes how idols are made by people (10:3–5, 8–9, 11, 14–15), but the true God is like no other (10:6–7, 10, 12–13, 16). The words *delusion* (10:3, 8) and *worthless* (10:15) are the same word that is used in 2:5. The word means vanity, emptiness, vapor, nothingness.

Chapter 10 closes with a lament about the coming destruction of Jerusalem. The prophecy describes the people as having bundles, warning them to be prepared to leave because the exile is at hand (10:17). The last four verses in this chapter show Jeremiah's distress, but he uses the language of nomadic shepherds to indicate that he speaks of the pain of loss of civilization and community for all the people of Judah (10:19–21). The judgment is coming from the north as prophesied (10:22), and the judgment is a necessary action from God to restore righteousness to His people (10:23–25).

Take It Home

Chapter 10 closes with Jeremiah's prayer that God will pour out His wrath on all of the people of Judah. Jeremiah no longer seeks God's mercy and forgiveness for the people, because the prophet knows that the people have regressed so far into their sin that they deserve the punishment of God's justice.

JEREMIAH 11:1–13:27

JUDAH'S BREAKING OF GOD'S COVENANT

Jeremiah Dialogues with God   11:1–12:17
The Warnings Begin   13:1–27

Setting Up the Section

Chapters 11–13 of Jeremiah detail the consequences in store for Judah as a result of having broken God's covenant. The covenant being referred to is the Mosaic Covenant, in which God promised to bless the Israelites if they obeyed Him. Their idolatry is a severe disobedience and breach of the covenant. This section also includes two of Jeremiah's laments about the gravity of the nation's sin and God's pending judgment.

📖 **11:1–12:17**

JEREMIAH DIALOGUES WITH GOD

Jeremiah communicates to the people that they have broken the covenant between them and God that was made with Moses on Mount Sinai. This covenant was to be foundational to the people and dependent upon them hearing and obeying the words of the true God (11:1–8). Instead, they have chosen to follow other gods, and their punishment is now inescapable (11:9–11). God predicts that the people will not find refuge from this destruction in Him and will thus turn to the idols for help (11:12). Verse 13 helps the listener understand how pervasive this idol worship had become (11:13; see 3:24). God insists that the people are so far gone in their sin that having Jeremiah pray for them or performing rituals in the temple will not restore the people's hearts (11:14–15). Jeremiah had previously likened Judah's state to a diseased or wide vine that emerged from a healthy or chosen vine, and that image is revisited here. In this case, the formerly productive tree will be burned down in judgment (11:16–17).

Critical Observation

In verse 16, Jeremiah reminds the people that God had called Judah to be "a thriving olive tree with fruit beautiful in form" (NIV). The psalmist also likens God's chosen people to an olive tree (Psalm 52:8–9). For the psalmist, such imagery describes total trust in and worship of God, which is what God desires from His people.

Throughout the book of Jeremiah thus far, the listener has heard Jeremiah's emotional and spiritual anguish over the condition of his people, but this is the first time the listener understands the physical danger Jeremiah is in because of his prophecies. Jeremiah knows of this danger because God reveals it to him (11:18). The tree in verse 19 refers to Jeremiah, and the fruit is the prophetic message he delivers. The people want Jeremiah dead so that they don't have to listen to his warnings any longer. Jeremiah asks God for justice, since he is working on God's behalf (11:20). God reassures Jeremiah, but not before it is revealed that these plotters are from Jeremiah's own hometown, which means that the plotters are possibly family members or priests (11:21–23).

Demystifying Jeremiah

God responds to Jeremiah's plea for protection from his enemies by declaring that He (God) will punish them. The punishment God declares is death by the sword to the young men and famine to the harassers' children (11:22). By killing their descendents, God makes sure no one will remember Jeremiah's enemies, just as the enemies want to make sure no one remembers the prophet.

Jeremiah hears God's reassurance, but he has more to say to God and more questions for Him. Through prayer, the prophet enters God's metaphorical courtroom, carrying a complaint against God. Desiring to plead his case and discuss matters of justice, he appeals to God's righteous and just character (12:1). Jeremiah's statements here capture age-old feelings and questions: Why do good things happen to bad people (12:2)? *Prosper* means to succeed, to be able to accomplish what is intended. *At ease* means to be secure, unconcerned, undisturbed, carefree, and at rest. It is disturbing to Jeremiah that these people are wicked and yet successful. And because God withholds any sense of justice, they are allowed to grow and even produce fruit. Jeremiah argues that their success is no accident.

But there is also an implied corollary complaint. Why is God allowing this to happen to people who love Him? Not only is Jeremiah outraged that the wicked prosper, but he can't understand why righteous people like him are suffering. He argues that God's name is on the lips of the wicked but is far from their minds. The wicked believe God is indifferent, meaning they can get away with their evil ways because He will not see what they actually do. Jeremiah reminds God that he is doing everything that is expected of him and that God knows and sees that this is true. The prophet wonders why there are not more signs of blessing in his life. It seems the scales of justice are out of balance (12:3–4).

God's first response indicates that things will get worse for Jeremiah before they get better (12:5–6). Second, God says to consider His grief (12:7–13). God laments over His people, His inheritance. Judah roared at God like a lion (12:8). She became like a speckled bird of prey whose plumage attracted the jealousy of other nations (12:9). The shepherds of Judah—the invading army—ruined God's vineyard (12:10). God's gift of a land flowing with milk and honey became desolate, and no one cared (12:11). So God has no choice. He forsakes and abandons Judah in the same way that she has forsaken Him (12:7). God gives His people over to their enemy (12:12–13; 46:6–7). In the midst of Jeremiah's confusion and anger, God is saying, "Have you ever thought about how I feel?" The words *my* and *me* are repeated a dozen times. Jeremiah's tragedy is God's tragedy in miniature. Jeremiah's rejection by his family parallels the nation's rejection of God.

Third, God tells Jeremiah to consider the extended view (12:14–17). *Uproot* is the key word (used five times) in these verses (12:14–15, 17). The word describes a plant being pulled out of the ground. It takes us back to God's mission statement to Jeremiah (1:10). God says that He will take care of every nation in its turn (12:16–17). He will uproot Judah and all of her enemies—Syria, Ammon, Moab, even Babylon. Then God will show compassion and bring Judah back. Not only will He have compassion on Judah, but He will have compassion on all the other nations and bring back each to His inheritance and to His land. If these former enemies who led Judah into idolatry learn the ways of God, then God will build them up. But if they do not listen, they will be destroyed. Every nation will be treated just like Judah.

📖 13:1–27

THE WARNINGS BEGIN

First, Jeremiah is commanded to buy a belt—or waistcloth, waistband (13:1). The linen belt was an intimate piece of apparel that clung closely to the body of the wearer and served as a thigh-length underskirt. Jeremiah obeys and puts the article of clothing around his waist (13:2). Second, Jeremiah is commanded to go to the Euphrates and hide the belt in the crevice of a rock (13:3–4). This would have meant a very long journey for Jeremiah, and the people of Judah may have been aware of his actions. In any case, Jeremiah obeys the Word of God (13:5). Third, Jeremiah is commanded to retrieve the belt (13:6). Once again he obeys, only to find that the belt is ruined (13:7). It is totally worthless and useless and no longer fits to accomplish its intended purpose.

Critical Observation

The *linen belt* in verses 1–11 is the first of several symbols and acts Jeremiah uses as a tangible way to portray God's message. There is a loose structure to the description of Jeremiah's symbolic act. The Lord issues three commands to Jeremiah, and after each command Jeremiah acts in obedience to what he is told. Following the three commands, there are three statements from God, which match the three commands, in reverse order.

The belt is a spiritual symbol of Judah's relationship to God. God gives a word that matches each action in reverse order. First, God says He will destroy the pride of Judah and Jerusalem in the same way the belt was destroyed.

The words *ruin* and *destroy* (13:7, 9) are the same. Second, God points out the reason for Judah's destruction: She refuses to listen to His Word. The people "follow the stubbornness of their hearts" (13:10 NIV). This is a favorite phrase of Jeremiah to describe the sin of Judah—he uses it eight times in this book. The people had ignored and neglected their relationship with God in the same way that Jeremiah had neglected the belt, and the people of Judah had hidden themselves from God in the same way that Jeremiah had hidden the belt. Third, God says that His original intent for Judah is that His people cling to Him in the same way that a belt clings to a man's waist (13:11). This last statement in verse 11 matches Jeremiah's first action in verse 2. The word *cling*, meaning to adhere or be glued together, describes the kind of dependent relationship that God intends His people to have with Him (see Genesis 2:24).

Verses 12–14 tell a parable of wine jars. There are several references to wine in the book of Jeremiah. The wine jar (or wineskin) referred to here is a large earthenware container, and it symbolizes the people of Judah (13:12). These jars are to be filled with wine, but God adds a twist: The inhabitants of Judah will be filled not with wine, but with drunkenness, which is symbolic of their addiction to idolatry (13:13). In the coming time of crisis, the inhabitants of Judah will be so inebriated by their sin that they will destroy one another like wine jars that collide and break, and God will not intervene to stop them (13:14).

Verses 15–17 are a warning against arrogance. It is impossible to miss the imagery of verse 16: darkness, dusk, deep darkness, and gloom. The figure of dusky mountains can refer to either twilight or dawn and of travelers on a mountain path overtaken by the gathering gloom before reaching their destination. *Deep darkness* refers to overwhelming darkness or grief. *Gloom* speaks of heavy clouds or thick darkness. The increasing darkness is a metaphor for the judgment coming upon Judah for her pride and haughtiness. The exhortation is that the light is fading, but there is still hope if Judah will listen to God. Exalting God and giving Him glory will dispel the darkness. Notice the agony of the poet in 13:17. If Judah doesn't listen, Jeremiah will be overcome with grief.

Demystifying Jeremiah

The king of verse 18 is King Jehoiachin of Judah, mentioned several times elsewhere in conjunction with the queen mother Nehushta. Jeremiah prophesies events in the year 597 BC, when Jehoiachin and Nehushta are banished into Babylonian exile with the first group of Jews.

The king and queen mother are commanded to take a low seat because their beautiful crown has been removed (13:18). They are used to privilege, but will become exiles. They might seek refuge, but Jeremiah warns that all the cities of the Negev, the area to the south of Jerusalem, are barricaded so that fleeing fugitives will not be able to find a place to hide (13:19). Dethroned kingship is a metaphor for judgment. God opposes the proud: Those who exalt themselves will be brought down. No one is exempt from the Lord's hand of judgment and discipline, which is coming from the north as prophesied (13:20).

The final picture is a lament over the disgrace to come upon Jerusalem (13:21–27). The judgment will come by the hands of the Babylonians, the very people whom Judah courted as companions, and it will be painful, like the pains of labor (13:21). In the midst of their sin, the people have forgotten God and resorted to falsehood (13:22). And worst of all, they have no hope of change. Judah can no more change its evil ways than the Ethiopian the color of his skin or the leopard its spots (13:23). Babylon will scatter the people like straw in the wind, a reference to exile, because of their behavior (13:24, 26–27).

Take It Home

Not even Jeremiah's warnings of captivity by an intruder and exile to a foreign nation can motivate the people of Judah to repent of their sins and return to worshiping Yahweh alone. Even though verse 23 records God's words that the people are beyond hope to change, the fact that Jeremiah continues to prophesy, in this case, means they still have the opportunity to repent. As the book continues, however, it becomes increasingly evident that the people do not intend to change.

JEREMIAH 14:1–20:18

GOD'S WARNINGS

Setting Up the Section

The next section of Jeremiah begins with a detailed prophecy of the drought and famine that will accompany the coming invasions. From there, it moves into a series of confessions from Jeremiah about his personal hardships as they relate to his ministry among the people of Judah, followed by another section of metaphors symbolizing the nation's relationship with God. This section ends with an example of the persecution Jeremiah faces because of the message he delivers. Interspersed throughout are additional warnings against Judah's idolatry and their need to repent to avoid the coming judgment.

📄 14:1–15:9

WARNINGS AND RESPONSE

A drought will come over Judah that is so powerful that all classes of people, all animals, and even the earth will be affected and cry out in anguish (14:1–6). Jeremiah connects this drought to God's judgment and intercedes with God on behalf of the people, appealing to his own sense of justice despite the nation's sinful ways, asking God not to forsake them (14:7–9). God rejects Jeremiah's plea, citing the people's consequences for their own wandering feet. Although they may be feeling pain and remorse now, based on their history it is likely they will wander away again (14:10).

God tells Jeremiah to stop interceding for the people, because by this point no amount of intercession or sacrifice will change God's mind about the judgment due the nation (14:11–12). Jeremiah points out that other prophets are testifying to the people about peace and being spared, but God calls them false and insists that both the false prophets and the people listening to them will face His justice (14:13–16).

God and Jeremiah continue to dialogue for several verses about Judah's situation. Jeremiah again weeps over the physical and spiritual state of the nation (14:17). His tears represent the hopelessness of the people of Judah if they don't repent of their sins. Death is all around Jeremiah, both in cities and in the country as a result of the famine and the diseases that accompany it (14:18). Seeing the death and destruction around him, Jeremiah questions God's rejection of the nation (14:19). Jeremiah confesses the sins of the nation and pleads with God that He not forget the covenant He made with their ancestors (14:20–21). In the midst of pleading with God, Jeremiah admits that God alone controls creation and has the power to make it rain; the false idols the people worship can do nothing to remedy the situation (14:22).

God's wrath continues to burn against the nation of Judah. Even though Jeremiah's generation attempts to repent, God's justice requires that the flagrant sins of past generations be vindicated. Perhaps Moses, who interceded for the nation at the giving of the law—can appeal to God for mercy. Or Samuel, who interceded for Israel as they cried for a king. But God knew that the repentant words from Jeremiah were no match for the hearts of the people, and He says neither Moses nor Samuel can make Him change His mind (15:1). Verse 2 describes the four different judgments that people will face: death, the sword, famine, and captivity. Then verse 3 lists the four different destroyers that will bring about this judgment: the sword, dogs, birds, and beasts. Judah will not avoid God's discipline and will become an object of horror and a symbol of God's wrath among the nations (15:4). Though God holds us all accountable for our actions, the Bible consistently claims that teachers and leaders are to be more accountable. In the case of Manasseh, the son of King Hezekiah, his evil exceeds even that of the nations that God appointed to destroy (15:4–6).

Critical Observation

The reign of King Manasseh, and the evilness he orchestrates and allows, is described in 2 Kings 21:1–16. Manasseh is described as being the most corrupt king of Judah, which is ironic considering he was the son of one of the most righteous—King Hezekiah. Verse 4 implies that the nation continues to follow in Manasseh's evil ways long after his reign. As the perpetrator of the people's wickedness, Manasseh is responsible for God's coming judgment.

The winnowing fork (15:7) was a primitive pitchfork used to scoop up the harvest and pitch it into the air, allowing the wind to blow away the lighter chaff while the heavier wheat remained. In this case, the winnowing fork has a dual purpose of separating the ungodly and inflicting death. God threatens to make widows as numerous as the sands of the sea (15:8). The reference to a widow of seven sons is likely a symbolic reference to the city of Jerusalem itself, a proud reference to the past glory of the nation of Israel (15:9). The glory of the nation is soon to be destroyed, as God does not relent in His quest to punish His beloved.

15:10–17:27

GOD DIALOGUES WITH JEREMIAH

Jeremiah is perplexed by Israel's condemnation of him. In spite of the fact that he is not a lender or a borrower, he is deemed to be a contentious leader; he pities his own mother for giving birth to one who has become such a curse upon the name of Israel (15:10). But God speaks words of comfort (15:11). God's reference to iron and bronze from the north is symbolic of the prophetic sweep of force by Nebuchadnezzar's armies as they converged upon Jerusalem to steal away Israel's dreams of glory (15:12). As with any domination of one nation over another, the buildings are leveled and the temple is destroyed. The people are humiliated and carried off to Babylon to serve their new king and his many pagan gods (15:13–14).

Verses 15-21 of Jeremiah's lament can be divided into four parts: address, petition, statement of innocence, and complaint. Jeremiah begins with an address to God (15:15). Although his words can seem to be words of trust, given his distress at his current situation it is more likely that they are a statement of reproach. Jeremiah claims that God knows what is happening to him but isn't doing anything about it. The prophet cannot believe that God is allowing him to suffer even though he is innocent.

Jeremiah's petition consists of four imperatives: remember, take notice, take vengeance, and do not take away (15:15). He is not asking for revenge but for justice and lawfulness. Expressing his anxiety about death, he fears being taken away. He tells God not to be too patient, too slow to anger. He wants God to unleash His judgment against Judah right away. Second, Jeremiah reminds God that he has filled his stomach with God's words (15:16). He is probably referring to the discovery of the law in the temple during Josiah's reign. When God's Word was found, Jeremiah devoured it. He is satisfied with God's Word in the same way we are satisfied by a delicious meal. But now, being called by God's name is like swallowing a bitter pill.

Third, Jeremiah reminds God that he has not gone the way of the crowd (15:17). Literally, he doesn't sit in the secret counsel of the partygoers. He sits alone because God's hand is upon him. He is filled with anger at the sin of Judah and perhaps his own afflictions. Finally the prophet issues his complaint and voices the deepest emotions of his soul (15:18). The prophet's pain is without end. Similar statements are often used in conjunction with sin and ensuing judgment. Sickness follows sin. But Jeremiah's pain prompts him to ask another penetrating question: "Will you be to me like a deceptive brook, like a spring that fails?" (15:18 NIV). Jeremiah paints a picture of a dried-up creek that fills with water only when it rains. In chapter 2, Jeremiah says that God is a fountain of living water, but that living water seems to have quit flowing. God no longer seems reliable to Jeremiah, whose focus has shifted off of the wicked nation and onto his own suffering. Jeremiah wonders if God has lied to him when He promised to be with him during his ministry. He is claiming that God is the cause of his misery.

What does God have to say to Jeremiah? Before He gives an encouraging word, He gives a bracing word (15:19). The first part of God's reply is a condition. God tells Jeremiah that he must repent of his attitude. In effect, God asks Jeremiah to do the same thing that he is urging upon the people of Judah. The prophet is pouring out his heart to God, but his words are tinged with self-pity and blame. God tells him to turn away from that. God wants Jeremiah to be faithful to his calling. To "extract the precious from the worthless" (15:19 NASB) refers back to chapter 6, when God tells the prophet to be an assayer and remove the dross of idolatry from the precious metals. The second part of God's response is more reassuring (15:20-21). These words reiterate what God tells Jeremiah in chapter 1, when Jeremiah was a young boy. God reaffirms that He is with him. Three powerful verbs—save, deliver, and redeem—describe God's presence. God is reliable and will stand by His messenger.

Demystifying Jeremiah

Verses 16:1–9 include another object lesson in which Jeremiah's life situation mimics the state of the nation. God uses Jeremiah's call to celibacy and bachelorhood as a picture of the relationship that is ending between God and the people, and the sorrow and loneliness that the people will soon experience.

Chapter 16 opens with the instructions that Jeremiah is not to marry or have children (16:1–2). Not only has God promised to sentence the people to lives of captivity in another land, but He also prophesies horrible deaths that many will face (16:3–5). Those who die, both great and small, will be left in the streets to be scavenged by the vultures in the air and the roaming beasts on the ground (16:6).

Families will not be allowed to honor the dead. The days of children playing and villages celebrating are long gone. In God's judgment, He is going to take from Israel its voice of gladness (16:8–9). By obeying God's instruction to avoid participating in mourning or in celebratory events, Jeremiah's life is a model for the people of how God feels toward them.

God prepares Jeremiah for the questions he will field in response to the gravity of his message (16:10). His answer is to be that Israel's forefathers forsook Him and turned to wooden idols. But the idolatry didn't stop with their ancestors; the people are also guilty of their own sins (16:11–12). God prophesies to them that they will be cast out of their sacred promised land, a land they have now inhabited for almost a thousand years (16:13). At each Passover meal, they speak of how God delivered them from Egypt into the land of milk and honey. Now, their history will be modified to say that God also delivered them from the lands of the north (16:14–15). Despite their sins, He will once again show them mercy. But that is in the distant future. First, they must pay the price for their wickedness, and the price has doubled: They now must pay the penalty for their forefathers and for their own iniquities (16:16–18).

The coming judgment is again offset by the promise of hope, restoration, and future blessing. Jeremiah prophesies a season when people from all nations will return to God, realize the absurdity of their idolatrous practices, and recognize God's power and might (16:19–21).

The next section, 17:1–18, is a continuation of the theme of Judah's sin and guilt as recounted in chapter 16. In Jeremiah 17, readers encounter the word *heart* four times, beginning in 17:1, when God insists Judah's sins are written clearly and permanently on their hearts. This sin is also written on items of their idolatrous worship (17:1–3). Again it is prophesied that punishment through exile and slavery is forthcoming (17:4).

Verses 5–8 set out a remarkable contrast between the person who places his or her trust in people and the person who trusts in God. Those who trust in human flesh and human strength are cursed (17:5–6). These words are addressed primarily to the people of the covenant. At the time, the nation was surrounded by superpowers—Egypt, Assyria, and the rising Babylon. Judah kept trying to make alliances with these nations, especially Egypt, to achieve national security. But God warns that the person who trusts in the strength and power of mankind and whose heart turns away from God will be cursed.

Such an individual will lead a dry, lonely, isolated, withered life. This is revealed in the three metaphors in verse 6: a bush in the desert, stony wastes in the wilderness, and a land of salt without inhabitants.

On the contrary, the one who trusts in God is wise and will see benefit from that trust. People who trust in the Lord turn their hearts toward Him. They not only trust *in* the Lord; their trust *is* the Lord. The curse of verse 5 is contrasted with blessing (17:7). The person who trusts in the Lord and turns his heart toward God will be like a tree that will always have a supply of water (17:8). He will not fear when the heat comes; he will not be anxious in times of drought. The leaves of this tree will be green and healthy. It will bear fruit and yield a blessing to others.

Critical Observation

The tree of verse 8 is in contrast to the desert shrub of verse 6. One is destined for life, the other for death. One has a root system that brings nourishment, the other does not. One has adequate water, the other does not. One sees the good, the other does not. One has no fear or anxiety, the other is always desperate. Those who place their trust in mankind to find security will find their source of comfort lacking. The only way to avoid these things is to trust completely in the Lord.

Misplaced trust is symptomatic of a deeper problem, the source of which God reveals in the next verses. The human heart is naturally bent toward sin, and it is the root of not only misplaced trust but every other way in which people sin against God (17:9). While people may not be able to discern why their hearts produce the type of deceit they do, God can discern and will judge according to the state of one's heart (17:10). The proverb of verse 11 is a reminder to all who hear it that coming upon wealth by unjust means does not earn the favor or blessing of God.

In 17:12–13 we are reminded of Jeremiah 2:13. God's throne is His place of honor. In the sanctuary, people worship and draw near to Him. He is the source of blessing, hope, and life. He alone has living water. But the people of Judah are deceitful. They turn away from God to place their trust in human resources, forsaking the fountain of living water. Their hearts therefore become dry and hard.

Jeremiah reflects on the condition of his own heart and makes his petition to God (17:14–18). He realizes that he needs God's help to cure his heart and deliver him from his sins (17:14). The people of Judah are coming to Jeremiah with questions about why the things he has prophesied have yet to come true (17:15). But Jeremiah knows that his prophecies are valid because they are not self-serving, and he has not shied away from proclaiming the Word of God (17:16). Although Jeremiah's trust in God wavers at times, in these verses he displays complete trust that God will not turn away from him (17:17). He also prays that God will act justly on his persecutors but keep him from harm (17:18).

In 17:19–27, Jeremiah delivers a sermon about the importance of keeping the Sabbath. Notice the repeated mention of the word *gate* in this passage. The public gate is the entryway into the city (17:19–20). It is from one of the gates to the city that Jeremiah preaches against breaking the Sabbath. The people have forgotten the Sabbath and are carrying on with their daily and weekly activities (17:21–23).

Notice the essence of God's instruction: If the people obey the Sabbath and cease their activities in order to honor God, then He will continue the Davidic reign and Jerusalem's strength as a city (17:24–26). But if the people refuse to obey this command and continue working on the Sabbath, then God will kindle a fire at the very gates of the city, and the palaces of Jerusalem will be destroyed (17:24–27). God uses the Babylonians to fulfill this promise to Jeremiah's generation.

📖 18:1–19:15

METAPHORS

God takes Jeremiah to the potter's house for His next message (18:1–2). Jeremiah observes the potter spinning a pot on the wheel, but then the craftsman takes the clay and crushes it and begins again (18:3–4). It is obvious that something isn't right with the pot; it has a design defect of some kind. However, the potter doesn't throw out the clay; he makes it into another vessel, working the lump until it meets his specifications. Most pots require several attempts before the potter is pleased. The meaning behind this scene at the potter's house is obvious to Jeremiah: God is the potter, and the house of Israel is the clay, but the clay has become spoiled through idolatry and sin (18:5–6). The people of Judah have forsaken God to pursue worthless and empty idols. As a result, the pot is not turning out the way God had intended. It has spiritual flaws and character defects. So He will crush the clay and begin again, remolding and reshaping His people.

God speaks a word of judgment on Judah in verses 7–12. God informs the people of Judah that their response is very important in determining His actions. While He may plan to destroy a nation, if that nation repents, He will relent or possibly change His mind (18:7–8). Likewise, if God plans on doing good to a nation but that nation does evil, then God will send judgment instead of blessing (18:9–10).

God informs Judah that He is planning on calamity, but His exhortation is to repent—it is not too late to change God's course of action (18:11). Sadly, the people of Judah have no intention of changing their evil ways (18:12). They want to follow their own plans and are unwilling to turn from the stubbornness of their evil hearts.

God continues speaking through Jeremiah, asking the people rhetorical questions and making statements reminiscent of chapter 2. God asks how His people could have forgotten their true identity, but He also laments that they have done so by worshiping idols and other gods (18:13–15). He will leave them to endure His absence during their judgment (18:16–17).

The people attempt to discredit Jeremiah's message from God and plot to kill him (18:18). Although the threat is only verbal, Jeremiah has had enough. The lament that ends this chapter is different from the previous ones (see 11:18–23; 15:10–21; 17:14–18). Jeremiah had interceded for the people before, but this time he asks God to do justice, honor His loyalty, and punish the people (18:19–23).

The metaphor of the potter and the clay resumes with God having Jeremiah buy a piece of pottery (19:1). The first several verses of chapter 19 again illustrate the people's idolatrous sins against God and the judgment that God will enact as punishment (19:2–9). After these reminders of the message God has sent through Jeremiah, God has Jeremiah go out in front of the elders and some senior priests and break the pottery he purchased (19:10). Judah has become so hardened there is nothing left for God to do but to break the pot (19:11–15). A spoiled vessel can be reshaped on the potter's wheel (18:1–6), but once it becomes hardened it is beyond reconstruction and is fit only for breaking. Jeremiah's act is a sign proclaiming that just as he broke the pot, so God will destroy Jerusalem and its inhabitants.

📖 20:1–18

PERSECUTION OF JEREMIAH

Jeremiah's prophecy in 19:1–15 foretells a grave future for the people of Judah. When one of the religious leaders, Pashhur, hears what Jeremiah has said, he has Jeremiah physically abused (20:1–2). Upon his release, Jeremiah renames Pashhur *Magor-missabib*, which means "terror on every side," an indicator of how Judah will soon be surrounded by Babylonian invaders (20:3–6). Jeremiah's message from God is clear: Because the religious leaders no longer recognize the words of the true God, judgment will come harshly and completely.

Verses 7–18 of chapter 20 include another of Jeremiah's laments to God. The cost to Jeremiah for his boldness is great, and his confidence gives way to despair.

Verses 7–10 set out Jeremiah's complaint. On one level, he complains about his unjust treatment. He is the object of public ridicule, a laughingstock. He is mocked, and his obedience has resulted in reproach and derision all day long (20:7–8).

Jeremiah trusts God, but in these verses he admits feeling like God has taken advantage of him. The prophet feels he is in a no-win situation. If he speaks God's word of judgment, he is the object of mockery, ridicule, and hostility. If he doesn't speak, then God's Word is like a burning fire in his body that he is unable to contain (20:9).

The remainder of this chapter includes an assertion of trust, a petition, and a doxology (20:11–18), though it ends with a surprising twist. Jeremiah feels God's presence, its meaning for his survival, and the success of God's mission through him (20:11–12). Verses 11–12 are a genuine assertion of trust, but they are also an attempt to motivate God. Jeremiah asks God to be God and be just (20:12). In asking God to take care of his enemies, Jeremiah seeks from God the very vengeance his enemies seek for him. He feels that he has proven his case and that God should act accordingly.

Critical Observation

The key word in verses 7–12 (used four times) is *prevail*, which means "to overcome." In verse 7, God prevails over Jeremiah. In verse 9, Jeremiah cannot prevail in holding in God's Word. In verse 10, Jeremiah's enemies are looking to prevail. But in verse 11, it is determined that Jeremiah's enemies will *not* be able to prevail.

Jeremiah's lamenting is broken for a moment by a doxology (20:13). The prophet gives way to praise and breaks into song. How can Jeremiah sing in the midst of his afflictions? Jeremiah states that he sings because God delivers the soul of the *needy* one. This word is used to describe the destitute, the day laborers of the ancient world who were completely dependent on others for their survival. What is delivered is the needy soul, not the needy body. In the midst of afflictions people must depend on God.

The odd juxtaposition of texts is intriguing. One would expect the lament to end with the doxology, but it continues and intensifies in 20:14–18. This represents the tension of the life of faith. The themes of lament and praise do not cancel each other out; both are honest emotions. Jeremiah had previously complained about his unjust treatment from people and his unfair treatment from God. But here, in a cry of hopelessness and futility, he complains about his very existence. He wishes he had never been born. He begins verse 14 with a curse, which is not addressed to God or to anyone in particular. It is a curse for the day he was born and the man who brought the news of his birth (20:15). He wishes there had been no announcement and no celebration. As he has been rejected as a messenger of God's Word, so he would reject this messenger (20:16). He wishes that this messenger would suffer the agony of God's wrath, like the inhabitants of Sodom and Gomorrah, because he did not kill Jeremiah in the womb (20:17). He wishes that the womb had been his grave (20:18).

Take It Home

The reason Jeremiah laments so deeply lies in the question of verse 18: Why was I ever born if all I experience is trouble and sorrow? What a contrast to God's statement to Jeremiah in his youth, when He promised He knew Jeremiah in his mother's womb (1:5). At one time Jeremiah had hope, purpose, and direction, but his life has become a series of afflictions. Sorrow is the only thing he knows.

JEREMIAH 21:1–25:38

MESSAGES ABOUT LEADERS AND CAPTIVITY

Kings	21:1–23:8
Prophets	23:9–40
Captivity	24:1–25:38

Setting Up the Section

Previously in the book of Jeremiah, the prophet delivered a series of prophecies detailing the future judgment by God on the nation of Judah. In chapter 21, Jeremiah transitions into more specific prophecies directed at Judah's kings and spiritual leaders. This section of prophecies culminates in the prophecy of the seventy years of Babylonian captivity (Jeremiah 25).

📖 21:1–23:8

KINGS

Chapters 21 through the beginning of 23 address the corrupt kings of Judah and pronounce the judgment that all will suffer because of their ungodly rule. These oracles detail some of God's qualities necessary for right leadership.

Critical Observation

The following is a brief review of Judah's kings during Jeremiah's prophetic reign. King Josiah began his reign over Judah in 640 BC, when he was only eight years old. His rule ended in 609 BC, following his death in a battle with the Egyptians. During this great king's reign, a part of the law was found in the temple, and Josiah led a reform movement to encourage his people to turn back to God. Josiah and Jeremiah, partners in this endeavor, sought to restore true worship in Judah. Following the death of Josiah, things quickly deteriorated. Prior to the fall of Jerusalem, Josiah was succeeded by four kings: Jehoahaz, Jehoiakim, Jehoiachin, and Zedekiah. However, none of these kings sought the Lord with all their heart. Zedekiah was installed as a puppet king by Nebuchadnezzar, king of Babylon, in 597 BC. Zedekiah continually tried to overthrow the rule of Babylon, leading to the destruction of Jerusalem in 587 BC.

With Babylon threatening, Zedekiah sends a messenger to Jeremiah in hopes of a word from the Lord that will give him assurance and confidence against Nebuchadnezzar (21:1–2). Instead, he receives a word of judgment: The God who did wonderful things for Israel in the Exodus will now stand against the nation (21:3–6). Furthermore, Nebuchadnezzar will kill Zedekiah and the rest of the war's survivors (21:7). It will be up to the people whether they stay in the city and die or are exiled to Babylon to live (21:8–9). God makes His plan for Jerusalem and its inhabitants clear—it will be overtaken by the enemy and burned (21:10). Following the word of judgment there is an exhortation for the king (21:11–14). The king is supposed to uphold justice and righteousness and the rights of the poor, the needy, and the afflicted. He is to uphold the integrity of the court system so that innocent blood will not be shed.

God sends Jeremiah directly to the palace to deliver clear directions to the nation's leaders: dispense justice and righteousness and care for the socially weak and powerless (22:1–3). The king's conduct is decisive for the wealth or woe of the entire social system. If he acts according to God's command, then his royal power will be guaranteed (22:4). If he fails to do so, the house of David will be terminated (22:5).

God contrasts two images to explain the result of both following His instructions and choosing to disobey them. The kingdom will be plush and fertile if the leaders obey, or it will be like a desert if they do not (22:6–7). The result depends on what the leaders choose to do (22:8–9). But the royal house forsakes God's covenant, and a description of the judgment to come follows in the text.

The first king to succeed Josiah is his son Jehoahaz, but his reign lasts only three short months before he is exiled to Egypt (22:10–12). The second king to follow Josiah is Jehoiakim, another of his sons (22:13–19). Jehoiakim fights against Babylon and enters into a dangerous political exploitation that evokes the anger of that nation. His chief sin is conducting his business without justice and righteousness (22:13, 17). He uses people and exploits the poor to surround himself with comfort and luxury (22:14). Jeremiah contrasts him with his father Josiah, who was just and righteous (22:15–16). After his death, Jehoiakim will be treated like a donkey because of his sin (22:18–19). There will be no funeral and no expression of grief or lament (22:19).

The next verses remind listeners of how God has continually tried to reach out to leaders, but they refuse to listen. They prosper and live in comfort (the mention of "cedar" refers to houses made of the finest timber available), but their judgment is forthcoming (22:20–23).

The third king to follow Josiah is Jehoiachin (also called Coniah and Jeconiah), the son of Jehoiakim and grandson of Josiah (22:24–30). Jehoiachin begins his rule in 598 BC, but he is exiled to Babylon in 597, reaping the curse of his father's corrupt politics. God claims that if Jehoiachin was a ring on His hand, He would pull it off, ending the relationship between the two of them and, consequently, the house of David (22:24). Ultimately this separation happens when Jehoiachin is exiled (22:25–26). With his exile, the royal line comes to an end and the land is forfeited (22:26–29). Although Jehoiachin has several sons, he might as well have been childless since none of his descendants will succeed him as king (22:30). These four kings not only forsake the Lord; they are also guilty of not doing the things they were supposed to do according to the law and the Word of God. These leaders of Judah exalted themselves and exploited their people for their own personal gain.

The leaders of Judah are supposed to care for their people, as a shepherd cares for his flock. However, the kings and other leaders of Jeremiah's day were not good shepherds. Rather, they destroyed and scattered the sheep of God's pasture (10:21; 23:1–2). Their leadership falls to such inappropriate levels that God Himself has to intervene (23:3–4).

Verses 5–6 are a word of hope in the midst of great sorrow: Jeremiah prophesies that God will bring a leader who will exemplify godly leadership and rule in stark contrast to the four kings previously mentioned (23:5–6). In the midst of failure, the Lord makes a promise to Judah: One is coming who will sit on the throne of David and rule with wisdom, justice, and righteousness (23:5). The phrase "a righteous branch" is one that in the Old Testament signals the idea of a Messiah who will fulfill the salvation God intended for His people. The name of this coming king will be *The Lord Our Righteousness*, and under his rule, both the northern and southern kingdoms will prosper in peace and safety (23:6). Future generations will not celebrate God as the One who brought His people out of Egypt—the way God was described previously in Jeremiah—but as the God who restored His people after their destruction by the northern invaders (23:7–8).

23:9-40

PROPHETS

In verse 9 of chapter 23, the focus shifts from the kings to the prophets of Judah, the nation's spiritual leaders. These men occupy a very important position in Israel. They speak in the name of the Lord. As seen in 18:18, Judah's prophets are proclaiming one thing about the spiritual state of the nation, but it conflicts with the words of the Lord that Jeremiah delivered. Jeremiah will be vindicated in time, but in these verses he has a painful message for the brothers who share his vocation: Their bad leadership has fostered immorality in the nation (23:9–10). Both prophet and priest are polluted, literally twisted and defiled, and the holy temple has become the site of sexually oriented fertility rites (23:11). Following other patterns throughout Jeremiah, at the end of this statement of sin, God assures He will judge the false prophets (23:12).

False prophets strengthen the hands of evildoers rather than turn people back from sin (23:13–14). They are more concerned about aligning themselves with people than they are with proclaiming God's truth. The comparison with Samaria in verse 13 is designed to shame the southern prophets. Judah is worse than Samaria because the idolatry of Jerusalem is more shameful than the Baal worship of Samaria. In fact, the evil so repulses God that in His eyes Judah is no different than Sodom and Gomorrah (23:14). God must punish the prophets the same way He said He would in 9:15 (23:15). The sin of the false prophets is so severe because they use God's name to speak a message that is not His (23:16, 25, 30). False prophets draw their messages from their own imaginations, literally, their own hearts. The content of their message is filled with lies and false assurances (23:17).

How are the people to respond to the false prophets? God commands the people to simply not listen to them (23:16). (He also provides criteria for judging the veracity of a prophet in Deuteronomy 13 and 18.) Counterfeit spiritual leaders lead people into futility, into things that are worthless and profitless. They claim authority from God, but they have no authority (23:18–22). The scene in verses 18–22 describes a council meeting that takes place behind closed doors. The false prophet is like a journalist who speculates over some matter of government which is discussed in private. The true prophet is the government spokesman who emerges from the meeting to speak with the ruler's authority. Had the false prophets sat in the council, they would have preached repentance and sought to turn people from their evil ways. Therefore these false prophets have no mission, no message, and no authority. Contrary to what the false prophets teach, God is capable of being both active in the midst of the people to save and protect them, and holy and just in His dealing with sin (23:23–24).

God's response to the false prophets in Judah is clear: He is against all false prophets and anyone who misrepresents what He has said in His Word (23:25). One characteristic of false prophets God points out is that they simply repeat what they hear each other say (23:26–27). False prophets contrast to the Word of the Lord like straw to grain (23:28). The idle dreams and self-induced visions of the false prophets are like straw—they lack substance. But the Word of God is like grain: it has a nourishing quality. The Word of God is powerful, like a refining fire that burns within us. It is also like a sledgehammer that shatters selfish dreams and stubborn hearts (23:29). God wants His people to know His rejection of those who speak falsely in His name (23:30–32).

In the closing verses of chapter 23, God addresses the false prophets' telling of oracles. He reiterates that anyone proclaiming a message in God's name that isn't from God will face His punishment (23:34). With so many people claiming to be delivering oracles from God, no one is able to discern His true message, so God tells Jeremiah to stop using the common phrase, "the oracle of the LORD," in order to discern the true prophets from the false (23:35–37). God's word to Jeremiah concerning the false prophets closes with the assurance that all false prophets will be cast from God's presence in exile and shame (23:38–40).

📄 24:1–25:38

CAPTIVITY

The opening verses of chapter 24 reveal that some captivity has taken place. Sources show that this captivity refers to Nebuchadnezzar taking captives in 597 BC (24:1). Jeremiah sees a new image that serves as a message from God to His people: a basket with good and bad figs (24:2–3). The good figs are the people who have been promised restoration, and the bad figs are the ones who have not (24:4–10). The frightening message the fig image symbolizes is that for some people, even exile and imprisonment will not return them to God.

The fourth year of Jehoiakim is 605 BC (25:1). By this time, Jeremiah has been a prophet for twenty-three years, so many people have had the opportunity to hear him (25:2–3). Jeremiah has been consistent in the prophecies he has delivered against the people's bad behaviors and their worship of false gods, but they still refused to listen (25:4–7). Because of their disobedience, God will send Babylonian forces, led by King Nebuchadnezzar, to invade Jerusalem from the north (25:9). This event is the fulfillment of the invasion Jeremiah has been prophesying about repeatedly throughout the book of Jeremiah. The destruction to the city will be so bad that significant life events, such as marriages and harvests, will cease (25:10).

Verse 11 contains the prophecy that the exile will last for seventy years. After the seventy years of punishment, God will also punish the captors and other nations for the same sins for which Judah is guilty (25:12). Conquering another nation and exploiting their citizens for labor is not just treatment, so even though God uses the invading nations for His purpose, their actions will not go unpunished (25:13–14).

In verses 15–38, God invokes another image to symbolize His judgment of nations other than Judah—a cup filled with God's wrath (25:15). God instructs Jeremiah to take the cup to a list of nations for them to consume (25:15–26). Unlike the clay pots Jeremiah broke in front of Judah's leaders (19:10), this vision most likely symbolizes the message God wants to send the sinful nations. The message of drinking to excess is interesting, almost as if there is a connection between the leaders being unable to control themselves and the punishment that they have brought upon themselves (25:16, 27). God makes it clear, though, that the choice to drink is no longer theirs; because of their past actions, God will force them to drink so that they will face the fullness of His wrath (25:28–29). The next verses depict God roaring and stomping people like grapes and expanding His judgment to all humankind (25:30–32). Again, the destruction will be so great that it will be impossible to bury the dead, much less mourn for them (25:33). This judgment appears to be particularly centered on leaders, those who are shepherding their followers (25:34–36).

Demystifying Jeremiah

In Jeremiah 3:15, God endows Judah with a special gift when He says, "I will give you shepherds after my own heart, who will lead you with knowledge and understanding" (NIV). The shepherds of Jeremiah 25, however, are not the same. These shepherds are the leaders of the offending nations. Beginning with the Egyptian empire and then the Assyrian empire and then the Babylonian empire, these nations surrounded Judah and sought her destruction. God invites humiliation upon these proud, arrogant leaders. Their penalty is watching the Lord destroy the shepherd's pasture—the land, agriculture, and prosperity they sought.

The final two verses of chapter 25 remind people of how dependent they are on God: It is His decision when people experience peace or horror (25:37–38).

Take It Home

Chapter 25 marks the end of Jeremiah's prophetic warnings of God's judgment against the people of Judah, which began in chapter 2. By this point, the Babylonian invasion has taken place, and God's judgment is being poured out on the nation.

JEREMIAH 26:1–29:32

JEREMIAH AND JUDAH DIALOGUE

Setting Up the Section

The central theme of chapters 26–29 is dealing with the false prophets who continue to speak lies in the name of God. The focus shifts from what Jeremiah is proclaiming to how the people react to his prophecies. Jeremiah represents the genuine prophet, and the false prophets are contrasted to him and his message.

📖 **26:1–24**

JUDAH RESPONDS TO JEREMIAH

God has Jeremiah again take His message to the public and the religious leaders by returning to preach in the temple courtyard (26:1–2). God wants the people to hear and repent and avoid the judgment He will impose if they do not turn away from their sin (26:3). God repeats all the ways He has tried to communicate with His people: through His own voice, through His law, and through prophets He sent again and again (26:4–5). The message here is clear: God wants peace and a relationship with His people, and He will wait until the last resort to punish them back into obedience. If they refuse to listen, then they will endure a fate like a city before them: Shiloh (26:6).

Critical Observation

Shiloh was the first place of worship in the land. This was where the tent of meeting was set up and the inheritance divided. The yearly feast was held there, and the ark of the covenant resided there. Shiloh was where Hannah went to pray for a son and where Eli and his two evil sons, Hophni and Phinehas, were priests. Because of the evil of Hophni and Phinehas and the people who followed them, the Philistines defeated the Israelites, captured the ark, and God's glory departed from Israel. Shiloh lost its significance when the ark of the covenant was captured by the Philistines; and later, the temple there was destroyed (1 Samuel 4:18; Psalm 78:60).

Jeremiah prophesies the same fate for Jerusalem (26:6). Judah possessed the temple, God's dwelling place. But this very temple is destroyed in 587 BC. The second temple is destroyed in AD 70. God's message to His people again and again is that their protection is not bought through religious activity. God will destroy even His most holy places—Shiloh, Jerusalem, Eden—in order to discipline His people and restore His relationship with them.

Verse 7 is powerful in its specificity. The message Jeremiah delivers to them is, in their minds, sacrilegious and insulting, and demands his death (26:8). All who gather—leaders included—agree that Jeremiah should die for his message (26:9–11). Jeremiah responds by saying that their salvation from this prophecy depends on their choice to repent and behave differently, a repeated theme throughout Jeremiah's sermons (26:12–13). But regardless of their choice, Jeremiah insists that the message he speaks is God's, not his own (26:14–15). With this perspective, the people change their minds—leaders included—and acknowledge that Jeremiah does speak on behalf of God (26:16). The elders remind the people of similar prophecies in the past when God demanded they repent or face judgment. Sometimes the people listened and repented (26:17–19), and sometimes they killed the prophet (26:20–23). In this case, the wisdom of the elders prevails. They choose to look at the history of how God has acted in the past, and they decide that repentance is God's wish and message to His people. Jeremiah's life is spared (26:24).

📖 27:1–28:17

JEREMIAH RESPONDS TO JUDAH

In chapter 27, Jeremiah receives another word from the Lord, this time instructing him to speak out against the nations that are planning to fight back against Nebuchadnezzar's invading forces (27:1). Jeremiah's message to the people is this: Get ready to put yourselves into submission. God has Jeremiah use yet another visual aid to symbolize His message, this time, a yoke (27:2). The prophet is commanded to wear a yoke around his neck, similar to the wooden yokes worn by oxen. Jeremiah becomes a walking illustration of the bondage the nations will endure by coming under the yoke of Nebuchadnezzar.

The audience for this message is a group of kings from surrounding nations who are trying to come up with a way to respond to Nebuchadnezzar (27:3). Despite their desire to resist the invasion, God makes it clear that He has orchestrated Nebuchadnezzar's attack and is delivering His people over to Babylon (27:4–8). God again warns against false prophets. Anyone who proclaims the nations will avoid Nebuchadnezzar's rule is lying, and any leader who believes those falsehoods will be completely destroyed (27:9–10). Those who obediently submit to Babylon's yoke will serve Nebuchadnezzar for a time but will survive the period of servitude (27:11).

Jeremiah reiterates God's message to Judah's king Zedekiah, because it is imperative that he hears the true message over the false prophets (27:12). Verses 13–15 repeat the distinction between the messages both sets of prophets are preaching. Jeremiah has the same warning against false prophets for the priests to hear (27:16). Some have been saying that items from the temple seized by the invaders will quickly be restored to the people (27:16–18). These items are valuable—not to mention sacred—and will be scattered in the chaos of invasion and enslavement. However, God declares that even the remaining temple relics will not join the people where they are in exile (27:19–20). Perhaps this separation of the people from their objects associated with God, their holy relics, is part of their discipline and chastisement. The true prophets, God says, will not be worried about what is left behind and where those relics end up; eventually all will be restored to Jerusalem (27:21–22).

Chapter 28 breaks from the prophecies to recount a specific confrontation Jeremiah has with a false prophet by the name of Hananiah (28:1). Hananiah claims to hear God saying the captivity will last only two years instead of seventy, and he speaks specifically about the same two things in Jeremiah's last prophecy: yokes and vessels (28:2–4). However, Hananiah's prophecy directly contradicts Jeremiah's, and Hananiah is sharing it publicly with all the religious leaders (28:1, 5). Jeremiah supports Hananiah graciously, saying he wishes Hananiah's words were true, but they aren't. Jeremiah restates the prophecy he received from God (28:6–9). Hananiah reacts fiercely, taking the yoke off Jeremiah's neck and breaking it (28:10). He is not backing off his false prophecy (28:11). Notice that Jeremiah does not resist, protest, or make a scene. But later, he receives a rebuke from God to pass on to Hananiah. He may have broken the yokes of wood, but his angry outburst has severe consequences: yokes of iron (28:12–13). God insists that Judah's captivity will continue (28:14). Jeremiah condemns Hananiah's prophecy as lies (28:15). He also predicts that Hananiah will die, and his word is fulfilled later that year (28:16–17).

📄 29:1–32

JEREMIAH'S LETTER TO THE CAPTIVES

This segment of the book of Jeremiah ends with what is commonly called "The Letter to the Exiles." The text is a letter Jeremiah composed in Jerusalem and sent to the leaders and the people in exile in Babylon (29:1–3). These are, again, God's words to His people through Jeremiah (29:4). Some have explained this is how Jeremiah instructed the exiled Judeans to live in the midst of their captivity.

God wants His people to make families and become members of their communities, seeking God's will for the city of Babylon and its welfare (29:5–7). Apparently, Babylon has its own fair share of false prophets who claim to speak for God. Like other false prophets, they, too, claim that the exile will not last long, and this perspective causes discontent among the Israelites (29:8–9). Those who believe the captivity will only last two years instead of seventy are only living from day to day and are not making commitments or plans. They don't plant and they don't build.

God's message for them is clear and powerful: The exile will be seventy years, but He has plans to be with them during that time (29:10–11). Although their exile and captivity is a result of their own sinful ways, they still belong to God, and He sends them this word of hope through His prophet. The Israelites will survive their situation, and their relationship with God will be restored, allowing them to once again communicate with Him and hear His voice (29:12–13).

Demystifying Jeremiah

Repeatedly in Jeremiah's earlier sermons, God voices His frustrations that the people of Judah no longer hear their Creator and that they turn to false gods and prophets for guidance and worship. God now tells the people that eventually they will again hear and respond to Him, and He will restore to them everything they lost (29:14). In the midst of God's judgment and punishment, the mercy and redemption He planned for His people is slowly coming into view.

In Babylon, the people are susceptible to false prophets promising them quicker relief from the seventy-year punishment God promised (29:15). God reminds them again not to listen to them. Further, God explains that the people who remain in Judea, who were not taken captive, will still face punishment (29:16–19). The punishment declared for them is familiar: sword, famine, and plague (see 14:12). God names two particular false prophets who are misleading the exiles in Babylon: Zedekiah and Ahab. Jeremiah prophesies that both will die, and the memories of their fate will live on in the lives of the exiles as a reminder of their blasphemy and sin (29:20–23).

Jeremiah writes a letter to the false prophet Shemaiah, as recorded in verses 24–28. Shemaiah had written letters to the people still in Jerusalem and to Zephaniah the priest (29:25). As part of his letter to Zephaniah, he reminded the priest that part of his role included taking prisoner every madman who acts like a prophet (29:26). At the root of Shemaiah's question to the priest is why the prophet Jeremiah has not yet been taken prisoner, since he is continuing to deliver God's messages to the exiles—messages that contradict those of Shemaiah and other false prophets (29:27–28). Zephaniah reads this letter to Jeremiah (29:29).

After he hears Shemaiah's letter, Jeremiah writes to the exiles again, this time delivering God's message of condemnation against Shemaiah for his attack on God's prophet (29:30–31). As punishment for his false prophecies against God, neither Shemaiah nor any of his descendants will live to experience God's mercy and the return from the exile (29:32).

Take It Home

As is evident from chapters 26–29, speaking falsely in the name of the Lord has dire consequences. As part of his role as one of God's true prophets, Jeremiah is tasked with delivering messages of warning not just to the people who sin against God but also to those who lead the people awry.

JEREMIAH 30:1–33:26

THE BOOK OF CONSOLATION

Some Restored and Saved   30:1–31:26
The Future   31:27–33:26

Setting Up the Section

Hundreds of years after enslavement in Egypt, the children of God are once again experiencing captivity in another land. As Judah braces itself for seventy years of anguish, the God of comfort wants His children to know that there is hope. Chapters 30–33 include text that reiterates the hope of a coming day when normal life will return for God's people—Judah and Israel—and they will return to activities like building and planting. While in exile, Judah can read these words and find comfort in the midst of barrenness. This is why Jeremiah 30–33 is often referred to as the Book of Comfort.

📄 30:1–31:26

SOME RESTORED AND SAVED

Two phrases in chapters 29–33 merit close examination. The first is "days are coming" (30:3; 31:27, 31, 38; 33:14–15), and the second is "restore the fortunes" (repeated eight times: 29:14; 30:3, 18; 31:23; 32:44; 33:7, 11, 26). God announces that days are coming and with them the promise of restoration. To restore the fortunes literally means, "to turn the turning." The implication is that everything will be reversed. Restoration is certain. Sin, exile, barrenness, and even the exiles' desire to turn away from God will be reversed. God wants His people to know this is coming and instructs Jeremiah not only to tell the people but also to write the message down (30:1–3).

Immediately following God's proclamation of a coming day when fortunes will be restored, there is a word of judgment (30:4–7). The coming Day of the Lord is a day of both salvation and judgment. It is going to be a day of glory for some but one of dire judgment for others. This is what Jeremiah means by the "time of trouble for Jacob" (30:7 NIV): There will be intense pain, pictured here by a strong man buckled over like a woman in childbirth (30:6). But God's people will be saved; exile in Babylon is not the final chapter of their story. For God's people, judgment precedes salvation.

Several images describe this salvation for Judah. There will be a new freedom from captivity and slavery. The God who put the yoke of Babylon on Judah's neck will remove it (30:8). Instead of worshiping Baal, Judah will serve the Lord her God (30:9). Notice that she will serve David her king as well. Instead of the unrest described in verse 5, there will be a new peace (30:10). A new security will replace the fear and dread of verse 5—the presence and protection of the Lord (30:11). *Discipline* means "to chasten or correct, instilling values and norms of conduct by verbal means or, after the fact, by rebuke or even physical chastisement." God chastens Judah while they are in Babylon, a necessary punishment to cleanse them from their sins.

In verses 12–17, God's character and will for His people is amplified through the metaphor of sickness and healing. Judah's condition is portrayed as an incurable wound or injury (30:12). *Incurable* is the same word that is used to describe the desperately sick heart in 17:9. The prognosis is not good. In human terms, there is no chance of healing and no recovery; no human physician can help cure or even ease the pain (30:13, 15). Judah's lovers have forgotten them, and they have no friends who care (30:14). This is a reference to Egypt, whom Judah sought as an ally to help save them when they should have turned to God. God is the source of the nation's sickness. The reason for His judgment, repeated twice, is clear: Her guilt is great and her sins are numerous (30:15).

God asks the question, "Why do you cry out?" (30:15). By now, God emphasizes, His judgment should not come as a surprise. Judah should have expected to pay a penalty for their sins. But God says He will judge Judah's enemies (30:16). Instead of benefitting from their attack on God's people, they can expect a similar fate. All who devour, enslave, plunder, and prey upon others will be devoured, enslaved, plundered, and given as prey. God's people will be miraculously healed and restored (30:17).

Sickness and healing are metaphors for what happens to God's people in exile. The restoration comes and a miracle occurs—a terminal condition is reversed. Why does God do this? He restores and heals because His name is at stake. In many ways, verses 12–17 parallel verses 4–11. The same principles are reiterated. Judgment and discipline are necessary in the sanctifying process. Sickness is not the end; there will be complete healing. God's goal is salvation, even though it is completely unmerited and undeserved.

Demystifying Jeremiah

Interestingly, the incurable wound inflicted by God in verse 12 is described with the same language Jeremiah uses in his personal lament in chapter 15, when he cries out to God, "Why has my pain been perpetual and my wound incurable, refusing to be healed?" (15:18 NASB). The same words are used to describe the pain of suffering and the horror of judgment. In other words, it doesn't matter whether we are unfaithful like Judah or obedient like Jeremiah; both the experience and the results of what God does in our lives can be exactly the same. He uses our sin or our suffering to draw us to Himself, to show us His deep compassion and commitment, to mold and shape us into what He desires us to be.

The final verses of this chapter reiterate God's power and character. He specifies how He will bring healing. In addition to health, God will also restore community, including civil life and religion (30:17–18). The people, knowing their help comes from the Lord, will express thanksgiving and increase their numbers (30:19). These offspring will serve the true God, and God will protect them (30:20). Instead of being oppressed or invaded, they will be led by one of their own, someone humble enough to be called by God—exactly the opposite of the false prophets God calls out in previous chapters (30:21). Verse 22 references God's original covenant with Abraham (as does the promise of offspring in verse 20). The fulfillment of God's covenant is possible because of the cleansing, refining work God has done for His people. The future tense of the verse is a reminder that God can bring about the same restoration again (30:22). God's people will come to understand that He acts as needed until His purpose is fulfilled (30:24).

The words of hope continue in chapter 31, as God specifies what restoration will look like for the Israelites. Some commentators emphasize the phrasing of this language as signifying a future time. As stated in chapter 30, the people will again know the true God as their God. With God stating that He will be the God of all the families of Israel comes the hope of restoration of all the remnants—both the northern and southern kingdoms—and all those who are scattered in exile. They will be reunited as one family under God (31:1). The first half of this chapter (31:1–22) refers specifically to the northern kingdom, Israel; the next part (31:23–26) refers to the southern kingdom, Judah; and the final verses refer to both (31:27–40).

For Israel, those who survive the Egyptian captivity find God (31:2). His love for them, described in verse 3, is the same as the marriage kind of love He mentions in 2:2. God again describes Israel in marriage terms and promises that she will be returned to a state of celebration and happiness (31:4; see 18:13). Before too long they will again farm and harvest their own land, and regular worship of the true God by all in the community will be restored for the first time since the division of the northern and southern kingdoms (31:5–6).

Verses 7–9 describe a time of great joy. Whereas earlier in the book of Jeremiah God commands people to repent, He now tells them to sing, shout, proclaim, and give praise. After all the messages of woe and punishment, the time for rejoicing has come. The object of that joy and praise is God, and the reason is for the salvation of the remnant of Israel, or Jacob, another name for Israel (31:7). The active, present tense in which Jeremiah speaks God's words is exciting for the people who had suffered for so long. God is bringing Israel back; they will return from every place they have landed during the ravages and consequences of war and exile. And they will be reunited with their brethren, healed, and will bear children together (31:8). Although they were persuaded through their trials, God will nurture and support them with every step toward restoration (31:9).

The restoration will be so whole and permanent that Israel will be able to share the truth of it with other nations as evidence of God's choice to restore His people (31:10). Ultimately, God is the one who controls Israel's fate, not leaders of other nations (31:11). The restoration will last long enough for harvest and bounty (31:12). Civil and family life will return—a powerful indication of healing after the complete collapse of such things earlier in the book (31:13). And remember the religious leaders who lost their way and were specific objects of God's wrath? Even they will be infused with the Spirit of God again (31:14). The healing and restoration will be so complete that the people will be satisfied and have no need to look beyond the true God (31:14).

Critical Observation

Ramah was a town north of Jerusalem, where many of the Israelites saw home for the last time before being deported. The crying of the mother for her children signifies both weeping over lost exiles and the northern kingdom weeping over the loss of some of its tribes (31:15). All those who heard Jeremiah's prophecies—whether they actually lived them out or not—could imagine the torment one would feel in these circumstances.

God has a word for those who weep in despair: Their toil and pain is not in vain. The ones who are lost will return (31:16). Reality seems dire, and truly it is, but God's Word promises restoration and hope (31:17).

The voice shifts in verse 18 to focus on the specific tribe of Ephraim. In these verses, Ephraim acknowledges its former arrogance and present humility (31:18–19). God asks a rhetorical question in 31:20: Does Ephraim still belong to me? This is reminiscent of God's earlier question about Judah: Is she still my wife even though she acts like a harlot? The answer is an emphatic *yes*. God still knows, owns, and yearns for His children, and He will act with mercy toward them (31:20).

The final verses of chapter 31 relate to the northern kingdom, Israel. God is offering wisdom and guidance to His people, encouraging them to remember their journey away from God (31:21). By doing so, Israel can remind both herself and future generations of this critical experience of sin, exile, repentance, and restoration.

Demystifying Jeremiah

Verse 22 generates much conversation among scholars and commentators. One opinion is that "a female will shelter a man" (HCSB) is a prophecy of the coming of Christ's birth to the Virgin Mary. Another understanding is that it is simply a metaphor for the coming time when things are so peaceful that women can protect men—an uncommon view at that time. More likely, however, is the opinion that the image describes a repentant Israel (often described in the feminine) returning to God (the male imagery).

The next four verses (31:23–26) refer to the southern kingdom of Judah, the recipient of the bulk of Jeremiah's prophetic messages. Like Israel, Judah will again worship God in truth in the same place their ancestors did (31:23–24). They will once again be a city of righteousness, and the community of God will be together again. The trials they just endured will not be forgotten, but God will refresh them (31:25). Jeremiah includes a personal note in verse 26: Upon waking from this latest vision, he reports that his sleep is pleasant. This must have been refreshing for the prophet, who had conveyed many heart-breaking messages from God to his own community and endured the harsh responses from the people upon being faced with God's truths.

THE FUTURE

Chapter 31:27–40 records a new message from God to the Israelites concerning their relationship with Him. These verses have since been labeled The New Covenant. Previously in Jeremiah, the prophet explained to the people that keeping religious rituals and attending temple services didn't matter to God if their hearts were disengaged. Relationship and faithfulness—which Jeremiah often describes with marriage language—is what God wants from His people, not sacrifices of animals and burning of incense. The new covenant described in these verses will accomplish what the old covenant could not.

Verse 27 opens with a reminder that just as God allowed calamity to come to Israel and Judah, He will also allow restoration (31:27–28). Furthermore, God does not punish people for the sins of their ancestors; people are only responsible for their own actions (31:29). Generations won't suffer because of what their ancestors have done, but they will suffer for their own sins (31:30).

God established a covenant with the Israelites' ancestors, but He has plans to establish a new one with them (31:31–32). The old covenant centers on the people's obedience to the Mosaic Law. But Jeremiah reveals that God intends to have an even more intimate relationship with the people He brought back from exile. He wants His wisdom and His ways to be a part of the people themselves, so much so that He will write it on their hearts, making it a part of their very being (31:33). The consequence of this new, more intimate way of knowing God is that people will no longer have to rely solely on the intercession of priests, leaders, and prophets to call them to God. All Israelites—regardless of rank or class—can enter into relationship with God on their own volition (31:34).

Critical Observation

Even though the notion of the new covenant is woven throughout the Old Testament, the only time the actual words are stated is here in Jeremiah 31:31. The next time this phrase is used, it comes from the mouth of Jesus, when He speaks to His disciples in the upper room: "And in the same way He took the cup after they had eaten, saying, 'This cup which is poured out for you is the new covenant in My blood' " (Luke 22:20 NASB). The writer of Hebrews further explains how the new covenant accomplishes what the old covenant could not (Hebrews 9).

The first characteristic of the new covenant is a new heart, and thus a new obedience (31:33). The people did not obey the old covenant, and thus their hearts were not changed. With the new covenant, God writes His character on the hearts of His people, using the pen, or influence, of the Holy Spirit. Then, once hearts are transformed, actions follow—God Himself lives through His people.

The second characteristic of the new covenant is the often-repeated promise of God: "I will be their God, and they will be my people" (31:33). The new covenant creates a new community, a restored humanity, and a new way of relating. This is a unique relationship between God and His chosen people, the Israelites. The third characteristic of the new covenant is a new intimacy and access to God (31:34). Under the old covenant, the life of God was mediated through the offices of priests and prophets. This verse will see its fulfillment in Christ's death, when the veil is removed from the entrance to the Holy of Holies (Matthew 27:50–51), giving all who believe a direct relationship with God through Jesus, the Mediator.

The fourth characteristic of the new covenant is a new sense of acceptance and freedom (31:34). Under the old covenant, the sacrificial system provided the means for confession and forgiveness for sins. In the new covenant, however, true forgiveness is achieved through God's promise to not remember the sins of His people. This forgiveness is later achieved through the atoning death of Jesus, the Son of God.

Verses 35–37 echo the new covenant poetically and remind readers of God's character. God, the Author of both the old and new covenants, is Creator and Sustainer of all creation, upon whom all creation is dependent (31:35). Verses 36–37 emphasize the security of God's people by expressing the impossible—God cannot stop being the Creator and Sustainer, and His creation cannot fully be measured. Because of who God is, His people are eternally secure in Him (31:36–37).

Chapter 31 closes with a final pronouncement. The city of Jerusalem will be rebuilt, and it will be larger than before (31:38–39). The ground upon which such suffering and destruction had occurred at the will of God will remain sacred to Him and to His people (31:40).

Demystifying Jeremiah

Chapter 32 slows down Jeremiah's rapid-fire prophecies to tell about a single event in the life of the prophet—his purchase of a plot of land in Anathoth. At the time of Jeremiah's purchase, the land was already under Babylonian control, meaning he bought land that he couldn't live on. But God instructed Jeremiah to buy the land as a prophetic message to the people that one day they would return to Judah, and the land they once owned would again be theirs.

The joy and hope of the future depicted in the previous chapter quickly returns to the harsh reality of punishment in chapter 32. In the years 587–586 BC, the city of Jerusalem is close to defeat by the Babylonians (32:1). Jeremiah is under arrest for proclaiming God's message of judgment regarding Judah and its king, Zedekiah, who doesn't take kindly to Jeremiah's predictions (32:2–5). Jeremiah, falsely charged with collaborating with the enemy, is shut up in the court of the guard, but he is permitted certain freedoms, one of which is receiving visitors.

God informs Jeremiah that his cousin Hanamel is going to offer to sell him a field in Anathoth, Jeremiah's hometown, just outside of Jerusalem (32:6–7). God's prediction is fulfilled, and Hanamel approaches Jeremiah because, as a family member, the prophet has the right to buy the field and keep it in the family (32:8). Because Jerusalem is under siege, the value of the land is dubious due to the military occupation. However, Jeremiah is instructed by God to purchase the land. So despite the uncertainties surrounding the deal, he makes the purchase (32:9). The text records the entire transaction with great specificity: The purchase price is seventeen shekels of silver (roughly seven ounces), and witnesses are called in to verify the signing of the deed and the exchange of money. Then the deed is given to Baruch for safe storage (32:10–14).

Buying a field in Anathoth in the middle of an invasion seems foolish, and yet Jeremiah's response is one of obedience and confidence in the Lord. He is confident that houses, fields, and vineyards, the most common elements of economic life, will again be bought and sold in the land of Judah (32:15). He makes a long-term investment based upon a future hope. Furthermore, his purchase shows the people that God's prophet believes there will be life after the exile in Babylon.

Verses 16–25 record Jeremiah's prayer following his purchase of the land. The prayer begins with praise and a doxology to God's character and name (32:16–17). God created the heavens and the earth with His outstretched arm. Nothing is too difficult for this great and mighty God. The prophet recognizes God's fidelity and justice, which Jeremiah has been witness to time and time again (32:18–19). Jeremiah goes to speak of God's great power in the exodus and the conquest of the land (32:20–22). But God's people do not obey him, so the outstretched arm that saves Judah will judge her (32:23). The prophet concludes by conveying what is happening to Judah at that time: The land is being invaded, and in the midst of it God has Jeremiah purchase land in front of witnesses (32:24–25).

Jeremiah hints at an unasked question underlying his prayer: I know that you are a great and powerful God, but are you sure you have this right? Buy a field in Anathoth (32:25)? God answers Jeremiah by asking a rhetorical question: "Is anything too difficult for Me" (32:27 NASB)? The word *difficult* is often translated "wonderful." In the Old Testament it is always used to refer to the great and miraculous deeds of God (see Genesis 18:13–14; Joshua 3:5). God reminds Jeremiah that He is the God of wonderful things in the past and the God of wonderful things in the future.

God goes on to outline the terrible judgment that will come upon Judah and Jerusalem as a result of their aforementioned idolatry and Baal worship (32:28–35). Judah's guilt is certain, and her discipline must be severe. But again, God promises to not completely destroy His people and to eventually bring restoration and healing. The Babylonian invasion is not a random act of violence. It is the will of God, again described by the trilogy of sword, famine, and plague (32:36). But this time God also reassures Jeremiah with a familiar phrase: "They will be my people, and I will be their God" (32:37–38; see 31:33). Their restoration will include the renewal of their hearts and will be so powerful that it will last for several generations (32:39). God also guarantees a continued relationship between Him and His people (32:40–41). The coming renewal is as much a part of God's plan for the Israelites as the current punishment He is inflicting on them (32:42). God's response is His way of reassuring Jeremiah that buying land is exactly the right thing to do, both as God's prophet sending a message of faith to his people and as a member of a nation that will endure and eventually be restored to full civic life (32:43–44).

Chapter 33 opens with Jeremiah still imprisoned and still communicating with God (33:1). God again speaks to Jeremiah, reminding the prophet of His true character as Creator and Sustainer of all and inviting Jeremiah to an ongoing relationship with Him (33:2–3). God lets Jeremiah know He is aware of the destruction happening to the people of Judah (33:4). Reflecting on the pain of invasion and war, God reiterates that He allowed the Babylonian invasion to happen as a way of cleansing Judah of its wickedness (33:5).

Verses 6–13 comprise another message of hope for the future: God will restore both His people and their holy city, Jerusalem. God's specificity about restoration matches His specificity about destruction. He will bring both health, which can refer to one's physical condition, as well as healing, which can refer to one's emotional and spiritual condition (33:6). The injuries of war last longer than war itself and significantly alter the mindsets of those who have experienced them. God speaks to this reality, saying He will reveal an abundance of peace and truth to the people (33:6). God's message is that He will heal their bodies and their spirits. Furthermore, He will heal their civic life. War inevitably affects commerce and infrastructure, leading to significant economic hardship. But God promises that He will restore the fortunes of both Israel and Judah (33:7). He will do this not simply for the sake of civic life but in conjunction with the whole point of this punishment in the first place: They will be cleansed and forgiven, making them an example to other nations (33:8–9). The city of God that was destroyed and desolate will again be a place where people thrive and live abundantly, all because of the hand of God (33:10–11). God sends this message in the midst of destruction, implanting a vision of hope in the nation's future (33:12–13).

Verses 14–26 close the chapter with a reminder of the Davidic covenant, God's promise that all of Israel will be restored through a descendant of the line of David, foreshadowing the coming Messiah. God reiterates that He will restore both Israel and Judah (33:14). During that restoration, He will choose a particular familial line, the branch of David, from which the Messiah will emerge to bring justice and righteousness to the earth (33:15).

Critical Observation

In just three chapters, God's plan has unfolded from His relationship with the Israelites through the old covenant of the law to a coming new covenant first for the Israelites and then all nations to a new leader who will bring justice and righteousness to all the earth.

Judah and Jerusalem will know a new level of salvation and safety (33:16). Under this new reign, Israel will always have a leader, and access to God will be assured (33:17–18). God emphasizes His point in the same way He does in 31:36–37, by the unrealistic *if/then* statement. Since God is the Creator and Sustainer of all creation, and will be for all eternity, the promises He makes with His people are also eternal (33:20–21). Again, hearkening back to the original covenant between Abraham and God, God reiterates that His people will multiply (33:22).

Finally, God closes by addressing a claim that foreign nations were making about Israel and Judah—that God abandoned them (33:23–24). God explains that His attachment to His people is as certain and predictable as day and night and the turning of the seasons (33:25–26).

Take It Home

Repeatedly throughout the book of Jeremiah, God asserts Himself as Creator and Sustainer of the earth and all that is in it. By doing so, God not only reminds His people of His faithfulness to them and His inability to abandon them despite their sins, but it is also a means of contrasting His character with the false gods His people had experimented with.

JEREMIAH 34:1–45:5

INCIDENTS SURROUNDING THE FALL OF JERUSALEM

Setting Up the Section

Chapters 30–33, referred to previously as the Book of Consolation, provide a series of hope-centered prophecies for the nations of Judah and Israel in the midst of much suffering and struggle. The four chapters also serve as an intermission from Jeremiah's prophetic messages of God's judgment against His sinful people. Chapter 34, however, resumes where 29 leaves off—with a description of Jerusalem just prior to its captivity and fall.

📖 34:1–35:19

BEFORE THE FALL

Chapter 34 begins with God's message for His prophet Jeremiah at the time King Nebuchadnezzar invades Jerusalem (34:1). His message for Zedekiah, the Judean king at that time, is that the invasion he is experiencing is the work of God. Jeremiah prophesies that Zedekiah will be captured, come face-to-face with Nebuchadnezzar, die a peaceful death, and be buried with dignity (34:2–7). Given how God had warned the people of countless corpses they wouldn't be able to bury, much less with formal rites and rituals of mourning, this message must have come as a comfort to Zedekiah.

Verses 8–22 tell a story that highlights a significant broken promise (34:8–11). King Zedekiah had made a covenant to release the slaves, who were those Jews unable to pay their debts and therefore put into slavery (34:8–10).

Demystifying Jeremiah

Zedekiah's initial action in verses 8–10 is consistent with the requirements of the law to cancel a slave's debt after six years of service (Exodus 21:1–6; Deuteronomy 15:1–11). Although the reason behind his benevolent action is unclear, it may have been motivated by economics. Jerusalem is under siege from Babylon (Jeremiah 34:21–22), and masters probably don't have enough food to feed their slaves, so they release them rather than starve them. Regardless of the motive for the release, it is an act of kindness consistent with God's Word.

Slaveholders obey the king's command, but their initial action of loyalty is soon followed by a reversal, when leadership reneges and takes back the slaves (34:11). God responds by reminding Jeremiah's listeners of their agreement regarding slaves (34:12–14). God released the people of Israel from slavery. He was faithful to His covenant and did not turn back. Zedekiah, too, released slaves, but he was not faithful to his covenant (34:15–16). The words *turn around* and *took back* come from the same Hebrew word *to return*. These words have emerged multiple times in the book of Jeremiah. The double turning indicates fickleness and inconsistency. A promise is given and a promise is broken.

God does not take kindly to this breach of covenant, and Zedekiah and his officials will suffer a harsh judgment. God again refers to the triad of destruction He has promised—sword, plague, and famine—throughout Jeremiah's oracles (34:17). The implication is that God holds back the floodwaters of judgment, but there comes a point when He opens the gates. The consequences will be brutal, and to express how brutal, God refers to the ritual of confirming an agreement (or covenant) by cutting a calf in two and walking between the pieces (34:18). The ritual signifies that anyone who breaks the covenant should become like the calf that is split in two. All those involved in breaking the agreement about the freeing of the slaves—the officials of Judah, the officials of Jerusalem, the court officers, the priests, and all the people—are guilty (34:19). Their punishment will be as severe as indicated in the message of the halved calf (34:20–22).

Chapter 35 records another instance when God has His prophet make a point by acting something out. The story of Zedekiah from 34:8–22 is contrasted with the story of the Recabites. The context changes from the days of Zedekiah to the time of King Jehoiakim, his brother (35:1–2). Most of the accounts in Jeremiah 30–39 take place during Zedekiah's reign, but for the insertion of this story, the chronology is unimportant. This account, which occurred at least ten years earlier, is placed here to establish a contrast with chapter 34.

In chapter 34, the main characters are Zedekiah and the other leaders of Judah, public and well-known figures. But in chapter 35, the main characters are the Recabites, an obscure family clan (35:2). Jeremiah is instructed by God to call the Recabites to the temple and give them wine to drink, a beverage that will be in direct contrast to the Recabites' way of life. Jeremiah brings the entire family into the temple of the Lord, a very holy and public place (35:3–4). The entire family fits into one chamber, so this incident is witnessed by important leaders. There in this public setting, the prophet sets before this family pitchers of wine and tells them to drink (35:5). The Recabites refuse to drink

(35:6–11). Even though Jeremiah gives them permission to do so, and even though they have already compromised a bit by moving into the city for fear of the Babylonians, the Recabites remain faithful to the covenant vow of Jonadab.

Demystifying Jeremiah

The Recabites are mentioned in more detail in 2 Kings 10, where we read that Jonadab (or Jehonadab), the son of Recab, joins himself to Jehu when Jehu ruthlessly slaughters the worshipers of Baal. Jonadab, who is zealous for the Lord much like Jehu, institutes strict disciplines for his family. They are nomads living in tents, not houses, and they do not raise crops. They do not plant vineyards, and they do not drink any wine. The Recabites are metal workers, but we don't have enough additional information to know exactly why they took the vows of Jonadab.

The key words in the next four verses are *listen* and *obey*. Both of these words come from the same Hebrew word, *shema*. This term means more than merely hearing; it means to hear and then put into practice what one has heard. God interprets the story of the Recabites (35:12–16). In verse 13, the words *receive instruction* (or *learn a lesson*) mean to listen and act on what is heard. God is about to reveal the lesson by contrasting the Recabites and Zedekiah. The Recabites listened; Zedekiah does not. The Recabites made a promise and remained faithful; Zedekiah made a promise and broke it (35:14–16). The specific details of the Recabite way of life shouldn't be the focus of the story. What is important is the fact that the Recabites lived in obedience and integrity. God repeatedly spoke to Judah and sent His prophets to them with the message of repentance, but Judah did not listen. The Recabites, on the other hand, listened and continued to obey even after 240 years.

Not only is there a contrast in fidelity, but there also is a contrast in results (35:17–19). Here we observe two different destinies. For Judah, the result of failing to listen will be judgment and disaster (35:17). They will lose their land and cities and be carried off into exile. But the Recabites will never lack a man to stand before God (35:18–19). The Davidic line was cut off with Zedekiah, but the line of the Recabites will continue. Two different stories of covenant loyalty end in two different destinies.

📖 36:1–38:28

JEREMIAH AND THE SCROLLS

Chapters 36–38 include another remarkable story from Jeremiah's life, clues to the development of the writing of the book of Jeremiah, and accounts of more of the prophet's imprisonments. Chapter 36 opens in 605 BC, during the reign of the selfish, perverse King Jehoiakim. Under this man's leadership, life in Judah is unsettled and disordered socially, politically, and religiously. Despite Jeremiah's plea, however, the people of Judah do not turn from their idolatrous ways.

The story begins with God coming to Jeremiah during the time of Johoiakim's reign (36:1). God tells Jeremiah to record everything He says to him concerning Israel, Judah, and all the nations on a scroll (36:2). Scholars think these writings, as a result of God's commandment, comprise all of Jeremiah's preachings from 627 to 605 BC (chapters 1–25 of the book of Jeremiah). Behind the assignment is the hope that the people might hear God's Word and repent of their sins (36:3). This is not the first time in the book of Jeremiah that God encourages His people to think back on His history with them or reflect on His past words and actions toward them.

Jeremiah appoints Baruch, the son of Neriah, to be his scribe and deliver the final product to the temple (36:4–5). It is likely that Jeremiah's past messages in the temple made him unwelcome there (see chapters 7 and 26). But God wants the prophecies to be shared with the people in their religious setting in hopes that they will repent (36:6–7). Jeremiah and Baruch obey God's command: The text records three readings of the scroll that are dictated by Jeremiah, including one near the New Gate, the same gate mentioned in chapter 26 (36:8–10). Verse 9 states that the people are fasting, which likely indicates the Babylonian invaders have already made progress in overtaking the city. The particular chamber mentioned in verse 10 is associated with a powerful political family. Even though a large crowd is present, it is obvious that God is targeting the leadership of the nation.

Critical Observation

Baruch is mentioned first in chapter 32, when Jeremiah buys his cousin's field in Anathoth. Baruch, a political figure, is from a distinguished family. Associating with Jeremiah meant that Baruch was risking his life. Chapters 36–45 are framed with the mention of his name. This section of the text is frequently referred to as Baruch's document.

When Micaiah, son of Gemariah, hears the Word of the Lord being recited in the temple, he takes it seriously. He goes back to the king's house and tells all the officials, one of whom is his father. The officials listen to Micaiah (36:11–13). Wanting to investigate the matter further, they send for Baruch himself (36:14–15). Upon actually hearing Baruch read the prophecies, the officials react with fear and a sense of urgency, and they immediately want to report the words to the king (36:16). Perhaps the texts read by Baruch voiced their own concerns or gave words to feelings they had been having and observations they had been making.

Critical Observation

Jeremiah faces much trouble in his lifetime, but there are times when God sends people to rescue him. The officials mentioned in this passage may well have been the very ones who rescued Jeremiah in chapter 26. Gemariah and Micaiah are instrumental in protecting Jeremiah and Baruch when King Jehoiakim burns the scroll and seeks to kill Jeremiah. Then, after the fall of Jerusalem in 587 BC, Nebuchadnezzar himself gives word to the captain of the bodyguard to protect Jeremiah from harm. When the choice is given to Jeremiah to go to Babylon or stay in the land, he attaches himself to Gedaliah, the son of Ahikam.

The officials validate the document by putting questions to Baruch concerning its origin, authenticity, and credibility, and Baruch explains its origin (36:17–18). Then they instruct Baruch and Jeremiah to hide (36:19). By doing this, the officials become protectors of the subversive voice of Jeremiah, who is tasked with reporting God's Word. Knowing the king, these leaders and powerful people are aware his reaction will be harsh. But they want to remove any connection between themselves and the informants so they cannot be implicated as being responsible for the message itself (36:20).

After hearing the message, the king sends for the scroll and has it read to him (36:21). Verse 22 gives the reader a few additional details of time and place. A *brazier* (36:22 NASB) is a metal container for burning coal or charcoal, either for cooking or heating. Jehoiakim is likely sitting in the comfort of his home, warming himself before a fire in the wintertime, when he hears the words of God contained in Jeremiah chapters 1–25. God is specific about the failures of civic and religious leaders in those passages of scripture. Jehoiakim is convicted by the words read to him, specifically of sin against God. In response, Jehoiakim throws out God's Word (36:23). He yields nothing of himself to the claims of the scroll. He shuts it out and refuses to let it touch his life. Likewise, the people of Jehoiakim's household who also hear the words let them pass over them without conviction. The men who had brought the message and the scroll to the king try to persuade him to respond differently, but to no avail (36:25). After destroying the words of God, the king calls for the arrest of Baruch and Jeremiah, but the Lord hid them (36:26).

Critical Observation

Jehoiakim's response contrasts with the response of the earlier officials in this chapter. They hear the words of God and fear Him (36:16), but the king hears the same words but does not fear (36:24). His response also contrasts with the response of his father, Josiah, seventeen years earlier. Josiah had been presented by Shaphan (Josiah's secretary) with the scroll of Deuteronomy, rediscovered in the temple. Hearing the Word of God, Josiah tears his clothes (2 Kings 22:11). A generation later, the scenario is repeated between the sons. Josiah's son, Jehoiakim, is presented with a scroll by Shaphan's son, Gemariah. His response is completely different. Jehoiakim does not tear his garments. Instead he tears the pages of the scroll, and the text specifically notes his servants do not tear their garments (36:24).

In response to Jehoiakim's actions, God tells Jeremiah to take another scroll, rewrite the words that were burned by Jehoiakim, and then confront Jehoiakim about his actions (36:27–29). God has a new message for Jeremiah to deliver to Jehoiakim: Destroying the scroll did not destroy the message of God. Because Jehoiakim did not listen, he is going to die, and his family will suffer the effects of the Babylonian invasion (36:30–31). The final verse of the chapter describes Baruch and Jeremiah recreating and elaborating on the original scroll (36:32).

Chapter 37 returns to the reign of Zedekiah, the king who breaks the promise of the slaves' freedom. Verse 1 reveals that Zedekiah is made king by the invading king of Babylon, Nebuchadnezzar. The text also reveals that Zedekiah continues to ignore the way of the Lord, even after being reminded of God's words through Jeremiah (37:2). Despite the continued sin of Zedekiah and his people, he still asks Jeremiah to intercede for them (37:3). At this point in the story, Jeremiah is still a free man, and reinforcements are coming for Judah to help fight the Babylonians (37:4–5). God takes this opportunity to respond to Zedekiah's request for intercession: The reinforcements are not going to help, and Jerusalem is still going to fall to the Babylonians (37:7–9). Reinforcements cannot thwart the will of God (37:10).

The supporting army from Egypt helps for a time, and during that brief period Jeremiah goes out to take possession of the land he had purchased from his cousin (37:11–12). But as he is leaving, a member of the army thinks Jeremiah is deserting Jerusalem and going to join the Chaldeans (Babylonians) (37:13). Despite Jeremiah's protests, he is arrested and thrown in a jail in the house of a man named Jonathan, where he is mistreated (37:14–15). Jeremiah's harsh treatment might have been because he was suspected of being a deserter, but there is also the possibility that it is because of his role as God's prophet and the message of judgment he had been preaching for years. Eventually Jeremiah is moved to a dungeon, possibly a cistern (37:16).

King Zedekiah sends for Jeremiah and secretly asks him if there is a word from the Lord, to which Jeremiah answers yes, defeat is certain (37:17). Jeremiah continues, asking Zedekiah to justify his imprisonment (37:18). Why is he imprisoned, Jeremiah asks Zedekiah, while the so-called prophets who prophesy peace and contradict Jeremiah are free, even though the current circumstances in Judah prove the false prophets lied (37:19)? Jeremiah asks the king to not return him to the jail at Jonathan's house where he is treated badly (37:20). Zedekiah agrees and, although he keeps Jeremiah captive, he is imprisoned in better conditions as long as the siege in Jerusalem allows (37:21).

Chapter 38 provides further detail regarding the prophet's imprisonments. Scholars question if the events in chapters 37 and 38 are the same, or if they represent separate occasions. Regardless, the message for the contemporary reader is the same—participating in God's work can mean having to endure suffering and injustice. The chapter opens with a list of men who hear Jeremiah prophesying about the coming justice of God by sword, famine, and pestilence (38:1-2). According to his prophecy, joining the Chaldeans (the largest tribe of Babylonians at this time) is a way to keep one's life. Since Jerusalem is going to fall to Babylon, if the people go ahead and surrender, they may be allowed to continue to live in their homes rather than be exiled when they are defeated (38:2-3). The leaders ask the king to kill Jeremiah, reasoning that his latest message is hurting troop morale, which will increase the likelihood of Babylonian victory (38:4). King Zedekiah dismisses himself from the situation and leaves Jeremiah to the mob (38:5). The men imprison Jeremiah in a cistern, a muddy place with only fetid water (38:6; see chapter 2).

It is likely that many people knew of Jeremiah's situation. But the text is specific about the one person who acts to ease his suffering: Ebed-melech the Ethiopian, a palace official (38:7). Ebed-melech means "servant of a king." This man is a foreigner from Ethiopia and a government official with no legal rights in Judah. None of Jeremiah's own people care enough about him or his message to fight for him, but Ebed-melech goes against popular opinion and asks the king to pardon Jeremiah's life (38:8-9). When he is granted permission, he pulls Jeremiah out of the pit (38:10-13).

At the close of chapter 38, Jeremiah again finds himself face-to-face with King Zedekiah (38:14). Jeremiah uses the opportunity to bargain for his life, pointing out to Zedekiah that in the past, even when Jeremiah told the truth about God's prophecy, Zedekiah didn't take actions to repent or change his behavior (38:15). Zedekiah promises, in the name of the true creator God, to neither order Jeremiah's death nor leave him to the whims of the mob like he did previously (38:16). Apparently satisfied, Jeremiah reveals God's latest word (38:17).

Jeremiah informs Zedekiah that if he turns himself over to the officers of the invading army, he and his family will live and the city's destruction will not be as vast as it has the potential to be (38:17). However, if Zedekiah continues to resist, the Chaldeans (Babylonians) will destroy the city completely and even kill Zedekiah (38:18). Zedekiah confesses his distrust of the alliances that formed in war and indicates that he doesn't trust his fellow countrymen to deliver him to Nebuchadnezzar safely (38:19). Regardless, Jeremiah assures the king that he must follow God's direction or face specific consequences: The remaining harem in Judah—Zedekiah's wife and daughters—will be brought to the officers of the invading Babylonian army (including the largest tribe of Chaldeans), where they will be raped, forced into marriage, and possibly killed (38:20-22). Furthermore, Zedekiah will be killed, and the city will be completely destroyed by fire (38:22-23). Zedekiah instructs Jeremiah to keep this message to himself, because this information can be used against the king (38:24). The king does not want his court to know that he truly trusts Jeremiah's prophecy, so he asks Jeremiah to lie about the purpose of their meeting (38:25–26). Jeremiah seems to support the king's secrecy and ultimately survives this event (38:27–28). However, as the next chapters reveal, Zedekiah does not heed God's Word, and the city of Jerusalem does fall to the Babylonian forces.

📖 39:1–41:18

THE FALL AND AFTERMATH

Chapters 39–41 detail what happens to the exiles in Babylon and Egypt and gives the fates of specific people: Zedekiah, Jeremiah, Ebed-melech, and Gedaliah. The continuing theme is that God's judgment falls on both those who obey Him as well as those who do not.

The Babylonians storm the city of Jerusalem for thirty months before finally breaking through the city walls in July of 586 BC, marking the fall of the city (39:1–3). With the fall of Jerusalem, both nations of divided Israel have been conquered: Israel, the northern kingdom, is conquered by the Assyrians in 722 BC; and Judah, the southern kingdom, is conquered with this event in 586 BC. The king of Judah at the time of captivity is Zedekiah, who has been warned by Jeremiah of the coming calamity (39:4). Zedekiah, his sons, and the nobles of Judah flee into the desert, only to be captured and returned to Nebuchadnezzar, the great king himself (39:5). Conquering kings believed it served no good purpose to keep the conquered king and his family alive. Sooner or later, any vestige of leadership or family was likely to attempt to retaliate. For this reason, Nebuchadnezzar disposes of Judah's leaders and Zedekiah's sons, burns the palaces to the ground, and gouges out the eyes of Zedekiah before presenting him as a trophy before the Babylonians (39:6–7). The Chaldeans, the largest of the Babylonian tribes, destroy the city of Jerusalem (39:8). The strongest of the people who are still in the city after its destruction are captured as exiles and begin their thousand-mile journey on foot to the great city of Babylon in the modern-day country of Iraq (39:9). The poorest and weakest citizens of Judah are left behind in the destroyed city, where they are given what remains of the vineyards and fields (39:10). The next four verses provide readers with Jeremiah's whereabouts during the attack. Jeremiah is taken from his prison by a captain named Nebuzaradan (39:11). Nebuchadnezzar ordered that Jeremiah be kept safe and obeyed (39:12). Jeremiah's reputation as a prophet and a man of power among Judah's leaders—albeit an unpopular man—was likely known by Nebuchadnezzar, and Nebuchadnezzar probably considered Jeremiah's message helpful to his own cause. Ultimately, Jeremiah ends up in the care of a man named Gedaliah, who is the son of the man who saves Jeremiah in 26:24 (39:14). Gedaliah seems to be of a godly heritage and believes Jeremiah speaks the words of the true God. Jeremiah 40:5 states that he remains in Jerusalem after the exile, where eventually Jeremiah joins him.

Before Jeremiah leaves his guardhouse prison, God speaks to him (39:15). He instructs him to take a reassuring word to Ebed-melech. Even though an entire city went up in flames by God's hand, He wants this one individual, a foreigner who does not belong to the people of Judah, to know he will be spared (39:16–17). Ebed-melech is rewarded for recognizing and believing the prophet of the true God (39:18).

Nebuchadnezzar's bodyguard, Nebuzaradan, knows that Jeremiah is a prophet from the Lord who has spoken an advanced warning of calamity for Jerusalem (40:1–2). He takes Jeremiah to a place north of Jerusalem, where exiles are taken and assessed for their worth, and speaks with him there. Nebuzaradan acknowledges the work of God in the invasion and conquering that has just occurred (40:3). He then offers Jeremiah a choice: come to Babylon or stay behind with Gedaliah, the new leader of the land formerly known as Judah (40:4). Jeremiah chooses to return to Mizpah, near Jerusalem, to be with Gedaliah, whose name means "watchtower" or "lookout" (40:5–6).

The forces in the field, mentioned in verse 7, are groups of Jewish troops who have not yet been captured (40:7). When they learn that Gedaliah has been appointed governor of the land by Nebuchadnezzar, they go to him in the city of Mizpah (40:8). In verse 9 Gedaliah tells the Judeans not to fear the Chaldeans (the largest Babylonian tribe). Further, he instructs them to stay and raise crops (40:10). It seems that the people can resume their lives under Nebuchadnezzar's reign. When other people from Judah, who are neither displaced by the war nor exiled, hear of Gedaliah's community, they join them, remembering that Gedaliah is the son and grandson of godly men who had served Josiah (40:11). These people also begin raising crops (40:12).

While stability and community seem to be returning to the land, a threat is brewing. Some of the forces in the field come to Gedaliah and tell him of a threat against him by a man of royal descent (and a former member of Zedekiah's army) named Ishmael (40:13–14). Gedaliah dismisses the charge and actually calls the accuser a liar (40:15–16). Gedaliah must have been willing to trust that Ishmael did not wish him ill. It is an unfortunate trust that will lead to disaster.

Three months after Jerusalem's capture and Gedaliah's appointment as leader of the Jewish community, Ishmael brings ten men to Mizpah and kills Gedaliah and all the people who are with him (41:1–3). Ishmael kills Gedaliah during a hospitality meal, while eating bread together. The inclusion of this fact in the text reveals what a cowardly and unjust act Ishmael committed. But it only gets worse. On the day after the first murders, eighty men from Shechem (in Samaria) come to visit Gedaliah and to worship (41:4–5). Ishmael greets them, acting as if he is mourning Gedaliah's death. He lures the men into the city, where he kills them and dumped their bodies into a local cistern (41:6–7). Ten are spared because they bribe Ishmael, further evidence that Ishmael is nothing but a self-motivated killer (41:8). Verse 9 describes the cistern as being a particular one made by King Asa (41:9; see 1 Kings 15:22; 2 Chronicles 16:6).

Ishmael's atrocities continue. He captures all the Jews who are under Gedaliah's protection with the intention of carrying them across the Jordan River into the area known as Jordan (41:10). Ishmael plans to take them to the sons of Ammon, a reference to the ancient residents of the modern city of Amman, Jordan. To the rescue, however, is Johanan, the leader of what is left of a small Jewish army allowed to protect the city from further assault and one of the men who had tried to warn Gedaliah of Ishmael's threat (41:11, 13). He puts together a group and rescues the kidnapped (41:12–14). Verse 13 notes that the people are glad when they see Johanan coming, further indicating his status as a good community member. After he rescues the Jews from Ishmael, Johanan goes after him (41:15). Johanan and the other army officers lead the rescued Jews to a place called Geruth Kimham, near Bethlehem, as a place to stop on their escape to Egypt (41:16–17). Their plan is to escape to Egyptian land to avoid any punishment that might come from Gedaliah's death (41:17–18).

📄 42:1–44:30

EGYPT

The remnant of people from Jerusalem has been through one traumatic experience after another, and all they want is security. Faced with the absence of the only leader they have had since the invasion, destruction, and exile of their fellow citizens and family members, they turn to Jeremiah. They want him to intercede to God on their behalf because there are so few of them remaining and they need God's guidance (42:1–3). They know they can no longer trust Jerusalem to protect them—the city's walls have been torn down in the war. Jeremiah, who for many years acted as an obedient prophet to these people, also shows the leadership of a priest by ministering to them in this way. He assures them that he will pray to God for them, and he will not hold back a word of God's answer (42:4). The people's response to Jeremiah seems to indicate that at least this remnant has learned to be responsive to the Word of the Lord received through Jeremiah. They promise to obey the message no matter what it is (42:5–6).

After ten days, Jeremiah has an answer, and he calls all the people back together (42:7–8). Jeremiah opens his statement by qualifying that it is from the God of Israel, who Jeremiah petitioned on behalf of this remnant of people (42:9). God's message is consistent with what He has said all along: The worst is over, and God will nurture them as they restore and rebuild their city (42:10). Nebuchadnezzar is no longer a threat, and because of God's will for His people, He will work through Nebuchadnezzar to support the people in their restoration efforts (42:11–12).

However, this restoration is dependent on the people staying where they are in the midst of the destroyed remains of Judah and Jerusalem. God knows the people are considering leaving the land and moving to Egypt for an easier life (42:13–14). And though God said the people have a choice to remain or flee, He implies that their minds are already made up, and predicts the same three kinds of destruction present throughout the book of Jeremiah. They can expect to face swords, famine, and plague if they flee (42:15–18). God's message is clear: Don't go to Egypt (42:19). Jeremiah also seems to know that despite the promises the people make in verses 5–6 to obey God's message no matter what, they might as well have already left. Disobedience to Jeremiah's messages has become a pattern (42:20–22).

Demystifying Jeremiah

The people cannot let go of their old thoughts about God. Just as they thought rituals would save them no matter what the condition of their hearts (see 7:21–29), they think that because Jerusalem has been destroyed, God is no longer with them. They need to understand that Jerusalem is merely a symbol of God's protection. They look at their reality—the large majority of Jews in exile and their new leader, Gedaliah, murdered—and logic tells them it is time to give up on the promised land. In their immediate struggle, they fail to understand that God wants them to stay in Jerusalem to remain the faithful remnant, that He has not deserted them, and that He will not remove His hand of protection.

Jeremiah speaks words of truth and warning to the remnant of people from Jerusalem, and yet they do the exact opposite of God's command. Azariah and Johanan are the first to voice resistance to the Word of the Lord, calling Jeremiah a liar (43:1–2). They even accuse Jeremiah of letting Baruch talk him into delivering the small remnant to the Chaldeans (43:3). Despite Jeremiah's words of hope, the people flee to Egypt (43:4–7). Those who flee include all the leaders (even Johanan, who had acted so honorably in previous situations), everyone who had been rescued after Gedaliah's murder, and Jeremiah and Baruch (43:4–7).

Demystifying Jeremiah

Prophets were stoned if their prophecies did not come to pass. The very idea that Jeremiah has survived all these years is a testimony that his prophecies are true. This fact should have been proof enough for the people to listen to him. But instead, the Judean remnant retreats back to the land God had miraculously led them out of a thousand years earlier. They journey back to the Red Sea to the place called Tahpanhes, the modern-day Suez Canal. Pharaoh had a palace at this juncture of the Mediterranean and the Red Sea.

God sends Jeremiah with the people on this journey and has him perform another symbolic act once they reach Tahpanhes (43:8). Jeremiah places stones in the patio of the government building to mark the spot where Nebuchadnezzar will soon set up his own palace as his conquests continue (43:8–11). This prophecy is fulfilled in 568–567 BC. God promised to tear down the temples of Egypt and burn their pagan deities (43:12). He also promised to shatter the obelisks of Heliopolis (43:13). *Heliopolis* is another name for "sun city," a place dedicated to worshiping the sun as a god. In honor of the sun god, the people erect tall, slender stone monuments which become known as fingers of god.

Chapter 44 begins with two major players: Jeremiah and God. Even in Egypt, God continues to be with the people and with Jeremiah (44:1). But this chapter also begins the last message Jeremiah delivers to the people. In this message, we see the same elements that have been present throughout the book of Jeremiah. God summarizes where they have been: He punished His people in many ways because of their persistent sin, and He sent prophets again and again (44:2–4). But the result is the same: The people turn away from God and His Word, and follow their own ideas about safety and prosperity in other places with other gods (44:5). Because of this behavior, Judah and Jerusalem are in ruins (44:6).

Critical Observation

God says to the unrepentant remnant of Judah, "Again and again I sent my servants the prophets" (44:4 NIV). Over a period of three hundred years, God sent the following prophets: Elijah, Elisha, Jonah, Joel, Amos, Obadiah, Hosea, Micah, and Isaiah. And now Jeremiah stands before the people with words of conviction, warning them of impending doom if they do not turn from their idolatry. God's indictment to the people is very clear: They burn sacrifices to other gods. Through the ages people continue to defy God by finding new and different ways to create idols and worship those idols at creative new altars. We are not immune from the perennial sins that weave their way through every generation.

In verses 7–9, God expresses His anger with His people by asking a series of rhetorical questions about their actions up to this point. The people did not get God's message, did not realize their sin, and did not learn to commit themselves to Him (44:10).

In the same pattern seen throughout the book of Jeremiah, God follows the statement of reality with the consequences. This time, even though only a remnant of Judah remains, God abandons them to the consequences of their decisions (44:11). They will die in Egypt by sword, famine, and plague (44:12–13). None who went to Egypt will return to Judah, except for a few refugees (44:14).

The people respond to Jeremiah by telling him they are going to ignore him (44:15–16). At this point, one would expect deep and mournful repentance. But instead, they tell Jeremiah they will no longer listen to him. Their defiance has become an open act of rebellion, and they justify it by saying when they used to worship the other gods they did not suffer (44:17–18). They admit to preparing flat bread images of Ishtar (the "Queen of Heaven"), the Egyptian goddess of love and fertility (44:19). Their baked goods became a creative new act of burnt offering, and they topped off their bread by hosting wine parties dedicated to their favorite deities.

Jeremiah responds to the people's latest argument by saying God was watching the entire time (44:20–21). He endured their behavior as long as He chose to, and when He decided to teach the people their sins were unacceptable to Him, He allowed them to be punished (44:22–23).

Once again the people sin against God by worshiping the gods of a foreign land. "Go ahead then, do what you promised! Keep your vows!" Jeremiah yells (44:25 NIV). God proclaims that never again will the sacred name of Yahweh be used by the remnant in Egypt (44:26). In a reversal of the hopeful promise of 29:11, God assures the people He is watching over them for harm and not for good (44:27). The few who will emerge from Egypt will have no doubt about God's power (44:28). In his final words of prophecy, Jeremiah speaks of a sign. Egypt's Pharaoh Hophra will also fall under the growing dominion of King Nebuchadnezzar, which comes to fruition in 569 BC (44:29–30).

45:1–5

BARUCH

Jeremiah's message to Baruch, recorded at the start of chapter 45, was written in the fourth year of Jehoiakim's reign (see Jeremiah 36), almost twenty years before Baruch went to Egypt with Jeremiah. The letter addresses some of the complaints Baruch is having about his role in Jeremiah's ministry (45:1–3). Verse 4 echoes the phrasing of 1:10, with language of overthrowing, building, uprooting, and planting. The fact that these themes sustained themselves through all these years is evidence of the consistent message of God and the loyal obedience of Jeremiah. It is not surprising that, given Jeremiah's enemies and his own honest times of frustration with God, Baruch would also have such struggles. Jeremiah encourages his assistant by asking him a question to gauge Baruch's perspective: Are you seeking great things for yourself? Jeremiah then reminds him that flesh is temporary and life with God is the real reward, a lesson Jeremiah learns through enduring much (45:5).

Take It Home

The name *Baruch* means "blessing," and this is what Baruch is to Jeremiah. He came from a distinguished family. He might have had a moment where he sought great things for himself and questioned his role in Jeremiah's ministry, but he counted the cost and gave it all up in order to bless Jeremiah. Baruch's work ensured that Jeremiah's prophecies and story would survive for generations. Chapter 45 marks the close of the narrative regarding the fate of the remnant that fled from Jerusalem. The narrative will not resume again until chapter 52.

JEREMIAH 46:1–51:64

PROPHECIES AND THE NATIONS

Setting Up the Section

Chapters 46–51 chronicle Jeremiah's prophecies concerning the nations (46:1). Such prophecies are not unique to Jeremiah. All of the prophetical books of the Bible contain a similar collection of prophecies, with the exception of the book of Hosea. The themes of this section include God's judgment for idol worship and misplaced trust; the punishment that comes as a consequence of such sins; and the continuing theme that God either won't destroy completely or will destroy now but restore later, which can be seen as evidence of God's amazing mercy. The geographical catalog of nations moves from west to east.

📖 46:1–28

EGYPT

During Jehoiakim's reign, Jeremiah receives a word from God concerning Egypt. The first two verses reference the battle of Carchemish, fought in 605 BC by Egypt and Assyria against the growing power of Babylon and King Nebuchadnezzar (46:1–2). God instructs the people to continue preparing for war by readying their horses, weapons, and armor (46:3–4), and He indicates that the mighty Egyptians will lose terribly (46:2, 5–6). The rivers are referenced for their benefits but also for their uncontrolled power, and the leaders are encouraged in their futile battle (46:6–9). But ultimately God is in control, and because of His justice, He allows Egypt to be defeated at Babylon's hands (46:10). As in Jeremiah 8, God references a possible balm available for healing but calls any attempt at healing vain (46:11). Egypt's desire for power overcomes the nation, and it must fail (46:12).

God goes on to explain that Nebuchadnezzar is the king who will lead the Babylonians in Egypt's destruction (46:13). Egypt can prepare itself, but the invasion is going to come, and Egypt will suffer as the Lord decreed (46:14–15). As in 46:12, the warriors won't even be able to put up a unified front and will retreat (46:16). As is common in defeat, the defeated leader will be questioned (46:17). Just as God warned Judah many times that an invader was coming from the north, He warns Egypt that one is coming to destroy them just as others have been destroyed by invaders from Tabor and Carmel (46:18). The ones who survive will be taken prisoner and marched away from their homelands, which will be destroyed (46:19).

In this passage, Egypt is described as a beautiful heifer, symbolizing the nation's size, strength, and importance as a world power that had dominated the nations even before 1800 BC, until the rise of Assyria in 722 BC. God's description of Egypt is of one that prospered for a while, with the invasion beginning as simply an annoyance (46:20). A horsefly (or gadfly), a pesky little insect (compared to the heifer) is symbolized as the threat of Babylon. Horseflies, unlike other insects, have the ability to tear flesh, suck large amounts of blood, and infect the target with disease and parasites. When the invasion becomes serious, Egypt will not be able to defend themselves (46:21). The Babylonian army marches 550 miles, like a swarm of horseflies, attacking everything in sight, until they achieve the coveted title of world dominator. Destruction will be real, and Egypt will be subjugated to Babylon (46:22–24). The gods of the Egyptians will be punished, as will the Pharaoh, and then everyone will be turned over to Babylon. The destruction will not be complete or permanent, though; Egypt will rise again (46:25–26).

Despite this chronicle of devastation, the chapter closes with God's simple, yet sustaining assurance that the sons of Jacob will not be consumed during the ravage of war. God will continue to discipline, correct, and punish them, but He will not remove them from their coveted position as God's chosen people (46:27–28).

📄 47:1–7

PHILISTINES

Chapter 47 contains the prophetic oracle for the Philistines. The area of Philistia was located geographically near Egypt (47:1). God's message to them is similar in that the invader is also Babylon (47:2). The image of a flood indicates that the invasion will be severe and widespread. The prophet Jeremiah describes the onslaught of Babylonian siege as a mighty torrent of water, sweeping through the land and consuming everything in its path. Philistia will be so overpowered that parents won't be able to save their children (47:3). Neighboring nations—allies—won't be able to help save Philistia, because this invasion and destruction is the will of the Lord (47:4). Those who survive will become captives of the Babylonians and will be shaved bald as part of their enslavement. Likewise, cutting is an act of mourning for some pagans (47:5). It is unclear who is asking God to sheathe His sword—it could be the Philistines themselves wondering if such harsh justice is necessary, to which God responds *yes* (47:6–7). Or it could be Jeremiah, wondering how God could allow such devastation to take place. When will God step in to restore order and peace?

MOAB

As is similar to each of the prophecies for the nations, Moab's coming destruction is described in chapter 48 as if it has already happened. The oracle to Moab is lengthy because of Israel and Judah's long history with the country. The judgment begins with the word *woe*, indicating a time of mourning has come (48:1). All of the cities mentioned early in this chapter—Nebo, Kiriathaim, Heshbon, Madmen, Horonaim, and Luhith—would have been well known to the original hearers of this prophecy (48:1–4). The cities that have already been invaded warn others to flee (48:6). Similar to accusations against Judah and Egypt, God specifies that Moab trusts too much in its own achievements; and consequently, its false god Chemosh, priests, and princes will suffer (48:7). No city in the entire country will survive the invasion, and all the citizens of Moab will either die or be captured (48:8–9). God is so intent on fulfilling the nation's judgment that He takes a break from detailing their sins to motivate His instrument, the Babylonians, to act swiftly (48:10).

Critical Observation

The territory of Moab was a mountainous plateau on the eastern side of the Dead Sea, in modern-day Jordan. The Moabites were descendants of Lot, Abraham's nephew, who reportedly fathered Moab by his oldest daughter (Genesis 19:30–38). Perhaps the best-known resident of Moab was Ruth, who left her home country to embrace the land and culture of Israel. The Moabites received protection from the Egyptians in return for their allegiance to pagan gods.

Verse 11 uses the imagery of wine, one of Moab's resources, to compare the Moabites to wine that is left alone instead of separated into containers. Nothing changes for the wine—it is the same for a long time. God likens this to the Moabites themselves, who have been left alone and never separated among nations. But this is about to change (48:12). Like Judah, Moab is about to see the futility of its faith in false gods (48:13).

The idea that Moab's warriors will be able to defend against God's justice is laughable (48:14). When God decrees His judgment for Moab, it is time for the people to begin their mourning for the nation and expect to see examples of its destruction (48:15–17).

Cities on hills are often the safest and manage to avoid destruction, but God calls those in Dibon, who survived the initial destruction, to come down from the hill and experience it for themselves. God links the destruction of the country to that of the individual citizens (48:18). Word begins to spread that Moab is destroyed and the people disgraced (48:19–20). Verses 21–24 list all the communities in Moab that are destroyed. The imagery in verse 25 is that of a mature stag that loses its horns or a person whose arm is broken. Such will be the crippled state of Moab.

As in Jeremiah 25, God describes Moab as drinking uncontrollably from a cup. Their gluttony leads to their illness and destruction (48:26). When Israel was weak, Moab took advantage of that weakness (48:27). Now, God instructs them to flee their cities and take up refuge in hiding places like animals (48:28).

In addition to being idol worshipers and opportunists, the Moabites are also arrogant and prideful (48:29). But God observes that this pride is misplaced and futile (48:30). Consequently, the mourning for Moab will be thorough, as seen by the specific groups God is mourning for, and the mourning will be even more intense than others known in history (48:31–32). The winepresses that once kept Moab in economic prosperity will quit working, and no income will be produced (48:33). The destruction will be far-reaching (48:34). Jeremiah prophesies that Moab will be destroyed as a people because of their idolatry (48:35). God mourns as if at a funeral for a nation that once prospered but now is destroyed (48:36). The survivors wear the markings and the behaviors of slaves horrified at their state (48:37–39).

Verses 40–47 open with the image of an eagle, an often-seen image of destruction in biblical texts (48:40). The invasion brings great pain, and the country of Moab will be destroyed because of its arrogance (48:41–42). Anyone who lives there will experience punishment, and escape is impossible (48:43–44). The destruction moves from city to city throughout the country, and the destruction and harm is intense (48:45). The god that the Moabites had worshiped fails them, and the Moabite children are taken captive by the invading nation, a method of destroying an entire culture (48:46). History shows that the people of Moab will assimilate into other cultures and cease to have a genetic identity. Yet God promises to restore the fortunes of Moab in the latter days (48:47).

📖 49:1–6

AMMON

In chapter 49, God opens the judgment against Ammon in an oracle directed toward Ammonites who have occupied Gad's ancestral land. The oracle begins with a question about how His people's families teach their children and others about the true faith. Because the people have begun worshiping yet another foreign god, Malcam (or Molech), God wonders if Israel has any sons or heirs who have learned about the covenant with the true God and kept the true religion alive in its community (49:1).

Mourning has begun for Ammon, indicated by wailing and people dressed in sackcloth rushing inside the city walls (49:3). The false god Malcam is said to be in exile along with his priests and princes, similar to Moab's false god Chemosh (49:3; see 48:7). The people once boasted in the beauty of their lands, but Jeremiah prophesies that those lands will be destroyed. God points out the futility of that misplaced boasting, pride, and arrogance (49:4). Punishment for this country is certain, God says, and it will come from all sides and result in masses of exiles (49:5). But in a recurring theme of divine mercy, God says He will eventually restore the fortunes of the people of Ammon as He does with Moab (49:6).

Critical Observation

The sons of Ammon lived to the east of the Jordan River in a town called Rabbah. Today that town is called Amman, the capital city of Jordan, which neighbors Israel. Ammon, like Moab, was born to Abraham's nephew Lot. And the Ammonites, like the Moabites, had angered God with their pagan worship.

EDOM

The second oracle in chapter 49 is against Edom. Apparently this nation used to act with wisdom, but that has ceased, and God asks if the wisdom is gone (49:7). As with Moab and Egypt, Edom's residents are urged to flee, perhaps even into nooks and crannies (depths or caves) like animals (49:8). Jeremiah mentions Teman and Dedan in 25:23, specific areas within Edom. The reference to Esau in verse 8 is because Edomites are descendants of Esau.

Verse 9 refers to the common practice of leaving part of the harvest behind, called *gleaning*, which is a way for the poor to come behind and get some harvest for themselves. God says that even thieves only take until they have enough. But what God will do to Edom is strip it completely bare, leaving nothing behind, not even what people try to hide (49:10). But, as with Moab and Ammon, God promises to save a few, namely, the most vulnerable: orphans and widows (49:11).

God references His own righteous character to assert His next pronouncement, and He seems to be continuing with the theme of those who are responsible versus those who are innocent. The cup of wrath (25:15–38; 48:26–28) will be drunk by those who deserve God's wrath. But God says the orphans and widows will be safe. God then rhetorically asks the listener, are you innocent? Will you be acquitted? And the answer is an emphatic *no* (49:12). God again references His own righteous character in that Bozrah, another city in Edom, will become an example of God's wrath and punishment (49:13).

In the next five verses, Jeremiah inserts his voice again, saying he has heard a message from the Lord and that all the nations should gather together and prepare for battle (49:14). The voice switches back to God's, and God reminds the listeners of His power and hand in their success or failure. God has made them small and taken away the might that the nations once had (49:15). The people who experienced the benefits of the nation's might and power—which will be the same people who lived highest off the ground—will now be brought down by God (49:16). God again states that Edom will become an example of God's punishment and be so destroyed that no one will return to live there (49:17–18).

God lets listeners know that His wrath is coming like a lion approaching a well-tended pasture. In biblical times, this pasture would house vulnerable sheep. Upon God's approach, all will run and leave the sheep untended. Again, in biblical times, as in any agrarian society, anyone or anything attacking livestock would be dealt with. But no one can dispute or stand up against God's just wrath (49:19). Because of this, God urges all to listen to what is coming: Edom will be conquered, and people will be taken captive (49:20). The fall of the mighty city will not go unnoticed (49:21). At the end of this segment, the eagle image that appeared in the Moab prophecy appears again. The people will feel much pain (49:22).

DAMASCUS

The third nation prophesied against in chapter 49 is Damascus. The cities mentioned here, Hamath and Arpad, are both cities in the Damascus region. Shame and anxiety have come to these people because they have heard of the Lord's coming judgment (49:23). Even those who want to flee are paralyzed with fear, and fleeing is no longer an option, just as a woman who is in labor must stop until she has delivered the child (49:24). Because of this, people have not left the city, and they will die where they stand (49:25–26). Afterward, the Lord will completely destroy Damascus (49:27).

ARAB TRIBES

The fourth group of prophecies in this chapter is against two nomadic communities in Arabia, Kedar and Hazor. Verse 28 conveys that both tribes will come under Nebuchadnezzar's control. Where in other areas of Jeremiah destruction of cities includes tearing down walls, to destroy nomadic communities means taking their tents and their flocks (49:29). As with Edom and Moab, the people are told to flee to caves because Babylonian troops are coming (49:30). Again, nomadic tribes move from place to place simply by moving their poles and tents, so God points out that they are an easy target, with no gates or bars for protection (49:31). These people depend upon their flocks for travel, food, and trade. God warns that these flocks will be destroyed or taken by the invaders, and the people left will be dispersed (49:32). The area where these nomads used to congregate will be so devastated that only scavenging animals like jackals will be there (49:33).

ELAM

The final set of prophecies in this chapter is against Elam. Verse 34 indicates that this is one of the prophecies that Jeremiah shared when Zedekiah was still king of Judah (49:34). As with Moab, God's wrath is specific to the skill Elam is known for: archery. God describes His judgment as breaking Elam's bow and finest archers (49:35). The metaphor of four winds indicates how complete the destruction will be and how far flung the Elamites will be (49:36). God indicates no hope for anyone trying to survive (49:37). Rather than others being worshiped in Elam, God will be restored as the rightful leader and king, and eventually God will restore Elam itself (49:38–39).

Critical Observation

Elam is mentioned in Genesis as one of the sons of Shem, who is Noah's son (Genesis 10:1, 22). The Elamites were known as a warring people, constantly at odds with the Hebrews. The Assyrians claimed to have wiped out all the Elamites during the Assyrian's reign of terror, but there was still a remnant during the later time of the Babylonians. God promises to break their mighty men and scatter them to the four winds. But God's mercy prevails, and He promises to restore their fortune in the last days.

📖 50:1–51:58

BABYLON

Chapters 50–51 contain multiple pronouncements against Babylon, the instrument of God's wrath against Judah and other nations. As horrifying as Jeremiah's specific predictions of destruction against Judah and the other nations have been, the pronouncements against Babylon are going to be even worse. How is this possible, since this nation is applying God's justice? Remember that in pronouncing punishments, God also pronounces reasons. These reasons will be detailed in the next two chapters. The chapter opens with a clear statement that the Lord is speaking against Babylon. Some translations identify Babylon by its largest tribe at this time, the Chaldeans (50:1).

God pronounces to all the nations, probably through Jeremiah, that Babylon will cease to be the invader and will itself be conquered. Babylon's god, Marduk, has been destroyed (50:2). Just as Judah was invaded from the north, so Babylon will be invaded by the Persians (50:3). Just like the other nations prophesied about in the book of Jeremiah, Babylon will become a wasteland and no one will remain (50:3).

The destruction of Babylon will be endured by the citizens of Israel and Judah, who survived Babylon's invasion and are now living in Babylon as exiles. These people are now looking to restore their relationship with Yahweh (50:4). Their original shepherds had let them down back in Judah. As their invaders are now conquered, they long more than ever for their home religion and its covenant with the true God (50:5). God laments for them and what they are forced to endure: The ones who had become their leaders are now under siege themselves, and in the chaos of war, the Judeans are left to fend for themselves (50:6–7). In this chaos, God allows them to leave Babylon while He plans His wrath against that country (50:8–9). The Chaldeans, again, are linked with Babylon; they will not escape punishment (50:10).

In the next section, it becomes evident why God intends to punish the people who He had used to be His punishers. God has established throughout the book of Jeremiah that nations prosper when He allows them to prosper. When a nation forgets God as the source of blessing, peace, safety, and prosperity, and begins to look to themselves, their allies, and false gods as sources of those things, God must intervene. God is angry that Babylon enjoyed the role He gave them in refining His people (50:11). After God's action, anyone affiliated with Babylon will be ashamed and humiliated at what Babylon has become (50:12).

God's anger will result in the destruction and desertion of Babylon (50:13). Because of God's wrath, Babylon is now an easy target for anyone who wants to conquer the nation (50:14). The city's civic life no longer exists, and its defenses are literally gone (50:15–16).

Attention now turns back to God's people within this chaos. Again referring to His people as sheep, God reminds the listener that His flock has been conquered before (50:17). God will punish this last invader, just as He did the first one (50:19). As this happens, Israel and Judah can rest easy; the cleansing God wants for them has occurred, and God is pardoning those who have survived (50:20).

In verse 21, God uses two sarcastic names for areas of Babylon: *Merathaim*, which means "double rebellion," and *Pekod*, which means "visitation" (50:21). It is no surprise, then, that God uses such names in ordering their destruction. Consequently, war breaks out against Babylon just as God intended (50:22–24). God speaks as if He personally is outfitting the invading Persian army and inviting it to do whatever it wants to Babylon and Chaldea (50:25–27). The consequences of war have come to Babylon: Its own citizens are now fugitives and refugees. This is the justice of God (50:28).

The next four verses reiterate what God is allowing to happen to Babylon. Now is the time to conquer this nation that has been so destructive to so many (50:29). Invading armies will succeed, and Babylon's people will suffer (50:30). This harsh justice is specifically because of the arrogance with which Babylon conducts its affairs (50:31–32).

In verses 33–34, God reminds the listener of His work on behalf of His people. God needs to perform a work on His people, and He does so through Babylon's armies. But those soldiers themselves are also subject to the will and the work of God (50:33–34). In verses 35–38, God again asserts the destruction that will come against the Chaldeans and the Babylonians, but this time He is specific about who will suffer: officials, wise men, priests, horses, chariots, and foreigners. God even states that drought will come. God adds here that this punishment is coming also because of Babylon's love of idols. Consequently, only scavenging animals will remain where Babylon used to be (50:39–40).

God states again that the instruments of His wrath against the Babylonians will come from the north (50:41). The people who work against Babylon will do so with gusto (50:42). Nebuchadnezzar is now reaping what he has sown for many years (50:43). The same image God uses for Himself in 49:19 appears again here in verse 44. God has spoken: The people of Babylon will be destroyed, and those who survive will become captives (50:45). The entire world will see the humiliation and suffering of the nation that has been so mighty for so long (50:46).

Critical Observation

The Chaldeans lived in the southwest corner of the Babylonian Empire. Abraham left Ur of the Chaldeans (or Chaldees) to journey westward, as God directed him toward the land of the Canaanites, later to become the land of Israel (Genesis 11:26, 31). The chronicles of Jeremiah have focused on the time leading up to the siege of Nebuchadnezzar. Chapter 50 looks forward to the execution of God's judgment on Babylon as the new empire, the Persians (power from the east), now inflicts their own version of terror and domination. The national god Marduk will soon be replaced by the national god of the Persians. The empire of Babylon that sowed destruction will now reap that same destruction as another ego seeks to replace the splendor and majesty of the Babylonian empire. Babylon has become arrogant before the Lord, and God promises to punish them by cutting down the young men in the streets and silencing the men of war. Terror is on every side.

God promises to raise up a spirit of destruction against rebellious Babylon and those who are called in the Hebrew *Leb Kamai*, which means "the heart of those against me" (51:1). God promises to raise up the tribal groups ("foreigners") of Ashkenaz (Germanic/Slavic), Minni (Iran), and Ararat (Turkey), all parts of the Medo-Persian Empire which will soon crush the regime of Nebuchadnezzar (51:2; see 51:27)). Verse 3 begins with God talking to the Babylonians and then instructing the invading Persians. As stated before, Babylon will be destroyed (51:4), and any injustices that occurred to God's people while they were being refined by God are now avenged (51:5).

Again, God instructs some people to flee Babylon because the wrath of God is coming. But why are some instructed to flee as if they are innocent? God is speaking to His people from Judah and Israel who have been captured and kept as slaves in Babylon. The destruction of Babylon is certain, and He doesn't want them to endure such wrath twice (51:6). In the next few verses we again see the cup of God's wrath, which, when drunk to excess, renders the drinker arrogant and sinful (25:15–38; 51:7–8). Any attempt at recovering from God's actions toward them will be futile (see 10:19; 15:18; 30:12–13), because it is God's will that they be destroyed beyond healing (51:9). The remnant of Israel and Judah see this as vindication for injustices they endured from the Babylonians during their own punishment from God (51:10).

Even more forces are awakened against Babylon to perform the Lord's work, and this particular people, the Medes, fulfill an earlier prophecy that they will participate in Babylon's fall (51:11–12). Babylon's placement near rivers has allowed it to amass great fortune, but the end has come by the hand of the Lord (51:13–14).

In the next two verses, God again reminds the listener of His work as Creator and Sustainer of all creation. This section is highly reminiscent of not only Genesis but also of earlier passages in Jeremiah, where God contrasts His nature as true God against the false, created gods Judah has turned to (51:15–16). God is the Creator, and people are the created; when human beings try to create as God creates, they reveal their foolishness (51:17). The idols and gods they create from their own limited minds are worthless, and those who do such things will be punished (51:18). God is the one true God (51:19).

God uses anyone He wishes to do His work (51:20–23). In this case, He must punish those Babylonians and Chaldeans who let themselves act of their own wills instead of the will of God (51:24). Verses 25–26 reveal that the ones who have been so mighty are now at the mercy of God and will not survive their punishment.

In this version of the war party against Babylon, three new groups are recruited: Ararat, Minni, and Ashkenaz (51:27). Their task on behalf of the Lord is as clear as the others have been: Destroy Babylon in the name of the Lord (51:28–29). The warring is taking its toll on the Babylonians (51:30–32). God notes that it is almost over (51:33).

The voice here shifts to that of a survivor of Judah, detailing what has happened at the hands of Nebuchadnezzar (51:34). God willed and allowed Judah to be invaded by Babylon, but chapters 50–51 have shown that Babylon acted as much out of its own arrogance and greed as it did out of respect for God's will. For the injustices that occurred in the midst of God's punishment, the survivors want retribution (51:35–36). Their desire is fulfilled; Babylon will be utterly destroyed (51:37–40). The next four verses detail how the mighty, fearsome Babylon has been brought down (51:41–44). Many of the same phrases of destruction that have been applied to other nations in the book of Jeremiah now apply to Babylon.

Similar to earlier in this chapter, God instructs the Judeans and Israelites who are living in Babylon as exiles that He is about to punish Babylon (51:45). He has prophesied this so word will get to His people in the coming years (51:46). The fact that God is speaking to His people personally and trying to comfort them with these details indicates that, as seen earlier in Jeremiah, the prophet and priest function still exist even after war and exile (51:47). God wants His people to know that the coming wrath is targeted toward Babylon (51:48).

The reason for God's punishment of Babylon is restated: They were excessive in their treatment of Judah (51:49). Now, vengeance must be had for the Judeans who were killed. Those Judeans who survived must now flee and remember the Lord and Jerusalem (51:50). In the meantime, Babylon's punishment is coming because of its arrogance and its worship of false idols. Her former power cannot save her (51:52–53).

The prophecy against Babylon closes with verses about the impact God's wrath is having on the Babylonians (51:54). They now know God's intent is real, and everything they've done to others will now be done to them (51:55–56). The leaders become drunk with arrogance and power, so much so that they will not survive (51:57). The city itself will not survive either; its walls will be destroyed, and its remains will be burned down (51:58).

📖 51:59–64

SERAIAH

This chapter closes with a specific message from Jeremiah to a man named Seraiah (Baruch's brother). Chapters 50–51 detail Jeremiah's delivery of the prophecies regarding Babylon. He is communicating to the Babylonians while traveling with the exiled Judeans (51:59). Jeremiah writes all these messages on a single scroll and instructs Seraiah to read every bit of it as soon as they got to Babylon (51:60–61). Jeremiah, fulfilling his role as prophet, wants God's message to get to the people (51:62). And just as he has so often done as a prophet, he creates one final visual image: He instructs Seraiah to tie a stone to the scroll and, when he is finished reading God's message, throw the scroll in the Euphrates so it will sink to the bottom. Babylon's fate is the same as the scroll's (51:63–64).

JEREMIAH 52:1–34

CONCLUSION OF THE BOOK OF JEREMIAH

Jerusalem Fallen	52:1–11
The Temple Sacked	52:12–23
To Babylon	52:24–30
Jehoiachin Released	52:31–34

Setting Up the Section

In this section, the reader gets an overview of how all of Jeremiah's prophecies look from a historical perspective. This section is almost exactly like 2 Kings 24:18–25:21. Most importantly, though, is the inclusion of the fall of Jerusalem as the final chapter of this book of Jeremiah's prophecies, revealing that the city's destruction happens just as Jeremiah said it would—validating Jeremiah's prophecies.

📖 52:1–11

JERUSALEM FALLEN

The reader is taken back to a time when the king who ended up accompanying Judah into Babylonian exile, and who was brutally killed as a prisoner of war, is just coming to the throne at age twenty-one (52:1). Despite Jeremiah's prophecies about God's anger and coming wrath, Zedekiah, like his predecessor, Jehoiakim, continues to lead the nation in sin (52:2). God then punishes Judah as He promised. Apparently, for a time, Zedekiah rebels unsuccessfully against Nebuchadnezzar (52:3).

The next verses explain in detail how Jerusalem falls to the Babylonians. In the ninth year of Zedekiah's eleven years as king, Nebuchadnezzar arranges his army around Jerusalem, cutting off traffic in and out of the city (52:4–5). After six months, the people are out of food, and the Babylonian troops break through the city walls (52:6–7). Babylonian troops are supported by the Chaldeans, who capture Zedekiah and bring him to Nebu-chadnezzar for sentencing (52:8–9). In a brutal fashion not uncommon in war, Zedekiah is forced to watch as all his sons are killed. He is then blinded and imprisoned in Babylon, remaining there until he dies (52:10–11).

📖 52:12–23

THE TEMPLE SACKED

About a month later, Nebuchadnezzar sends his chief into Jerusalem to burn not only the temple but also all the large houses he can find, including Zedekiah's (52:13). This is the culmination of progressive actions Nebuchadnezzar has been taking to conquer Judah. This is the end. The Chaldeans destroy the city walls (52:14). As seen earlier in Jeremiah's prophecies, huge numbers of people who haven't already been captured are taken prisoner (52:15). But also mentioned before, the poorest and the weakest are left behind (52:16). The next seven verses list in detail items that are taken from the temple. These are the items the exiles are longing for in 27:16–22.

📖 52:24–30

TO BABYLON

Verses 24–30 give additional information about some of the people who are cap-tured: They are of religious and civic importance—leaders of the people who have just been conquered (52:24–25). Like Zedekiah, they are taken to Nebuchadnezzar and killed (52:26–27). With these leaders dead, the exile can begin (52:27). At least three waves of exile are listed here (52:28–30).

📖 52:31–34

JEHOIACHIN RELEASED

The final verses of the book of Jeremiah show that despite the destruction of Jerusa-lem and its temple, and the death and exile of so many of its citizens, a king of Judah remains alive. This king (though in name only) is Jehoiachin, and Nebuchadnezzar's son Evil-Merodach takes him out of prison (52:31). Probably as a gesture of good will, Evil-Merodach improves Jehoiachin's living situation by giving him new clothes, allowing him to share meals, and providing him an allowance. Even amongst prisoners there is hierarchy, and the improvement in Jehoiachin's situation is an indication of hopefulness that closes this powerful book.

Take It Home

The closing words of the book of Jeremiah disclose that 4,600 of Jerusalem's finest are bound into slavery to serve out their lives in subservience to King Nebuchadnezzar. Little do they know that God will use them as an object lesson to the world, to prove His uncompromising mandate for sovereignty in their lives, and to prove the severe and widespread consequences of bowing in worship to false gods. In every generation, we disappoint God with new ways of disobeying Him. Yet in new ways every generation, He proves His faithfulness to us and proves that His loving-kindness is everlasting.

LAMENTATIONS

INTRODUCTION TO LAMENTATIONS

Wedged between two of the major prophet works—the books of Jeremiah and Ezekiel—is the short, five-chapter poem titled Lamentations. The book's name reveals what it is—a poem of lament. It records in grave detail and sorrow the aftermath of one of the lowest points in the history of the Israelites. But it also provides one of the greatest testimonies of God's justice and mercy.

AUTHOR

There is a tradition that the prophet Jeremiah wrote this book, and thus it has its place in the Bible following the book of Jeremiah. However, no author is named in this specific book itself, and there is no place in the rest of the Bible where this writing is attributed to Jeremiah.

PURPOSE

Lamentations is a poem that reflects on the nation of Judah's suffering. The author witnessed the fall of Jerusalem and the exile of many Israelites, and in this work he is grieving the nation's fall and the demise of his people. God punished His people for their unfaithfulness to Him and His covenant, and the author and poet who wrote this poem wrote it from that place of suffering as both a reflection on the people's sins and its consequences and a prayer to God for His mercy and redemption.

OCCASION

Lamentations was most likely written soon after 586 BC, shortly after the fall of Jerusalem at the hands of the Babylonians. The author is reflecting on what he sees around him, making it most likely that the city's fall was recent at the time the book was written. In this work he alludes to the future redemption God promised His people, but that redemption has not happened yet, and the wounds of their sins and consequences are still fresh.

THEMES

The themes of the book include the following: sorrow and grief, as evidenced by the book's title; the consequences of sin; and God's judgment, mercy, and sovereignty. However, the strongest theme, which is largely unexpected based on the historical context of the book and its genre, is that of hope. Hope in God and His mercy is the foundation on which the author's lamenting takes place.

HISTORICAL CONTEXT

In 586 BC, the Babylonian army under the command of King Nebuchadnezzar attacked the city of Jerusalem, Judah's capital and the holy city that housed the temple of God. The city and temple were destroyed, and the people who weren't killed were exiled to Babylon. These events are recorded in 2 Kings 25 and 2 Chronicles 36. The people would remain in exile for almost fifty years. The author witnessed the city's fall and wrote this book shortly thereafter.

CONTRIBUTION TO THE BIBLE

Lamentations is one of the poetic books of the Bible. Chapters 1–4 are written in the very specific literary structure of an acrostic, with each verse beginning with progressive letters of the twenty-two letter Hebrew alphabet. Chapters 1, 2, 4, and 5 have twenty-two verses, and chapter 3 has sixty-six. Each Hebrew letter is used in three verses in chapter 3.

LAMENTATIONS 1:1–22
THE ELEMENTS OF GODLY GRIEF

Setting Up the Section

The introductory chapter to the book of Lamentations focuses on the depth of the author's grief over Jerusalem's destruction. The fall of the city marked the fulfillment of what had been prophesied for years—that eventually the people's idolatry would be their downfall.

📖 1:1–7

THE AUTHOR'S LONELINESS

Chief among the grievous feelings the author has is loneliness—the first observation he makes is how deserted the city is. The loneliness he feels when observing his fallen city is compounded by all of the losses he notices. Verses 1–7 catalog some of these losses. Among them are abundance, allies, a home, worship, prestige, courage, and prosperity. But despite all the tragedy the author notes, he quickly acknowledges that the destruction isn't undeserved (1:5). Rather, in the poet's own words, "The LORD has brought her grief because of her many sins" (1:5 NIV).

📖 1:8–11

THE CAUSES OF JUDAH'S GRIEF

Judah's sin has devastating consequences, not just for the state of the nation, but in the lives of its inhabitants. The author's grief is rooted largely in how much he cares for Judah's people and the sorrow he feels regarding their downfall. In verse 8, he notes the shame the people feel after their idolatry is exposed. The people's sin also leaves them defiled (1:9), and the unclean aren't allowed to enter the presence of God. Because of their sin, their worship is tainted. One of the worst consequences of the Babylonian invasion for the city of Jerusalem as a whole is the desecration of the temple. The most holy place on earth has been invaded by a group of pagans who would never have even been allowed in it (1:10). Verse 11 notes that another devastating consequence of the nation's sin, probably one of the most strongly felt by the people of Judah, is the famine caused by how long the city was held captive before being overtaken.

Demystifying Lamentations

The cause of Judah's grief and destruction isn't a mystery—it is a direct effect of the sin in which they had been living for many years. God was gracious to the nation by sending prophets to speak truth into the people's lives, but they repeatedly refused to listen. Even the most holy places of the temple were corrupted by priests practicing idolatry. This is the ultimate example of disloyalty to the one true God.

1:12–17

THE PURPOSES OF JUDAH'S GRIEF

While the suffering of the nation is undoubtedly deserved, and long overdue because of their sin toward God, God doesn't exact suffering on them for punishment's sake alone. At this time idolatry was rampant, and God had to remind the people who their true God was. The severity of their punishment is to get their attention and turn them back to Him (1:12–13). Their suffering also serves the purpose of making them slaves to their sin (1:14). God gave His people the freedom to make their own choices, but they became slaves to their sins' consequences. But no matter how much one suffers inwardly as a result of sin, nothing is as humbling and serves as adequate a wake-up call as being crushed in the presence of one's enemy. And that is exactly what Judah experiences when its capital city is destroyed (1:15).

1:18–22

JUDAH'S CONFESSION

The nation comes face-to-face with the consequences of their sin, and this stark reality leads them to some confessions: God is righteous and acts rightly, and we were wrong to rebel against His Word (1:18–19). Having confessed the foundation of their sins and their recognition of God's holiness, the people appeal to God to hear their cries of sorrow and act mercifully toward them (1:20–21).

LAMENTATIONS 2:1–22

JERUSALEM'S SUFFERING

Setting Up the Section

The second chapter of Lamentations describes God's anger at the sin of His people. For too long, the people of Judah have lived in a state of continual sin through the idolatry they both practiced and tolerated.

📖 **2:1–10**

GOD'S RIGHTEOUS ANGER

The results of God's righteous and just anger are described in a series of powerfully descriptive verbs that capture the severity of God's anger against Jerusalem (2:1–8). Verses 9–10 describe the reaction of the city and its people to this outpouring of God's wrath. The gates and walls of the city literally crumble, mimicking what happened to the people as well.

Critical Observation

Lamentations 2:1–10 mentions more than forty times how God was personally involved in Jerusalem's downfall and what happened to the people within its walls. This repeated mentioning of God's control reiterates that although King Nebuchadnezzar may have commanded the attack on the city, it was ultimately God's judgment that orchestrated the events.

📖 **2:11–13**

THE AUTHOR'S RESPONSE

Having just described the response of the city and its people to God's anger, the author describes his own reaction—one of both torment and a sorrowful understanding of the justice of God. He understands that God's discipline is appropriate for the sin of the people of Jerusalem, but that doesn't make it any easier for him to stomach the city's destruction (2:11). He is admittedly without words of comfort in the face of the people's suffering (2:13).

📖 2:14–17

FALSE PROPHETS REVEALED

There were many false prophets who were telling the people that they had nothing to fear (see Jeremiah 27–28). In the wake of the city's destruction, however, it becomes evident that these prophecies were false (2:14). Although Jerusalem's enemies gloat in the face of its downfall, the enemy's involvement in Jerusalem's destruction is secondary to God's (2:15–17).

📖 2:18–22

THE NEED FOR GOD

Verses 18–19 include a command to the people to let their grief overtake them. They are encouraged to wail and mourn at the consequences of their sin, the worst of which is the suffering of the innocent, especially their children (see 1:5, 16; 2:11–12). In the aftermath of Jerusalem's destruction, horrific atrocities occurred such as women eating their children, priests slain in God's sanctuary, and both young and old people dead in the streets (2:20–21).

Take It Home

The author admits that God's actions are a direct consequence of His Word (2:17). Deuteronomy 28 warns the Israelites of the consequences of disobeying God's commands and prophesies a time when they will be taken captive to a foreign land. God proves that His character is steadfast and that His Word is true.

LAMENTATIONS 3:1–66

HOPE

Setting Up the Section

Because of the faithlessness of the people of Jerusalem, this holy city has been destroyed. The people who survived the attack were taken off into Babylonian captivity. Their situation is one of complete hopelessness. But God is a faithful God. It is in this truth that hope for the nation of Judah rests.

📄 3:1–24

GOD'S LOVE AND MERCY

Lamentations 3:1–24 reveals the measure of God's love and mercy to His people. Verses 2:1–18 paint a picture of just how desperate the situation in Jerusalem has become.

The chapter opens with an identification of a man who is afflicted (3:1). Most scholars see this man as a personification of the city of Jerusalem, much like the widow mentioned at the opening of the book. Others think, however, that the author is simply referring to himself and his own desperation.

Throughout the first part of chapter 3, the author uses a variety of analogies to build a picture of hopelessness. But it is from this place of suffering that he voices a profound word of hope. Verse 21 begins with the word *yet*, which marks the powerful transition from the desperation all around to the hope of God. This hope is rooted in the fact that God didn't destroy everyone, therefore He hasn't completely abandoned His people (3:22). Verses 23–24 attest to God's faithfulness. Just as He was faithful to bring the judgment and destruction He had promised, He will also be faithful in the mercy and renewal He promised.

📄 3:25–39

GOD'S GOODNESS AND CONTROL

Despite the suffering the author has witnessed, the goodness of God is still evident (3:25–26). The people's suffering doesn't change this aspect of God's character. Being able to recognize the characteristic of God's goodness doesn't happen overnight, but it is rather a testimony to living continually under God's instruction and discipline, so that when in the midst of affliction, one cannot deny that God is good (3:27–30). Verses 31–39 are a reminder that God is in control, even during times of grief.

GOD'S FORGIVENESS

Judah rebelled against God, and they have been punished for their repeated sins of idolatry. However, their punishment produces repentance, and they find themselves pleading for God's forgiveness (3:40–42). In verses 43–49, there is a catalog of a series of sufferings, but they now seem out of place following the author's statements of hope in God's goodness, faithfulness, and control. This suffering is still the reality, but the author trusts that the characteristics of God he knows to be true will soon return and bring relief to those who seek God's forgiveness (3:48–50).

Critical Observation

For those who consider Jeremiah the author of this book, verses 52–58 seem to be an obvious description of an event from Jeremiah's life when he was attacked, thrown into an empty water tank (or cistern), and left to die (Jeremiah 38:6–13). Just as God rescued him from that situation, he prays that God will rescue the nation from its suffering.

As if the sufferings of the nation aren't enough, the author once again finds himself being attacked and persecuted by his enemies (3:59–63). He knows the Lord is capable of delivering him, and he prays that God will rescue him and punish his attackers (3:64–66).

Take It Home

God's mercy and forgiveness are limitless to those who believe in Him and repent of their sins. The book of Lamentations serves to encourage the people of God to repent so they, too, can experience God's forgiving grace.

LAMENTATIONS 4:1–22
EVIDENCE OF JERUSALEM'S DESTRUCTION

Setting Up the Section

Lamentations reaches its climax in chapter 3, when the author responds to God's unwavering mercy, goodness, faithfulness, and control. In chapter 4, he looks more closely at what caused God to judge Judah in this manner by comparing the state of the city of Jerusalem before and after the Babylonian attack.

📖 4:1–12

THE COSTS

The fourth chapter opens with a description of the costs of the people's rebellion against God in imagery they would understand. Although their lives had once been as valuable as gold, they are now as dispensable as everyday pottery (4:1–2). Their rebellion has physical costs as well. The children are starving, and people who were once considered royalty are sleeping in ash heaps on the streets (4:3–5). In verse 6 there is a comparison of the situation in Jerusalem to that of Sodom, but in this case the author says Jerusalem is worse off in that her suffering lingers (see Genesis 18–19).

Verses 7–12 paint a picture for the reader of what the suffering in Jerusalem is like following the Babylonian siege. Bejeweled princes are sickly and roam the streets unrecognizable and covered in filth (4:7–8). People are constantly dying of starvation due to famine (4:9), and the author again notes the horrific scene of women cooking their children to survive (4:10). All of this is a result of what is referred to in verse 11 as God's fierce wrath.

📖 4:13–20

THE CAUSES

Having detailed some of the results of God's judgment, this section gives more specifics about its causes. The first is in verse 13: Those who were supposed to be the example of holiness and the mediators between the people and God were leading the people astray with lies and corrupt practices. The priests who survive the Babylonian attack are left to wander the streets and are shown no honor (4:14–16). But unfortunately, the priests' damage had been done, and the nation paid for their sins.

Not only do the people of Judah follow their religious leaders in idolatrous practices; they also falsely trust the hope of a political leader and ally nation to save them from Babylon when they should have been trusting in God (4:17). They put misplaced hope in their king, Zedekiah, who was heavily influenced by the false prophets and even tries to escape from Jerusalem after its fall (4:20; see 2 Kings 25:3–7).

Demystifying Lamentations

Jeremiah 37:5–7 records how the people of Jerusalem look to Egypt and Pharaoh Hophra to ally with them against Babylon. In Lamentations 4:17, the author notes that this prophecy has come true. Even after the attack, some of the people who survived and weren't taken into captivity sought refuge in Egypt, where they would be free to continue their idolatrous practices (Jeremiah 44:7–30).

📖 4:21–22

THE CONCLUSION

But for the people of Judah, there is good news, and the author wants to make sure they hear it. Their enemies, the Edomites, who took delight in what happened to Jerusalem, will face their own day of judgment from the Lord (4:21–22). Even better, though, is the prophecy that the Israelites' punishment will end (4:22).

Take It Home

Although the aftermath of the fall of Jerusalem is horrific, God still proves faithful to His promise of forgiveness and mercy. For those who maintained hope, how great these words must have sounded: "O beautiful Jerusalem, your punishment will end; you will soon return from exile" (4:22 NLT).

LAMENTATIONS 5:1–22
THE POET'S PRAYER

Setting Up the Section

Having grieved for the suffering of the nation, cataloged the related tragedies, voiced words of hope and a reminder of God's mercy, and prophesied an end to the suffering and the downfall of the enemy, Lamentations closes with a prayer for God's swift mercy.

📖 5:1–13

RELIEF FROM PHYSICAL SUFFERING

The prayer opening chapter 5 is a petition to God to remember the suffering His people are experiencing (5:1). The suffering is deserved, but many are repentant and God will not turn away from them forever. Verses 2–10 describe the people's condition at the time of the prayer. Their property (inheritance) is gone, they are exiled to a foreign land, and they are impoverished and at the mercy of their enemies. Everyone has suffered in some way. Verses 11–13 mention six different people groups, all of whom have experienced extreme suffering. The entire nation feels God's punishment on an individual level.

📖 5:14–18

RELIEF FROM EMOTIONAL SUFFERING

Verses 2–13 focus on the nation's physical suffering, but in verses 14–18, the prayer shifts to the topic of emotional suffering. There is no joy among the people, and their hearts are faint because of what they have endured (5:17). More importantly than physical healing, the people's spirits need to be restored to the joy of the Lord they once knew.

Critical Observation

Prior to the fall of Jerusalem, the nation was ruled by the line of David in fulfillment of the Davidic covenant (2 Samuel 7). But the fall of the city marks the end of Davidic rule. The covenant is ultimately fulfilled in Jesus Christ's reign, but the reign of Davidic earthly kings is finished (see 5:16).

PLEA FOR REDEMPTION

Verse 19 is the crux of this prayer and reveals the foundation of the author's hope. God is the only One with power to right the people's punishment and bring physical and emotional healing to the nation. The author prays for restoration and for God, in His mercy, to turn the people's hearts back to Him if mercy is in His plan (5:21–22). He admits that God, in His sovereignty, may not choose to lift the punishment and show mercy, but it is his prayer that that is not the case.

Take It Home

The underlying theme in Lamentations is that of hope. God had promised restoration, just as He had promised the punishment the people suffered, and it was this promise of salvation that the author clung to. He knew God's character to be good and merciful, and he hoped that with repentant hearts, God would soon lift His punishment from them and return them to Himself.

EZEKIEL

INTRODUCTION TO EZEKIEL

Ezekiel was a prophet caught up in the turmoil of his time. He was among ten thousand exiles carried off to Babylon in the second of three deportations from Judea (2 Kings 24:14). He and his wife settled in a Judean community established near Nippur, on the Kebar Canal. God's people needed a prophet in Babylon because, with some wonderful exceptions, they carried all the spiritual baggage from the years of idolatry and apostasy that began their ruin.

AUTHOR

Ezekiel was a priest, and his priestly orientation comes through in his prophecies. More than any other prophet, he depicts the consummation of the kingdom of God in terms of a new temple and revitalized worship. His prophetic call came at age thirty, which would have made him a young eyewitness to the spiritual reforms during the reign of King Josiah. Unable to serve as priest in a traditional capacity due to his relocation (and subsequent destruction of Jerusalem's temple), his spiritual preparations are still put to use as God calls him to be a prophet during a crucial time of Israel's history.

PURPOSE

Ezekiel has a clear voice from God during a difficult time. He prophesies several years in Babylon before the Babylonians actually destroy the temple and the city of Jerusalem, warning his people of what will happen. He then continues to minister several years afterward to assure them of God's continued sovereignty throughout their bleak circumstances.

OCCASION

God's people were caught in the maw of conflict between world powers Egypt and Babylon. International tensions overshadowed the circumstances of many smaller states and turned the lives of countless individuals and families upside down. Ezekiel's world was turbulent, which makes his message surprisingly relevant for today.

THEMES

Ezekiel's book contains a number of themes:

- *Visions.* No other Old Testament prophet is given as many visions as Ezekiel, and no other Old Testament book devotes so much space to visions.
- *"Then you will know that I am the LORD."* This phrase is found again and again throughout Ezekiel's writing. Israel has forgotten the Lord her God. Ezekiel repeatedly passes along God's reminder to assure the people that God is still at work to put Israel's culpable ignorance right.
- *Individual Responsibility.* The people tended to blame their problems on their ancestors or circumstances beyond their control. Ezekiel stresses the importance of one's individual relationship with the Lord.
- *God using Ezekiel as a sign.* Many other prophets were orators, and Ezekiel did his share of preaching. Yet he is distinctive in how frequently God uses the prophet himself as a sign. Much like Jeremiah, Ezekiel acts out or symbolizes what he is saying on several occasions.

HISTORICAL CONTEXT

When Ezekiel began his prophetic work, Babylon had gained the upper hand and was holding sway over the entire ancient Near East. Judah's King Jehoiakim had first submitted to Babylon, but later rebelled (with the encouragement of the Egyptians, but against the advice of Jeremiah). As a result the Babylonian leader, King Nebuchadnezzar, dragged him to Babylon in shackles where he was apparently executed. Jehoiakim's eighteen-year-old son, Jehoiachin, succeeded him as the Babylonian appointee, but he, too, was summoned to Babylon a few months later.

CONTRIBUTION TO THE BIBLE

Much of what Ezekiel teaches is similar to the writings of Jeremiah or other prophets. But unique to his writing is the fascinating vision of the valley of dry bones (37:1–14) and his vision of a temple unlike anything that has yet been constructed (chapters 40–48).

IMPENDING JUDGMENT AGAINST THE NATIONS

25:1–32:32

AFTER GOD'S JUDGMENT OF JUDAH

33:1–36:38

DRY BONES AND NEW LIFE

37:1–39:29

A NEW TEMPLE

40:1–46:24

THE RIVER MEASURED AND THE TERRITORY DIVIDED

47:1–48:35

EZEKIEL 1:1–3:27

THE CALL OF A PROPHET

Setting Up the Section

The first section of Ezekiel (chapters 1–24) is devoted to prophecies of judgment and divine wrath to befall the citizens still remaining in Judea and Jerusalem. The first subsection of this large division concerns the call of Ezekiel.

1:1–28

EZEKIEL'S VISION

Ezekiel is among a group of expatriate Jews living in Babylon along the Kebar River at Tel Abib (1:3; 3:15). It is his thirtieth year (1:1), the age at which a priest should be beginning his official service to God (Numbers 4:3). He is far away from the temple in Jerusalem, but God has not forgotten him.

Critical Observation

Verses 2–3 shift from first person to third person, likely the insertion of an editor to provide objective dating for Ezekiel's call and/or to make the opening more consistent with other prophetic books. The date would have been July 31, 593 BC. It may seem strange that this account is dated according to the reign of Jehoiachin (1:2), a king who ruled only three months and accomplished nothing. Yet Jehoiachin is perceived as the last of the kings in the Davidic line.

There in the land of Israel's enemies, while God's people are in captivity, Ezekiel receives a magnificent vision. A sudden storm blows in, accompanied by wind, lightning, and fire. In the center of the fire are four creatures, each with four faces (Ezekiel 1:4–6). They will be identified later (10:2) as *cherubim*, a specific rank of angels.

Each of the four faces of the creatures is significant: The lion is chief of the wild animals, the ox chief of domestic animals, the eagle the primary bird, and human beings chief of all animals (1:10). The four faces orient the beings in all directions, so they therefore have no need to turn while navigating (1:9, 12). They move, literally, like lightning: They are both brilliant and quick (1:13–14).

Demystifying Ezekiel

The description of these cherubim may have appeared less bizarre to Ezekiel's original audience than to modern ears. The iconography of the ancient Near East included figures that had more than one head, multiple sets of wings, human bodies with animal heads, etc. However, no symbols have been discovered that exactly match Ezekiel's depiction.

Just as fascinating and puzzling is the prophet's portrayal of the wheels by which these creatures move from place to place (1:15-21). The beings could move in any direction, including leaving the ground. In Hebrew and Greek, the same word can be used for wind and spirit, so the *windstorm* (1:4) is associated with the movement of God's Spirit. No prophet writes of the Spirit as much as Ezekiel. This energizing power of God directs him from place to place, at least in his visions. And the movement of the four creatures is in response to the Spirit (1:20).

We shouldn't be surprised if Ezekiel's description leaves us unsatisfied. He is attempting to describe something that is beyond his power to understand, much less communicate to others. He uses a great number of analogies to try to explain what he is seeing, but it is still difficult to make sense of his account.

After the creatures and the wheels, Ezekiel describes a gem-like firmament—an expanse or platform above the creatures upon which the throne of God will rest (1:22-28). The throne of sapphire (1:26) is reminiscent of Moses' description of seeing God on Mount Sinai (Exodus 24:9-11). Even describing the sound the creatures made is a challenge for Ezekiel. He likens it to three different things: the roar of a great torrent, the voice of the Almighty, and the tramp of a great army on the march (Ezekiel 1:24).

Yet these amazing sights are only a prelude for what is to come. Ezekiel's attention is arrested first by a voice from above and then by a figure like that of a man, sitting on a dazzling throne. The shining brilliance of the figure prevents Ezekiel from seeing anything other than a general shape, yet the prophet leaves no doubt that he is witnessing the terrible majesty of Yahweh. In response, he falls facedown before the Lord God (1:28).

📖 2:1–3:11

EZEKIEL'S CALL

Throughout the entire book of Ezekiel, God never addresses the prophet by name. Instead, He uses the term *Son of man,* which highlights Ezekiel's humanity in contrast to the Lord's divine glory.

God is sending Ezekiel to speak to his own people, the Israelites. But at this point in their history, they are rebellious, obstinate, and stubborn (2:3-4). They are subjects revolting against their King and children rebelling against their Father. But according to verse 5, they are about to discover a real prophet among them. The problem with false prophecy is that it is invariably rosy and frequently proven false by real-life events. Ezekiel, on the other hand, will provide stark promises of divine wrath, and the people will see his prophecies come to pass.

Demystifying Ezekiel

References to *Israel* can be confusing. The name originated with Jacob (Genesis 32:27–28). By the end of Genesis, phrases such as "the tribes of Israel" (Genesis 49:16) or "the children of Israel" (Genesis 50:25) indicate the people of God. Centuries later, after Solomon's death, the tribes divided. The ten northern tribes continued to be known as *Israel* while the southern tribes comprised *Judah*. Technically, the Jews exiled to Babylon were from Judah, but they were the only ones to return to their homeland after captivity. From that point, biblical writers again use *Israel* to refer to them, as Ezekiel does (Ezekiel 2:3; 3:5, 7). And while the term *Jew* is by definition someone from the kingdom of Judah, the term soon broadens to include any of the citizens of the remnant of Israel after the exile.

Ezekiel has a challenging assignment. Not only is he being sent to his own people, which is difficult enough, but there are many exiled priests in Babylon. Why should the people pay special attention to *him*? In addition, the people's rebellious attitude toward God will make Ezekiel's message especially hard for them to hear. No patriot wants to prophesy the doom of the nation he loves. But Ezekiel is up to the task.

In fact, God warns Ezekiel of the danger of getting caught up in the rebellious attitude of his people (2:8). He offers him something to eat, and Ezekiel no doubt expects some kind of food. Instead, he is handed a scroll. Jeremiah had written of eating the words of God (Jeremiah 15:16), but Ezekiel goes beyond metaphor into a more concrete (and most likely unpleasant) experience, as he is instructed to fill his stomach (Ezekiel 3:3). The message he is digesting is summed up by lament, mourning, and woe (2:10).

The message certainly isn't appealing, yet the taste of the scroll is sweet (3:3). The sweetness must have come from the prophet's encounter with the Word of the Lord itself. Opening one's life to God's Word and God's will is humanity's highest privilege and the greatest conceivable satisfaction.

Had Ezekiel been sent to some other people, they might be expected to respond, as the Assyrians had listened to Jonah. But the people of Israel had a long habit of rejecting God, so Ezekiel should expect the same response (3:4–7) and not take it personally.

Critical Observation

A soldier on the battlefield doesn't wring his hands or ask the enemy soldiers firing at him, "What did I do to you?" Rather, he understands that the opposition is the result of a deeper and larger cause. He is a target only because he is serving the cause of his government or nation. Ezekiel was to have a similar outlook in his ministry.

God promises to help toughen up His prophet. (The name *Ezekiel* means "God strengthens.") We speak in terms of "facing" difficult situations, so it is Ezekiel's face that is hardened to help the prophet cope with his listeners (3:8–9). And it is at this point revealed that Ezekiel's assignment is to preach to the community of exiled Hebrews (3:11).

EZEKIEL'S (POSSIBLE) RELUCTANCE

So how does Ezekiel feel about his call from God? We see no overt resistance, and we hear no objections from his mouth. Many assume, then, that he readily accepts the call to become God's prophet. But a close examination of the text and a combination of several observations suggest that Ezekiel may have responded much like Moses, Gideon, and Jeremiah in initially resisting God's invitation.

Much of scripture—especially in regard to the experiences of the life of faith—is communicated indirectly and subtly. The reader is expected to pay close attention with his or her imagination fully awake to the personal dimension. When reading this section of Ezekiel in such a way, the impression is that the prophet does not want to do what the Lord is calling him to do and has to be cajoled and persuaded, if not compelled, to undertake the assignment.

Following is some of the evidence to support such a viewpoint:

- The length and detail of Ezekiel's call narrative is almost 50 percent longer than that of Moses, who is clearly disinclined to respond to God at first.
- The power and scope of the vision preceding Ezekiel's call.
- In 2:8, Ezekiel is personally commanded not to rebel like the rest of the people. A similar warning is not necessary with Moses, Isaiah, or Jeremiah.
- He is told three times to eat the scroll before actually doing so (2:8–3:3).
- God gives Ezekiel two commissioning speeches (2:3–8; 3:4–11), with considerable repetition in the second.
- Ezekiel's first response that we know of is bitterness and anger (3:14).
- When Ezekiel returns from his encounter with the Lord to sit among his people, he is in a state of shock and spiritual desperation until God finally breaks the silence with a strong and uncompromising warning to get to work (3:15–17).
- It appears that God attempts to forestall any effort on Ezekiel's part to plead for or defend Israel.

Regardless of his other mental disposition at the time, Ezekiel is angry as he makes the transition from witnessing the glory of God to returning to his home and assignment (3:14). He has been forced to take a difficult assignment. He has suddenly moved from at least a measure of tranquility among his fellow exiles to the prospect of living with their rejection and hostility. His personal future has quickly become dark and foreboding. The Lord's hand is upon him to see him through the assignment, but he isn't happy about it (3:12–15). He did not volunteer; he was drafted.

But Ezekiel will not be evaluated based on the *results* of his prophecies—just his faithfulness in speaking for God. The image of the watchman in verses 16–21 will be repeated again in 33:1–6. Ezekiel's role as a prophet is like that of a watchman for a city. It is his job to sound an alarm after being made aware of an approaching threat. All Ezekiel has to do is pass along God's message to the people. They might respond and be spared a tragedy, or they might ignore the message and suffer the consequences. God's truth is a fragrance of life to those who are being saved and an odor of death to the defiant. The results are not under Ezekiel's control, but the prophet *will* be held responsible for speaking the truth clearly.

Ezekiel had previously been carried by the Spirit (3:14–15), but he later moves under his own power in response to God's command (3:23) before the Spirit again comes into him, lifts him up, and speaks to him (2:1–4; 3:24). But what the Lord tells Ezekiel in verses 24–27 has created no small degree of confusion among those reading and trying to interpret the text. We are left wondering how to understand Ezekiel's confinement and speechlessness. It is likely that this is the first of several instances throughout the book of Ezekiel where the prophet himself is used as a sign from God. Later examples will be more apparent as to their intent. In this case, the symbolic action may be primarily applicable to Ezekiel rather than the entire nation because the prophet has been stubbornly unhappy about receiving his assignment from the Lord.

Critical Observation

Ezekiel has already been told repeatedly and emphatically that he is to deliver a message to Israel, so he is clearly not being *totally* silenced (3:24–26). Nor is he being bound *entirely*, because he will soon be given specific assignments. Perhaps the reason for his being bound and muted is singularly in response to his initial unwillingness to undertake the assignment God gave him.

Ezekiel will not be allowed to plead for Israel, to argue the case for her escaping God's judgment. He will not be allowed to soften his message or shape it in a way that will make him less unpopular with the Israelites. He will speak what the Lord tells him to—that and nothing else! Ezekiel's binding and muteness are also demonstrations of the withdrawal of God's favor from His people that will last until the destruction of Jerusalem seven years later.

The final statement in the narrative of Ezekiel's call (3:27) seems to clarify, once again, that Israel's spiritual condition is fixed. Israel is once more characterized as hardened in rebellion and no longer eligible for appeal. This is the heavy burden of Ezekiel's assignment, to proclaim judgment and doom against Israel without offering hope of pardon or deliverance. While this may sound cruel or unreasonable in light of what we like to think about God's mercy and grace, the Israelites had long had faithful prophets warning them of God's wrath if they did not repent. The people of Judah had already witnessed the devastation of the northern kingdom, just as the prophets had warned. They had seen the dark clouds gather on the horizon as Babylon made her way westward. Yet they were so hardened, so spiritually dead, that they didn't get it, still refusing to acknowledge their own fault or God's perfect justice.

Yes, God is gracious and merciful, but the Israelites of this day indifferently rejected His repeated offers of mercy. Ezekiel is letting them know that the Lord has departed from them. When it becomes obvious that they will not be able to withstand the Babylonians, they cry out to God in a panic, but He is unwilling to listen.

Ezekiel is called to address Israel's distressing spiritual condition—that of settled rebellion, defiant unbelief, and the inability to interpret their situation correctly. It is evident that God anticipated that some of the rebellious Israelites would repent and return to a life of faithfulness (3:21).

Take It Home

Ezekiel opens with some big surprises. To begin with, in Near Eastern thinking, gods ruled over specific territories. It would have been totally unexpected—and significant beyond our understanding—for Israel's God to make a glorious appearance to Ezekiel *in Babylon*. Is there an equivalent to Babylon in your life, where you don't normally expect to experience God, yet where He could make a meaningful difference? Then, in a second surprise, God's opening statements focus not on hope and comfort but on doom and judgment. How do you think most believers today compare to the Israelites in regard to expecting primarily good news from God, even when they are slow to respond to His leading and reluctant to repent?

EZEKIEL 4:1–7:27

LESSONS IN DIVINE JUDGMENT

Setting Up the Section

The people of Judah are being taken in large groups to Babylon where they will live in captivity. Ezekiel was among one of the earlier groups, and while in Babylon, God called him to a prophetic ministry. He appeared to be initially reluctant, but in this section he begins to respond to God's instructions, even though many of his actions must have seemed quite strange to onlookers.

📖 **4:1–5:17**

EZEKIEL'S SYMBOLIC ACTIONS

Ezekiel received his call to be a prophet in 593 BC. The Babylonians would destroy the city of Jerusalem in 586 BC. Many of Ezekiel's first assignments were to predict the fall of Israel's beloved city. If the previous section (chapters 2–3) seems repetitive in its depiction of the Jews as hard of heart and obstinate in their refusal to humble themselves before the Lord, this section will prove equally repetitive in describing God's determination to punish Jerusalem for the Jews' betrayal of His covenant.

God first tells Ezekiel to construct a model of the city of Jerusalem (4:1–2). The prophet would have drawn a map of the city on soft clay and then allowed it to harden under the Middle Eastern sun. Jerusalem was on a hill, so any attempt to overtake the city would require ramps to transport battering rams and other weapons to the walls. Conquering a walled city was no easy task, so enemy armies would usually lay siege to the city first in order to weaken its resistance. Ezekiel's model of the city includes the ramps, weapons, and surrounding armies.

Iron was the hardest metal available at the time (4:3). God tells Ezekiel to use an iron pan, normally used to bake flat cakes over an open fire, as an impenetrable wall between the prophet's face and the model of the city. The message is clear: While Jerusalem is surrounded and suffering, anticipating defeat, God is hiding His face from the people.

Critical Observation

The text doesn't elaborate about Ezekiel's enactment of God's instructions, although it isn't likely that the prophet is doing these things in private. The object lessons are designed to be public and to incite first curiosity, and then a reaction. As people walked by Ezekiel's home, they saw the map of Jerusalem and the prophet's mock siege. It wouldn't be long before everyone in the community was talking about it.

Next Ezekiel is told to symbolically bear the sin of his people. He is to lie on his left side for 390 days, most likely representing the 390 years or so between the building of the temple in Jerusalem to its destruction (4:4–5). Presumably, his face would have been turned toward his model city. We are not to suppose his is a round-the-clock vigil. Just as someone might say that it took three weeks to read a book, never intending to infer that he or she read continuously for twenty-one straight twenty-four-hour days, Ezekiel probably assumes his position for only a segment of each day, perhaps during times when many people will observe him.

After spending 390 days turned toward the northern kingdom, Ezekiel reverses sides to deal with the sin of Judah—a forty-day commitment this time. The number in this case may have been symbolic of the generation that would suffer the consequences of exile on account of Israel's sin. Adding the 390 with 40 yields 430—the number of years of Israel's previous sojourn in Egypt (Exodus 12:40). And if the forty years is considered symbolic, it is close enough to harmonize with Jeremiah's prophecy of seventy years of exile (Jeremiah 25:11–12; 29:10).

Ezekiel's bare arm would have symbolized Yahweh's power and determination to act (Ezekiel 4:7). We aren't told exactly how Ezekiel is bound with ropes (4:8), although the purpose is to demonstrate the unalterable character of the prophecy of Jerusalem's destruction and Judah's punishment.

Ezekiel's next sign involves baking bread using an unusual combination of ingredients: grain and vegetables (4:9). The intent is to simulate a siege diet, much like those remaining in Jerusalem would be forced to eat (4:16–17). The shortage of available grain required making bread out of whatever could be found. The daily allotment is only eight ounces (4:10). Water is rationed as well, with Ezekiel only allowed about two-thirds of a quart each day.

Ezekiel doesn't balk at any of God's instructions until he is told to cook his meals using human excrement for fuel (4:12). This distasteful practice would also be part of life under siege. But Ezekiel had always striven to uphold his principles as a priest, so God is sympathetic to his request and grants the prophet a concession. Ezekiel's symbolic actions in Babylon are to reflect the horrific conditions of life in Jerusalem. It is important not to overlook the qualifying phrase in verse 17. The people are certainly suffering, but their situation is because of their sin. Ezekiel's symbolic demonstration continues with a severe haircut. In 5:1, he is instructed to remove his hair and beard. Normally, priests were forbidden to shave their heads (Leviticus 21:5), so the action would have drawn attention. But the haircut is just the beginning. More significant is what Ezekiel is told to do with the hair; he is to weigh it and divide it into thirds.

After his observation of the siege periods, he is to burn one-third of the hair inside the city (his clay representation). Another third is to be stricken with a sword and placed around the city. The final third is to be tossed into the wind (Ezekiel 5:2). But Ezekiel is to hold back a few strands (5:3). The explanation for these curious acts are provided in verse 12. No one in Jerusalem is going to weather the siege well. The people will either die from plague or famine inside the city, be killed outside the city, or be scattered by God to faraway places. Any survivors who may have remained complacent are represented by the few strands of hair first held back by Ezekiel but eventually added to the fire (5:3–4).

God's frustration with Israel is evident, and for good reason. The Israelites are supposed to be a light to the Gentiles, an example of higher standards. Yet they have degenerated to the point where they don't even meet the standards of the nations around them (5:5–7). Even after thousands of people have been carried away in two large deportations, the remaining Israelites continue to offer sacrifices to Canaanite gods (5:8–9). As one awful consequence, they are going to be driven to cannibalism as Jerusalem is besieged and their food supplies dwindle to nothing (5:10–11). Although the Babylonians are the instrument of their fall, God makes it clear that He is the one responsible for what is happening (5:8–17).

The events described should have come as no surprise to the Israelites. They are the very punishments described in the Law for those who broke their covenant with God (Leviticus 26:23–39; Deuteronomy 28:15–68). However, since God remains in control of the situation, the terrible circumstances will not last forever. He will see His people through, even in their desperate situation (Ezekiel 5:13).

6:1–14

A PROPHECY FOR THE MOUNTAINS OF ISRAEL

After being told to make models of Jerusalem, lie on his side for weeks at a time, and cut his hair, Ezekiel is instructed to simply prophesy (6:1–2). He is told to address the mountains of Israel. (The phrase *mountains of Israel* occurs seventeen times in Ezekiel but nowhere else in the Bible.)

The phrase is significant for a couple of reasons. First is a topographical observation. The Israelites had been deported out of the mountainous region of Jerusalem and Judea and reestablished on the plains of Babylon. When they thought of home, they thought of mountains. Second is a spiritual concern. Ezekiel would be addressing Israel's embrace of pagan idolatry. Such idolatrous worship commonly took place in high places—usually on hilltops and mountaintops (6:13), although elevated sites could be constructed within cities as well.

So Ezekiel's oracle to the mountains of Israel begins with God's pronouncement of judgment on the high places around Jerusalem. While the people in Jerusalem will eventually hear what Ezekiel is preaching in Babylon, the Hebrews already exiled in Babylon realize they are implicated in Jerusalem's sins and have already suffered punishment for them. The Lord does not speak abstractly about judgment but rather talks about the punishment of real people in specific times and places. It is common for people to read biblical prophecies of judgment and assume the dire predictions apply only to people in other times and places. But by linking His wrath to real events in human history, God forces people of all eras to reckon with prophecy's meaning for them.

Other than the object of worship, idol worship in the high places is not dissimilar to worship at the temple. People burn sacrificial animals on an altar of dirt, stone, or wood that is usually overlaid with bronze. This offering for the benefit of the particular god at that site is accompanied by incense burned in incense altars, creating a pleasing aroma for the god (6:4).

But Yahweh is about to thoroughly devastate such idolatrous worship (6:4–7). The exposure of corpses as punishment is among the curses spelled out for those who betray God's covenant (Deuteronomy 28:26). Yet God will spare some of the people to bring them to a right mind and restore them to a life of faith. There is a terrible irony in that those who are restored first have to be cast out of the land the Lord has given them and stripped of all the privileges that have been theirs as His people (Ezekiel 6:8–10). But that's what it will take for some people to know that He is Lord (6:7, 10, 13–14).

Demystifying Ezekiel

Ezekiel is told to clap his hands, stamp his feet, and cry out in response to the wickedness of Israel and their subsequent fall, but the underlying emotion is unclear. Some have suggested the intended attitude is one of anger for what is happening. Others believe it is appropriate in this instance to express joyful delight in the misery of another—although God does not tolerate this attitude among Israel's enemies (25:6–7). Either way, Ezekiel acts in the Lord's place to express disgust over what Israel has become.

📖 7:1–27

A PROPHECY CONCERNING "THE DAY"

The next prophecy Ezekiel receives from God is no more optimistic than the previous one. Indeed, he is foretelling "the end" for the entire nation. "The four corners of the land" in verse 2 is an all-encompassing reference much like "mountains and hills, ravines and valleys" in 6:3. Disaster will befall the entire nation of Israel, but God's judgment is no more than God's justice. Israel has committed detestable acts and will receive only what is deserved (7:3–9).

When Ezekiel speaks of "the day," his listeners would have known what he is talking about (7:7). Other prophets (Amos, Isaiah, Joel, Zephaniah, and others) had already spoken and written of the Day of the Lord. Ezekiel's prophetic ministry falls squarely in line with these other prophets who warned of God's terrible judgment if His people did not repent and return to Him.

The rest of this passage describes the appalling effects of that day. However, the reader needs to be aware of the examples of hyperbole—the use of exaggeration for effect (the way we might say, "She lost a ton of weight"). For instance, Ezekiel says that no one will be left after God's judgment (7:11), yet he will soon speak of the survivors (7:16).

Ezekiel does not explain what he means about the rod that has budded (7:10). Perhaps it is a reference to Nebuchadnezzar or other oppressive rulers who will soon dominate Israel. What is clear, however, is that the economic consequences of God's judgment will be catastrophic. All the normality of daily life—buying and selling, for example (7:12–13)—will be forgotten as Judah is driven from their land.

Critical Observation

We should note that although Ezekiel speaks of "the day" in present tense (7:10, 12), it will still be about six years before his prophecy is fulfilled. Yet the likelihood of the event taking place in the future is just as certain as if it had already happened.

Sword, plague, and famine have been recurring themes in Ezekiel so far (5:12; 6:12; 7:15) as the three forms of death associated with siege warfare. And the few who escape death won't be able to rejoice. They carry with them their own guilt and God's anger toward them on account of their rebellion. They will be overwhelmed, powerless, and psychologically devastated (7:16–18).

Wealth will no longer provide comfort. Without food to buy or people to influence, money will have no purpose. Not only will personal assets become plunder for the enemy but also the temple in Jerusalem will be robbed and desecrated (7:19–22).

The city of Jerusalem has been spared for some time, and even under Babylonian control life is not particularly unpleasant at first. But Jerusalem will eventually be destroyed and associated with bloodshed. Those who don't die will be subject to chains—captivity and exile (7:23–25).

It will be a time of "calamity upon calamity" (7:26 NIV). Their prophets will have no visions. The priests will offer no teachings. The elders will provide no wise counsel. Not even the king will be spared indignity and despair. The people will have nowhere to turn as they realize that they are bereft of help (7:26–27). Jerusalem had been Israel's pride and joy. Its destruction will be their most agonizing memory.

Take It Home

Ezekiel chapters 4–24 are largely devoted to the same theme, affording readers the opportunity to develop a theory of divine wrath. The prophet presents the Lord as a God of vengeance as surely as He is a God of love. Humans tend to want to soften their image of God, yet God's wrath is not only a feature of divine nature and character but also the exercise of His justice. God is never shown as capricious, ill-willed, arbitrary, or unstable. Very much the contrary! God's wrath is His holy justice in operation. Think about your own beliefs in this area: Do you agree with Ezekiel's image of God? Is the wrath of God difficult for you to comprehend? Does the image of a wrathful God in any way affect how you live?

EZEKIEL 8:1–11:25

A VISION OF JERUSALEM'S TEMPLE

Wickedness within the Temple	8:1–18
God's Response to Israel's Wickedness	9:1–11:25

Setting Up the Section

Ezekiel has been delivering some hard-to-hear messages to the Israelites who have already been deported to Babylon. The city of Jerusalem will soon be conquered and the temple destroyed. In this section, Ezekiel is given a vision that makes evident the source of God's displeasure in regard to the temple.

📄 **8:1–18**

WICKEDNESS WITHIN THE TEMPLE

This vision takes place some fourteen months after Ezekiel's initial vision (1:1). The date is September 18, 592 BC, still several years prior to the fall of Jerusalem at the hands of Babylon. The fact that the elders are gathered at Ezekiel's home indicates that they recognize his prophetic authority.

As in his first vision, Ezekiel sees a general shape of a man, fiery and bright (1:26–27; 8:2)—another manifestation of Yahweh Himself. The details of this vision continue through 11:24, so one must wonder what the elders observed as Ezekiel witnessed what God was showing him.

The Lord assumes a form Ezekiel is familiar with (a hand) to lift him up. While remaining bodily in Tel Abib with the elders, Ezekiel is taken to Jerusalem *in visions* (8:3).

Ezekiel first sees the north gate of Jerusalem's temple. Three gates lead from the outer court to the inner court, the north gate being the one used by the king and likely the most prominent. An idol stands in full view. The pathetic sight of an idol in the temple is soon contrasted with the glory of God Himself in the fullness that Ezekiel had previously witnessed (1:26–28; 8:4). The Lord tells Ezekiel that he will see things even more detestable (8:6).

The prophet is instructed to look north, where he sees a curious hole in the wall. He is instructed to enlarge it sufficiently to pass through it. He discovers a doorway, and behind it he sees Israel's leadership participating in full-blown pantheistic idolatry, surrounded by all kinds of images.

Jaazaniah (8:11) is from a prominent family and probably known to Ezekiel before his removal to Babylon. His father had served under Josiah, the last of Judah's righteous kings (2 Kings 22:3), and one of his brothers had been a defender of Jeremiah (Jeremiah 26:24). How sad, then, that Jaazaniah is leading Israel astray in the worship of animals. His involvement, along with that of the other elders, indicates that the spiritual rot has thoroughly penetrated the highest reaches of Israelite society.

Critical Observation

Pantheism, the belief that everything is a god (or part of one) and that the gods are part of everything, was rife in the ancient world. With a belief that all life is divine, the practice had even reached the point where the Egyptians worshiped dung beetles.

The elders of Israel are attempting to appeal to the spirits of various animals, represented by images on a wall (Ezekiel 8:9–11). Incense is burned to appeal to the selfish and sensual natures of such gods. Worship of the Lord also included the burning of incense, but as an emblem of prayer—an act of personal confidence in a God of love who cares for His people.

The irony in this scene is almost too much to fathom. The elders, clustered in one of the temple's inner rooms (Nehemiah 13:4–9), wrongly assume that Yahweh has been defeated by the gods of Babylon and is no longer able to help them. They look for help wherever they can find it. But the accusations they make are not about God but rather about the very images in which they place their faith. Yet Ezekiel has still not seen the worst (Ezekiel 8:12–13).

Tammuz (8:14) is a Babylonian fertility god who is particularly appealing to women. They are mourning because tradition held that Tammuz had been banished to the underworld. Then, moving from the inner room to the entrance of the temple, Ezekiel sees about twenty-five men worshiping the sun. Sun worship is nothing new in Judah (2 Kings 23:5, 11), but it has never been more brazen than in this temple setting. The temple faced the east; so, logistically, to bow to the sun in the east one had to turn his back on the temple. Yahweh is being displaced in His own sanctuary!

Corrupted worship of God and crimes against other humans go hand in hand, so it is not surprising that Ezekiel notes the violence that fills the land in verse 17. The phrase "the branch to the nose" is not used elsewhere in scripture, and its meaning is uncertain. It may be a reference to some pagan ritual or perhaps a disrespectful (obscene?) gesture.

📄 9:1–11:25

GOD'S RESPONSE TO ISRAEL'S WICKEDNESS

The men who are summoned (9:1–2) are most likely angels sent to execute God's sentence. Six have weapons, the seventh a writing kit. The six executioners will accomplish their work through the Babylonian army. The seventh is assigned to mark the people of the city who lament the detestable acts taking place throughout Jerusalem. The mark (9:4) is the *taw*, the last letter of the Hebrew alphabet. Jeremiah would have been one of the inhabitants of Jerusalem at this time, so he and a minority of other citizens would not have been complicit in Jerusalem's apostasy. God's judgment will therefore make appropriate distinctions between those who participate in idolatry and sin and those who are grieved by such things.

Those with the mark are to be spared, but no one else. The widespread destruction, including women and children (9:6), is a feature of the holy war—a divine war against a wicked people. There is no mention of adult men because they will have been killed in combat.

Ezekiel fears that this judgment of God might do away with Israel altogether (9:8). Galilee and Transjordan had been lost in 733 BC. Samaria and what was left of the northern kingdom fell, and its people were carried off in 721 BC. Little territory was left around Jerusalem. But the section concludes with the reminder that every true believer has been marked—a remnant will be spared.

Israel has defied God in the most brazen and disgusting ways by forsaking Him for the ridiculous mythologies of other cultures. Their spiritual apostasy has led to a culture of violence and injustice. As severe as their judgment will be, it will be nothing they don't deserve.

The angel who had been given the task of marking the righteous is next assigned to bring the fire of Yahweh's judgment upon Jerusalem (10:2). It is at this point that Ezekiel identifies the creatures he had seen in his initial vision (chapter 1) as cherubim (10:20–22).

Demystifying Ezekiel

The Bible maintains a close connection between cherubim and the presence of God. Large images of cherubim stood above the ark of the covenant, the physical sign of God's enthroned presence in the temple (Exodus 25:18–22), and the temple was filled with carvings of cherubim (1 Kings 6:29, 35). In the Old Testament, Yahweh is routinely portrayed as borne by cherubim. Ancient Israelites expected that wherever cherubim were found, God would also be present (Psalms 18:10; 80:1).

The cherubim seemed to accompany the Lord's chariot (Ezekiel 10:9–14), which was parked to the south of the temple (10:3)—perhaps because of the idol that stood in the north gate. God is planning to depart from the temple. The cloud, representing the glory of the Lord, first moves from its established position in the Holy of Holies to the threshold of the temple (10:3–4). Soon it moves from the threshold to the place where the cherubim are assembled outside. It is significant that the temple is called the Lord's house at precisely the moment He is leaving it (10:19).

More evidence of the wickedness within the temple is seen as Ezekiel is shown another group of men. (The Jaazaniah in 11:1 is not the same as in 8:11.) They are arrogant and self-confident, presuming that, as meat in the pot (11:3), they are secure and protected in Jerusalem—unlike the exiles in Babylon. The repeated command to prophesy indicates urgency (11:4). Not much time remains.

As always, the Lord's gaze penetrates human motives. The group of men is placing confidence in Jerusalem, but the city will provide no safe haven. They will be driven out to suffer either death or captivity (11:5–12). In fact, the city's leadership will become the target of mass executions after the Babylonians overrun the city (2 Kings 25:18–21). The people *will* know that Yahweh is the Lord eventually (Ezekiel 11:12).

The death of Pelatiah, one of the men Ezekiel had witnessed in the temple (11:1, 13), is intriguing. It seems that he actually dies, not in the vision that Ezekiel is having, but *while* Ezekiel is prophesying. If so, his death would have symbolized what would soon come to pass for the rest of his peers. Ezekiel acknowledges the significance of Pelatiah's death and expresses fear that God will completely destroy the remnant of Israel (11:13).

But the people with Ezekiel in Babylon are a remnant, and God will eventually return them to Israel. Those who remained in Jerusalem had somehow come to believe that *they* were the favored few, even with their inferior leadership established by the Babylonians after two previous deportations of Israel's principal citizens. God contradicts their assertion. A new exodus will take place, this time comprised of the exiles returning to Israel (11:14–17).

As God had promised previous generations of Israelites (Exodus 6:7), He again affirms that they will be His people and He will be their God (Ezekiel 11:20). Ezekiel will have more to say about the renewed covenant later on. For now, however, judgment remains his primary theme (11:21).

The glory of God continues its progress out of the temple, ascending to a place above the Mount of Olives, east of Jerusalem (11:22–23). The vision concludes and Ezekiel is again set down in Babylon, where he reports to the exiles what he has seen and heard.

Take It Home

Humanly speaking, it was easy for the people in Jerusalem to believe that Yahweh had favored them and rejected those in exile. But Ezekiel's vision demonstrates that the situation, in fact, is precisely the reverse. God is departing His temple and leaving behind those who give Him no thought. Instead, He will restore those in exile who had a humble and submissive mind toward Him. Can you think of contemporary examples where people wrongly presume to have God's blessings simply because nothing bad is happening to them at the moment? Or instances where suffering people think God has given up on them, when in fact He is closer than they realize?

EZEKIEL 12:1–14:23

EZEKIEL SPEAKS OUT

Setting Up the Section

Having been shown the deplorable spiritual condition of Jerusalem in a vision, Ezekiel is now told to enact the exile of all those remaining there—or more accurately, the exile of the few who will survive the destruction of the city. He is also told to confront other so-called prophets who are telling the exiles only what they want to hear.

12:1–28

A VISIBLE LESSON

Ezekiel has just related a detailed vision to the exiles (11:24–25). But God knows the people remain resistant and rebellious, so He has Ezekiel act out what those in Jerusalem will soon undergo. As the exiles watch, the prophet packs his belongings, digs through the wall of his house to retrieve them, puts them on his shoulder, and carries them off (12:3–7). When people ask what he is doing, Ezekiel is to explain that it is a sign of what will soon take place in Jerusalem: Babylonians will break through the walls of the city, and most of the remaining survivors will be exiled.

Evidently, the exiles in Babylon still believe fervently in the security of Jerusalem, as do those who remained there. They do not accept that their exile has been divine punishment for their sins. The complete destruction of Jerusalem will not directly affect the circumstances of the exiles already in Babylon, but it will dash their hopes of a speedy return home.

Babylon will be the instrument of the fall of Jerusalem, but Yahweh is the Judge (12:12–16). The reason the prince (King Zedekiah) will not see is because he will be blinded by the Babylonians (2 Kings 25:7). Eventually, the remnant of people who survive will acknowledge their sin and God's hand in the matter (Ezekiel 12:16).

Continuing his symbolism of the situation at home, Ezekiel is to publicly eat and drink while trembling (12:17–20). His actions symbolize the anxiety and despair of the people not just in Jerusalem but in its surrounding towns as well.

Yet people are slow to acknowledge harsh truths. The prevailing attitude among the exiles is that Ezekiel's prophecies are not coming true and that he must certainly be talking about a distant time in the future (12:22, 27). God's response is that every vision (of His true prophets) will indeed be fulfilled, and there will be no further delay (12:23, 28).

CONFRONTING FALSE PROPHETS

True prophets of God receive a message from the Lord and repeat to the people what they have been told or shown. False prophets have no such message, so they must make one up. False prophets had long been by-products of Israel's deteriorating spiritual condition, but at this point Yahweh charges Ezekiel to confront his professional competition head-on.

Critical Observation

Although Ezekiel may appear to be singled out as a solitary spokesperson for God surrounded by false prophets, there are a number of other true prophets who are his contemporaries, including Daniel, Habakkuk, Obadiah, and Jeremiah.

The false prophets are portrayed as "jackals among ruins" (13:4 NIV), an image of destruction. They prophesy what people want to hear—peace and safety—so no one feels motivated to repent or to expect the coming judgment of the Lord. Ezekiel is trying to repair and rebuild Israel; other prophets are merely capitalizing on its spiritual ruin (13:5).

Divination (13:7) was a widespread practice posing as a science, by which the practitioner presumed to learn what the gods intended in the future by studying animal livers, the stars, or some other symbol. The practice was forbidden in Israel because the Israelites were supposed to maintain godly character and faithfulness to God's covenant, leaving their future in His hands.

The consequences of prophesying falsely are severe indeed. The false prophets will face loss of membership in the assembly, have their names stricken from the census register, and lose their right to the land, since they will not participate in the return of the exiles to Judah and Jerusalem (13:8–9). Theirs will be permanent excommunication.

It is characteristic of Israel's and Judah's false prophets to proclaim peace. Their income depends on contributions, and people are far less likely to pay to hear about gloom and doom. Such false preaching encourages lazy complacency. If the people never acknowledge their sins, naturally they don't anticipate judgment. Yet pretending that all is well when their nation is on the brink of catastrophe doesn't change reality. God compares the false prophets to builders who whitewash a flimsy wall and make it look good, but it can't withstand the violent wind, torrents of rain, and hailstones God will send (13:13). The wall will fall, and the facade of the false prophets will be exposed for what it is—nothing but lies. No matter how regularly or boldly they declare "peace," there will be no peace (13:10, 15–16).

Israel had female prophetesses as well as male prophets, so it stands to reason that there would be a number of female false prophets. It is surprising, therefore, that Ezekiel provides one of the very few judgments against women found in the Old Testament prophets (13:17–23).

The language Ezekiel uses is clear enough to verify that Israel's magic and divination practices are wrong and offensive to God, but obscure enough to prevent stating exactly what those methods are. It seems likely that some of the exiles had adopted Babylonian magical ideas. *Magic* is a negative term in a biblical sense, as it broadly refers to all efforts to influence events by manipulating unseen powers. It is utterly foreign to the teaching of scripture that emphasizes a person's character and his or her fidelity to the Lord.

Adherence to practitioners of magic can be alluring and addictive. In this instance, God is preparing to take strong action against those who are involved in order to set free people who have been ensnared and save their lives (13:20, 22–23). If the magicians had literally killed people, it is unclear. But they had profaned Yahweh by reducing Him to the level of Babylon's petty deities, so they had definitely killed people spiritually by undermining their faith in God.

📖 14:1–23

CONFRONTING THE ELDERS OF THE PEOPLE

Having faced the false prophets, Ezekiel's next communication from God concerns the elders and the people themselves. They have come to Ezekiel to get some direction from God. Perhaps they are worried about something Ezekiel has said and they want more information, but God speaks to the prophet before they can.

God knows that the elders of Israel in Babylon are still involved in idolatry, although it is perhaps more covert than before (in their hearts; 14:4). They found Babylon to be far more wealthy, prosperous, and powerful than their own nation, and they have been tempted to imitate Babylonian ways. But attempting to combine recognition of Yahweh's lordship with recourse to other gods is a bad idea.

Demystifying Ezekiel

Idolatry was the standard form of religion and religious practice in Babylon and surrounding areas at the time. People believed that any depiction of a god, however crude, partook of the essence of the god himself or herself. Anything offered to the image was thus offered to the god. It was also believed that the gods appreciated gifts and would respond in kind. They were relatively easily pleased; and the more generous the worshiper, the more prosperity he or she would receive from the gods.

The gods of the Babylonians could tolerate other loyalties, but not the one, living, and true God of Israel. The Ten Commandments lead off with, "Thou shalt have no other gods before me" (Exodus 20:3 KJV). The reason, of course, is because other gods are foolishness: false and unreal. The Babylonians had so many gods that it's difficult to know which particular ones might have been most appealing in Israel at this time. Excavations in Canaan have uncovered large numbers of small statuettes of Babylonian and Egyptian deities.

So the elders of Israel have come to Ezekiel, not planning to submit their lives to the Lord in true faith, but to consult the prophet as if he were merely a fortune-teller. They want an answer to a question, and then they fully intend to return to the lives they have been living. They aren't looking for their covenant God to speak His truth to them.

Considering their spiritual state, one might not expect God to reveal *anything* to them. In this instance, however, He promises to answer their inquiry directly, although it will not be the kind of answer they are hoping for. God's response (14:4–11) is made for the sake of the larger people of God and not for this particular generation.

This is the first of very few calls to repentance in Ezekiel that may seem to contradict the earlier statement that the prophet will not be preaching for repentance (3:26). Indeed, the die has been cast for Israel: This generation will be judged, and there is no hope left for it. Still, repentance remains God's desire for His people.

God will not tolerate an idolater continuing to pose as a member of His covenant people. His judgment of such a person will be designed precisely to disabuse the rest of God's people from committing the same sin (14:7–8). Any prophet who is complicit in such hypocrisy will also suffer accordingly, because his power to influence people is not to be misused. As a result of God's judgment, the people will learn not to take seriously the messages of prophets who do not remain faithful to the Word of God. The intent is for people to stop straying and again find satisfaction in belonging to God (14:11).

Beginning with verse 14, God assures Ezekiel in four successive paragraphs of the inexorable and merciless judgment that awaits those who rebel against Him. Although the Lord speaks generally, it is Israel who is being addressed here. (His judgments for other nations will come later.) The particular judgments listed are the typical curses of the covenant for those who prove unfaithful to God: famine, wild beasts, sword, and plague (Leviticus 26; Deuteronomy 32).

Noah, Daniel, and Job (Ezekiel 14:20) are all conspicuously godly men who live outside of Israel. The Israelites seem to presume that because there are heroically good people among them, they will be exempt from judgment. God had agreed to spare Sodom if only ten righteous people could be found (Genesis 18:26–32), but He did not intend to establish some kind of divine law or principle that would be observed in every case.

Demystifying Ezekiel

The Daniel mentioned in verse 20 may not be the prophet with whom readers of scripture are familiar. The Daniel of the lions' den was a contemporary of Ezekiel, and a young one at the time of this writing—too young, some think, to be listed with such ancient and venerated names as Noah and Job. In addition, Ezekiel spells his name differently than it is spelled elsewhere.

The sad fact that God addresses *Jerusalem's* great sin makes the judgment even worse. The people had known His truth and had His light shine upon them, so their judgment will be heavier (14:21). The one consoling consequence will be that the exiles in Babylon will see the new exiles come from Jerusalem (14:22–23). When they realize how faithless and wicked they were, they will also acknowledge that God is entirely just in destroying the city. The impiety of the newcomers will be evident to the entire Israelite community in Babylon.

Take It Home

Ezekiel is proven right in 586 BC, when Jerusalem is destroyed. The false prophets are exposed as charlatans and fakes, and the people of God feel the Lord's wrath. They had believed a message that was too good to be true. So do many people today. Consider the false prophets of Ezekiel's time and of ours. Why do people go to phonies and pay them for their advice? Why do you think fortune-telling is such big business today, as sophisticated as our culture imagines itself to be? On a personal level, do you tend to be more attuned to preachers of peace or to those who proclaim the reality of God's judgment?

EZEKIEL 15:1–17:24
THREE ALLEGORIES TO DESCRIBE ISRAEL

Setting Up the Section

As Ezekiel continues to address the spiritually defiant exiles in Babylon, passing along God's judgment for their recurring rejection of the Lord and pursuit of idolatry, he is given three allegories that illustrate Israel's condition. In each case the meaning is clear because the interpretation is provided.

📖 15:1–8

ALLEGORY #1: ISRAEL IS THE WOOD, NOT THE FRUIT, OF THE VINE

Grapevines have a single purpose: to grow grapes. The vine itself is woody, but the wood is virtually useless. It is too soft even to use for making pegs (15:2–3). At least it burns, even if it doesn't make particularly good firewood.

It is the fruit of the grapevine that makes it important, which was especially true in the agricultural life of ancient Canaan. Wine was a staple of life, and Israel no doubt had a flattering estimation of herself as the fruit of the vine. But in reality, the nation had ceased to bear fruit. As a vine, it then became good for nothing except fuel for the fire.

What the Israelites don't realize is that they are already in the fire. The nation has been burned at both ends and charred in the middle by the first two Babylonian incursions into the Holy Land (15:4). It was customary at the time for invading armies to burn the cities they captured, so this allegory merges into a literal account of Jerusalem's future. Nothing is left but to cast the remaining wood into the fire to be consumed.

ALLEGORY #2: JERUSALEM AS AN UNFAITHFUL WIFE

At about 830 words (depending on the translation), this single chapter of Ezekiel is longer than six of the twelve books of the Minor Prophets. It is certainly the longest allegory in the Bible. Like the previous example, its meaning is obvious, yet it is more elaborate and says much more about *how* Israel got into her present situation. It is also quite sexually explicit, employing the metaphor of prostitution to describe Israel's spiritual infidelity.

But the first image of Jerusalem is that of a baby, abandoned by Canaanite parents. Indeed, Jerusalem was originally a Canaanite city steeped in pagan roots. Abandoning a child has never been the norm at any point in human history, yet it is not unheard of for poverty and other considerations to drive desperate parents to abandon a newborn—especially a daughter.

This allegorical "child" has not even been washed or rubbed with salt (16:4), a custom still practiced by some Arab mothers to this day. The origin of the custom has been lost, although it may have been for hygienic reasons.

Yahweh is depicted as a passerby who spies the abandoned girl in an open field, helpless and near death, and chooses to make her live (16:5–6). The girl grows up to become a beautiful young woman. She is mature but still naked, creating a completely different situation. Yahweh preserves the young woman's purity and marries her.

The custom of spreading a corner of a garment over one's intended (16:8) is mentioned in Ruth 3:9. The Lord's relationship with Israel had long before been described as a marriage, and Ezekiel's hearers would have known he was speaking about Yahweh's covenant to be Israel's God. The allegory and the theology merge at the end of 16:8.

Yahweh dresses His bride and bedecks her in fine jewelry. The blood washing from her suggests virginal bleeding, the effect of the first lovemaking (16:9). At this point, Israel is an innocent maiden. As His wife, the Lord lavishes luxuries upon her. The previously abandoned baby girl is now a queen, and fed and clothed as one (16:10–14). Her beauty, status, and fame are all Yahweh's doing. She owes everything to Him.

Critical Observation

Some of the language of this section, such as *embroidered cloth* and *fine linen*, is also found in previous descriptions of the tabernacle, its curtains, and the priestly robes. The fine leather of her sandals (16:10) is mentioned elsewhere in the Bible only in regard to the tabernacle and temple. Even the special food can be compared to the Israelites' sacred offerings.

Yet despite His great generosity and love for His bride, Yahweh begins to speak as a betrayed husband (16:15–19). His wife has begun to use her beauty for purposes other than for the pleasure of her husband. The verb meaning "to act as a prostitute," or some derivative, occurs twenty-two times in this chapter and may be regarded as the key word of the passage.

As if prostitution weren't bad enough in itself, the bride of Yahweh also participates in child sacrifice, the ultimate cultic crime. Involvement in such a barbaric act requires both a pagan mindset and the most extreme repudiation of Yahweh's covenant. The practice seems to have first been introduced to Israel in the eighth century BC, in the northern kingdom (2 Kings 17:17), spreading to Judah during the reign of Ahaz (2 Kings 16:3) and becoming rampant during the reign of Manasseh (2 Chronicles 33:6). Josiah took steps to eliminate Israel's participation (2 Kings 23:10), but after his death the practice returned (Jeremiah 32:35). Israel, who had been rescued as an unloved and abandoned baby, is killing her children with her own hands (Ezekiel 16:21–22).

The details of Israel's promiscuous actions continue in verses 23–34. If the first portion of the description reflects her religious betrayal of the Lord, the second part deals with the political betrayal of her status as the people of God. Israel trusts her welfare to everyone but Yahweh.

Here prostitution is a metaphor for military and political alliances with other nations, each of which represents a failure to trust the Lord. The order in which other nations are mentioned—Egypt, Philistia, Assyria, and Babylon—reflects Israel's history. Each of these political relationships proved harmful, yet Israel moved from one such affair to another.

In the original language, Ezekiel's description is more explicit than what is interpreted in most Bible translations. Israel's effort to attract other lovers is brazen. Even the pagan nations around her are shocked by such behavior (16:27).

In spite of her repeated conscientious efforts, Israel doesn't make a good prostitute. The point of prostitution is to make money, yet Israel paid others to be involved (16:32–34). The money is a reference to the bribes and tribute Israel gave to foreign powers over the years. Israel would not have *wanted* to make those imposed payments, but Ezekiel sees it all as the result of her philandering.

After the husband's case is made and Israel's betrayal has been exposed, the sentence is pronounced (16:35–43). In an ironic twist, the wayward wife, who bared her nakedness without shame to entice her various lovers, will be stripped and shamed before them. Her fortune has come full circle. She who began naked and abandoned by her parents will find herself naked and abandoned by the Lord.

Adultery is a capital offense in the Mosaic Law. In this case, the sentence would be carried out by Israel's paramours (16:38–41). Yet once the punishment has been inflicted, God's holy wrath will be satisfied (16:42). Ezekiel often reminds his readers that God's judgment is not a fit of divine temper but rather the exercise of His holy justice.

Ezekiel can't seem to emphasize enough, throughout his writing, that what is happening to Israel is a result of her own actions. He makes the point again that Israel has ignored and forgotten the grace of God, His covenant, and His kindness to her (16:43).

God then compares Jerusalem to other notable cities in history. Samaria (16:46) had been the capital of the northern kingdom of Israel until the Assyrians conquered it during the previous century. What compounded Judah's sin was that the people had witnessed the fall of Samaria—punishment for the betrayal of Yahweh's covenant—and still did not repent (16:51).

Perhaps more surprising is the comparison between Jerusalem and the city of Sodom (16:48). God did not dwell on the rampant homosexuality in Sodom; perhaps it would have been too easy for Israel to deny such a comparison. But equally heinous were Sodom's sins of arrogance, self-centeredness, and lack of concern for the poor and weak (16:49–50). The noted city of sin had nothing on Jerusalem in those regards. It is hard to know what is meant by the restoration of Sodom in 16:53–55, although it is meant as a backhanded rebuke of Jerusalem. The point is that since Jerusalem's wickedness is greater than Sodom's or Samaria's, those cities should be restored if Jerusalem is.

Yet as is so common in the prophetic books, the Lord looks beyond judgment day to the new work of grace He will perform among His people (16:59–63). The restoration of Jerusalem will be a humbling experience. Sodom and Samaria are portrayed as being united with Jerusalem—a picture of universal salvation also common to prophetic books. The original covenant God made was with Israel, not with other nations, but the nations will not be left out in the end.

📄 17:1–24

ALLEGORY #3: A VINE AND TWO EAGLES

Ezekiel's third allegory approaches the style of a fable where animals and inanimate objects talk and act with human characteristics. And although its meaning is not as clearly evident as the first two, the explanation is eventually provided.

Demystifying Ezekiel

This allegory is much more like a riddle. In fact, the word used in 17:2, commonly translated as *allegory*, is the same word used to describe Samson's riddle to the men in his wedding party (Judges 14:12). The literary style would have had an impact on Ezekiel's listeners because they would not have been able to figure it out until he provided them with the meaning.

The allegory begins with a precise description of an eagle that breaks off the top of a cedar tree and carries it away (17:3–4). Babylon had long gone to Lebanon for wood, so the tree in Ezekiel's allegory represents Israel. The top of the tree (the leadership of the nation) had been carried away (deported to Babylon in 598 BC).

The seed in verse 5 is Zedekiah, the member of the royal family that the Babylonians placed on the throne as their puppet king in Jerusalem. For a time, Zedekiah was loyal to Babylon, indicated by the branches turned toward the eagle (17:6). But then a second eagle appeared, also powerful, yet not described quite as impressively as the first one (17:7). If the vine then sent its roots out toward the second eagle rather than the first, would it survive? Ezekiel's question is confusing, so he provides the answer first and then the explanation.

The vine will *not* thrive; it will wither (17:9–10). The second eagle represents Egypt. After a while, the galling yoke of subjection to Babylon begins to provoke thoughts of rebellion from Zedekiah. Egypt is nearby—a longstanding enemy of Babylon. As far as we know, Egypt never actually provided assistance to Judah other than selling them some warhorses (17:15). In this context, the east wind is the siroccos that heat Palestine from the desert (17:10).

Zedekiah had sworn an oath of loyalty to Nebuchadnezzar, and a treaty had been written spelling out his obligations. He knew that if he betrayed the treaty, he would invoke a curse upon himself (17:13). Yet Zedekiah violates his oath and breaks the treaty. His change of disposition toward Babylon seems to coincide with the accession of a new pharaoh in Egypt, although it is not known if the new Egyptian leader encouraged the revolt. Depending on the date of Ezekiel's prophecy, the Israelites in Babylon may have already heard of Zedekiah's overtures to the Egyptians. They may have entertained the hope that he would succeed in delivering Judah from Babylonian control.

But when Babylon returns to reassert its control over Judah, the Egyptians stand by and watch as Jerusalem is destroyed. Zedekiah's betrayal of the treaty is not just an offense to Nebuchadnezzar; it is an affront to God as well. God would have regarded such an action as the act of a traitor, even though Babylon had imposed the treaty on Israel. The offense is made clearer by the account in 2 Chronicles 36:13, where it is shown that Zedekiah had sworn loyalty *in Yahweh's name*. Zedekiah's enemy, the one that counts, is not Babylon. It is Yahweh Himself (Ezekiel 17:19).

Zedekiah's loyalty to the wrong eagle results in the Babylonian army bearing down on Jerusalem in 586 BC. After being forced to watch the execution of his sons, Zedekiah is blinded and taken captive to Babylon. His army, seeking to escape, is caught and destroyed (17:21). The rest of the population, with the exception of a few poor people left to tend the fields, is sent into exile. The details are found in 2 Kings 25.

But this third allegory has a surprise ending (17:22–24), as the Lord promises the eventual restoration of the remnant of Israel. He will choose and plant another shoot from the top of a cedar tree (provide another king). The positive influence of this new king will be felt around the world. The Lord will eventually cause Babylon to fall and restore life to the nation of Israel.

Take It Home

Jesus' New Testament command to love one's enemies is a novel concept, yet it has some precedent here in Ezekiel. God's people are to show integrity, even to their enemies. When Zedekiah broke an oath—even though the oath was to a pagan king and his intentions were to preserve his nation—the action was an offense to God. Do you tend to make distinctions on how you deal with others based on whether or not they share your faith?

EZEKIEL 18:1–21:32

A RETIRED PROVERB, A LAMENT, AND MORE WARNINGS

Setting Up the Section

Ezekiel 18 is one of the better-known sections of this mostly unfamiliar book. In this section, the prophet clarifies God's attitude toward sin and who is responsible. Afterward, Ezekiel returns to his message of judgment on Judah and Jerusalem.

📄 18:1–32

CLARIFYING A PROVERB

Ezekiel begins this section by illustrating that someone cannot begin to really understand human existence until he or she acknowledges that each life belongs to God. The emphasis throughout the chapter will be on the *individual* life.

The proverb in verse 2 suggests a world of fatalism, which is by no means true. Every single person will one day stand before a personal God, and He will judge each one accordingly. Jeremiah had cited the same proverb (Jeremiah 31:29), but both he and Ezekiel foretell an end to its popularity. The belief that God will hold future generations accountable for the sin of an ancestor is not accurate.

"As I live" (18:3) means that the Lord charged the nation by an oath taken symbolically upon His own life. God judges each person according to his or her holiness. It is evident that the use of *die* in this context is a reference to spiritual death—death that continues in the world to come (18:4).

God provides Ezekiel with some illustrations to help his listeners clarify their thinking. The first describes a righteous man who has an unrighteous son (18:5–13). The father not only avoids actions that are clearly sinful but he also chooses to act honorably in everything he does. The son, however, is violent and disregards both civil and spiritual laws. The unrighteous son will answer for his own sins; his father's righteousness will be of no help to him.

Critical Observation

The biblical language used in verse 9 and other places is often questioned. God isn't saying, through Ezekiel, that a person deserves life rather than death because he or she follows God's laws. Works of faith do not accumulate points for anyone. Rather, such actions are the proper response of anyone whom God has already delivered from the fear of death. It is due only to God's deliverance, not a person's actions, that he or she will live.

The second illustration is a reverse of the first one: The father is the sinful party, but the son refuses to follow in his father's offensive footsteps (18:14–18). The father will be judged for his wrongdoings, but the son will certainly not be punished for the father's sins. He will be treated by God as the righteous man that he is.

The Lord expects objections to what Ezekiel is proclaiming and prepares the prophet with a good response: "The soul who sins is the one who will die" (18:20 NIV). If a wicked person turns away from sin and starts obeying God, the Lord will show forgiveness and acceptance of the person (18:21–22).

The same principle applies in reverse (18:24). If someone repudiates a life of covenant faithfulness to God, his or her past "righteousness" will be no more a help than another person's past sins will be a hindrance. There is neither a treasury of merits nor of demerits. One generation cannot build up merits for another to trade, nor can the individual. And there is no measure of sin that reaches a point where the individual stands beyond hope of forgiveness and new life.

Demystifying Ezekiel

God isn't saying that children *never* suffer as a result of the sins of their parents and previous generations. The very reason the Israelites are in Babylon is because of the sins of Manasseh, several kings earlier (2 Kings 24:1–4). And modern statistics show, for example, that children of abusive parents tend to become abusers themselves. Children *can* suffer from the sins of parents, but Ezekiel clarifies that such suffering is not *inevitable*. Each person has the opportunity to answer the Lord's summons in faith, find forgiveness, and walk in the ways of righteousness. Repentance can mend anyone's past. Faith can open to anyone a new and bright future.

Still, the people are accusing God of being unfair (18:25–29). Ezekiel ends this particular oracle with a plea for his audience to accept responsibility for their own destiny. What may be true for the generation as a whole need not be true for any specific individual. His call for them to receive a new heart and spirit refers to the seat of thoughts, attitudes, and desires (18:31). God will have to make the change, but the individual must initiate the desire. Faith, repentance, and obedience are at one and the same time divine gifts and human duties.

Again, the references to death throughout this passage are in regard to *spiritual* death. Ezekiel is manifestly not talking about a longer life on earth (18:32). The exiles had dodged a fatal bullet when they were carried to Babylon instead of being killed on the spot in Jerusalem. They might, in fact, lead long lives, yet they will still *die* if they do not repent and turn to God.

📄 **19:1–14**

A LAMENT WHILE REVIEWING ISRAEL'S PAST

Several laments can be found throughout the Old Testament—dirges composed and sung at the death of an individual or over the destruction of a nation. (The book of Lamentations is a series of five laments.) One of the general features of a Hebrew lament is the "once. . .now" pattern that contrasts the glories of the past with the misery, indignity, and shame of the present. Such is the pattern of Ezekiel 19.

In addition to using the term *Israel* rather than the more accurate *Judah* in this passage, Ezekiel also uses *princes* to indicate their kings. The plural indicates that Ezekiel has in view not just Zedekiah but probably the whole series of unrighteous rulers who have led Judah to its final catastrophe.

The lion imagery in verses 2–3 refers to Judah, which had been true since the days of the patriarchs (Genesis 49:8–9). The lion was a symbol of rule, and Judah was the tribe that would rule over the other tribes of Israel, so Ezekiel's reference is to the kings of Judah.

The reference in Ezekiel 19:4 is to King Jehoahaz, the only one of Judah's last kings to be taken to Egypt (2 Kings 23:34). As to whom Ezekiel is describing in 19:5–9, a case can be made for any of three kings: Jehoiakim, Jehoiachin, or Zedekiah. Perhaps Jehoiachin is the most likely candidate because Ezekiel seemed to consider him the last legitimate king of Israel, and he had been taken to Babylon at the same time as Ezekiel, so the past-tense setting of the lament would have made sense. If Ezekiel has Zedekiah in mind, the passage is a *prediction* of the leader's downfall and exile.

In verses 10–14, Ezekiel's shift of imagery from lion to vine is yet another tie-in to Genesis. In Jacob's prophecy concerning his son Judah (more than fifteen hundred years before Ezekiel), the boy's future is portrayed in terms both of the power of a lion and the fruitfulness of the vine (Genesis 49:8–11). After God's subsequent covenant with David, Judah had seen twenty-two kings from David to Zedekiah. But during that time, the kings of the house of Judah and David had become arrogant. They ruled Judah without regard to their obligations to God or the people of Israel. Consequently, the line of royalty came to an end (temporarily) because there was no strong branch left on the vine "fit for a ruler's scepter" (Ezekiel 19:14 NIV).

It is important to note that this lament is for the people of Israel, not just the kings. It is *about* the kings, but it will be sung *by and for* the people (19:14).

📖 20:1–44

THE PROBLEM OF ONGOING IDOLATRY

After his lament, Ezekiel returns to the central theme of his writing: condemnation of the people of Israel for their betrayal of God's covenant, the anticipation of God's judgment about to befall them, and beyond that, the eventual restoration of Israel. However, in this section he emphasizes that the reason for the problem is Judah's idolatry.

According to verse 1, the date is August 14, 591 BC, almost a year after Ezekiel's most recent dated prophecy. Again, some elders of the nation have come to consult with the prophet about something, but Ezekiel doesn't bother to say what the group wants to know. God is unwilling to respond to their agenda, but He has a message for them nevertheless.

Critical Observation

Just because Ezekiel is obedient in passing along God's message to his peers in Babylon doesn't mean he isn't fazed by his duty. It would have been no easier for him to deliver a message of woe to his friends and neighbors than for anyone to announce to his or her loved ones that they are doomed and about to suffer the judgment of God. In addition, such people are typically objects of ridicule and scorn.

Ezekiel's contemporaries have a romantic recollection of their history. They take pride in their past accomplishments. It is a common assignment of God's prophets to review the past with a critical eye. Just as Stephen will later do before Israel's spiritual leaders (Acts 7), Ezekiel here begins to recall the history of Yahweh's relationship with the nation, underscoring the long pattern of Israel's unbelief and infidelity to God. By the time he finishes, it is evident that the current generation is committing the same offenses that their ancestors had made throughout their history.

God reveals information through Ezekiel that had not been provided earlier in the scriptural account. In making a covenant with Israel, God had made it absolutely clear that there could be no compromise with idolatry. Any such practice is a denial of the one, true, and living God and a repudiation of the revelation God had provided about Himself. However, Israel in Egypt was hardly a devoted and faithful people, waiting patiently for the promises of God to be fulfilled. Rather, they were idolaters who had adopted the religious practices of the Egyptians (20:5–8).

Yet Yahweh does not punish Israel as she deserves (20:9–10). Her idolatry notwithstanding, He is gracious and brings her out of Egypt. The Sabbath is a sign in that it is a regular weekly reminder of God's covenant (20:12). As it is confirmed in weekly worship, it became a perpetual reminder of Yahweh's goodness of delivering His people from the seven-day workweek by which slaves were exploited in the ancient world.

Demystifying Ezekiel

It is frequently proposed that the commandment to keep the Sabbath originated at Sinai, along with most of the other laws. By this way of thinking, God's people would have been under no obligation to keep one day holy prior to their wilderness experience. Yet Ezekiel clarifies that God gave *all His laws* to Israel in the wilderness (20:11–12)—that is, they were all formally codified at that time. Israel had already abided by certain civil laws (prohibitions to kill, lie, steal, etc.) and religious regulations (offering sacrifices, prohibitions to worship idols, etc). It is reasonable to believe, therefore, that observing the Sabbath was also among their already established practices, even though it is not mentioned specifically until Exodus 16:21–30.

Yet the observation of the Sabbath was soon regarded by Israel as a burden more than a boon, so even in the wilderness they failed to keep the Sabbath holy. The rebellion mentioned in 20:13 is most likely a reference to the incident with the golden calf at the foot of Sinai. At any rate, the first generation of Israelites to escape Egypt rejected God's laws, disobeyed His clear instructions, and desecrated the Sabbaths. In spite of everything God was doing in taking them from slavery to a promised land, they continued to put more faith in idols than in Him (20:13–17). Still, God does not destroy them, both out of His mercy and to prevent surrounding nations from profaning His name (20:14, 17). He gives their children (the next generation) another chance to follow Him more faithfully. That generation enters the promised land, but they prove to be hardly more faithful than their parents had been (20:18–26). Reading through the passage, it is impossible to miss the repetition Ezekiel uses as a literary device to emphasize God's patience in light of Israel's persistent denial of God's covenant, their disobedience to His commandments, and their ongoing profanation of the Sabbath.

At this point, Ezekiel begins to make a transition from the history of Israel to their current state. One might think that the one place where Israel would have been faithful to God was the promised land itself—a beautiful place God gave them in spite of the fact that they did not deserve such a gift. Yet they quickly adopted Canaanite idolatry as they had practiced Egyptian idolatry previously. Ezekiel's point is that the people of his time are descended from blasphemers, and idolatry is in their national DNA.

Now they are in Babylon, surrounded by yet another pantheon of idols. English speakers miss the relevance of the question in 20:29. *Bamah*, the word meaning "high place," is sounded several times in Ezekiel's phrasing. The implication is that the current generation of Israelites is still seeking out high places to worship other gods, even in Babylon, as their ancestors had repeatedly done.

Even more offensive than anything their forefathers had done, this group of Israelites has become involved in idolatry to the point of child sacrifice—a monstrous outrage against the holiness of God (20:31). Yet they have the audacity to come to Ezekiel hoping to get some specific answer from the Lord! Rather than serving God, they expect God to serve them.

The people are out calling on idols, and God is going to judge them (20:34–35). The Babylonian exile is, in a way, a repetition of Israel's history of slavery in the wilderness.

But in Babylon, the people will be purified and then restored to the promised land in a second exodus—a return from exile and new beginning (20:37–44). Their restoration will have nothing to do with their achievement or performance. As always, it will be entirely due to God's grace, mercy, and faithfulness to His Word.

20:45–21:32

PREPARE FOR BABYLON

As God continues to speak to the people through Ezekiel's oracles (20:45–48), it isn't certain that even Ezekiel is aware of the meanings at first. Clearly his listeners aren't making sense of the imagery because they accuse him of just telling stories (20:49). But God will soon supply the proper interpretations: Fire represents war; the south is Judah; the green tree symbolizes righteous people; the dry tree stands for the wicked people.

The Babylonian armies will be the sword God uses (21:2–5). The route they take from Babylon will result in Judah/Jerusalem being to the south (20:46). Consequently, there will be much reason to groan (21:6–7). Ezekiel's symbolic groaning will pique their curiosity and make a point, but the time is coming when they and all of Israel will groan for real. And a fact of war and other circumstances is that sometimes righteous people suffer in the punishment visited upon a wicked nation (21:4).

The proper interpretation of 21:10 is unclear. Perhaps the people first imagined that the image of Yahweh brandishing His sword would have been good news. In this case, however, He is not preparing to defend and avenge Israel. Just the opposite: God is preparing to destroy Jerusalem. The sword will soon be handed to Nebuchadnezzar (21:11). In response, Ezekiel's groaning escalates into wailing and beating his breast, for good reason (21:12–17).

Nebuchadnezzar will arrive at a crossroad and seek direction through divination, beseeching his gods, and other signs. Then he will choose the route that takes him to Jerusalem for conquest (21:19–23). But since God is telling Ezekiel exactly what will happen, it is clear that the choice is not Nebuchadnezzar's at all, but God's.

Critical Observation

Usually divination methods were used in cases where one of two choices needed to be made: go to war or not, attack this way or that, and so forth. Examining the liver of animals (hepatoscopy) was one standard technique of divination that was very popular with the Babylonians. Also, arrows would be marked with various symbols and drawn from a bag, not unlike drawing straws (21:21). And it was around this time that astrology—the effort to discover the future in the stars—was being developed in Babylon. The ancients were fascinated with attempting to know the future. But God's people were forbidden from such practices. The future was to be left to God; people were to concern themselves with faith and obedience in the present.

The Jews might have thought themselves safe from Babylonian attack because they had sworn loyalty to Nebuchadnezzar. But after the oath of loyalty was broken by Zedekiah (2 Chronicles 36:13), they should have had no expectation of security. Zedekiah was the profane and wicked prince (Ezekiel 21:25–27). The threefold repetition of *ruin/rubble* in verse 27 is the ultimate Hebrew superlative. The outcome will definitely not be pleasant.

Ezekiel's prophecies of judgment against other countries (besides Israel/Judah) will begin in earnest in chapter 25. But Ammon is the only one mentioned in chapters 1–24 (21:28–32). Perhaps it is the single exception for the contrast that could be made. Ammon had joined Israel in rebellion against Babylon, and their people must have heaved a sigh of relief when the Babylonian army attacked Jerusalem rather than their town of Rabbah (21:20). The diviners in Ammon were forecasting good news for their nation (21:29). But the truth of the matter is that the sword will soon strike them as well. And while Israel will eventually recover from their tragedy to receive a future that includes the blessings of God, Ammon is to disappear, never to rise again (21:31–32).

Take It Home

Review Ezekiel's lament in chapter 19. In today's religious culture that focuses heavily on God's promises and blessings, do you feel that people give adequate attention to lamentable things that aren't as they should be? Do you think God ever laments over the condition of His church?

EZEKIEL 22:1–24:27

SOME FINAL WORDS FOR JUDAH

Setting Up the Section

With this section, Ezekiel completes the first of three major sections of his book. He will finish his message of judgment directed to Judah/Jerusalem, after which he will begin to address other nations. But as he concludes this portion, his words will be punctuated with symbolic actions, even in regard to the death of his wife.

📖 22:1–31

JERUSALEM ON TRIAL

This section has the overtones of a courtroom scene where a defendant is found guilty by a judge. It first appears that Ezekiel is the judge, but it quickly becomes clear that he is only Yahweh's spokesperson. And although Ezekiel addresses Jerusalem, the city clearly represents the nation as a whole.

The prophet, like any good prosecutor, begins by indicting the people for their betrayal of God's covenant, and then he amasses the evidence of their crimes. He doesn't cite chapter and verse because he has repeatedly addressed this topic, but every violation he lists is clearly an act of disobedience to the law of God as it had been revealed to Israel. The result is that the great empire of David and Solomon declines into nothing, and other nations make jokes about it (22:4-5). Had Israel been faithful to the covenant God had established with her, the nation would have been exalted above all the other nations of the earth. Instead, their sins create the opposite situation, where they are humiliated before all the other nations.

A reference to blood, or bloodshed, occurs seven times in the first sixteen verses. The terms are not limited to literal physical violence committed against another person, but they also include, by extension, *any* harm done to another. Ezekiel begins his case with the sins of the leaders of the nation (22:6), but the problem isn't limited to them. The leaders only represent the more widespread problems that permeate the nation.

The list of specific accusations is only a sampling that represents a cross section of violations of God's law (22:7-12). Taken together as Israel's way of life, they reveal that the people have forgotten Yahweh. So the sins are not presented simply as specific violations of God's covenant but rather as evidence that the people have lost all interest in honoring the God who had brought them into covenant with Himself.

Still, this is among the longest lists of sins found anywhere in the Bible. The offenses cover a broad spectrum: religious idolatry, taking bribes, demanding sex from menstruating women, incest, and more. They are listed with no sense of one sin being more or less harmful than another, not an arrangement on a continuum of evil. They are all sins, so all are offensive to God. And sin *will* be punished.

Ezekiel, still speaking for the divine Judge, moves from the list of charges to the pronounced punishment. The image of Yahweh striking His hands together in verse 13 is a gesture to indicate both His anger and His order to put an end to all such behavior. Israel may have forgotten God, but He has not forgotten her (22:16).

All proper punishment has three purposes. First is *retribution*, paying back what is deserved and balancing the scales of justice. Human beings have a sense of retributive justice because they are created in the image of a just and holy God, who will by no means clear the guilty. The second aspect of punishment is *correction*, by which a person learns not to commit the same sin again. A driver who has just received a ticket is much more likely to slow down the next time he or she is on the same stretch of highway. And the third purpose of punishment is *purification*. God doesn't simply want His people to correct their errant behavior; He wants to create in them a new heart, a new mind, and a new attitude. Yet punishment is not pleasant. Here, as in other places, it is compared to a refiner's fire that will burn away the dross and leave what is valuable (22:17-22).

Although most of the people in Israel are guilty of the various sins cited, their leaders continue to be addressed. Ezekiel mentions five different groups of leadership: kings, priests, government officials, prophets, and wealthy landowners (the people of the land) (22:23-29). These are the cultural elite, the opinion shapers, the people with clout. They influence the beliefs and ethics of the people, so they carry the greatest responsibility for the society that forms under their leadership. Too few leaders realize that leadership is a call to responsibility, not a call to privilege.

The priests are indifferent to the Word of God. Government officials take advantage of people rather than protect them. False prophets outnumber faithful ones. God doesn't want to pour out His wrath on the people, but it has gotten to the point where He cannot find a single person committed to making a difference (22:30–31). The Judge has declared His people guilty and pronounced His sentence on them.

23:1–49

A TALE OF TWO PROSTITUTES

It is not uncommon to find instances of Israel or Judah compared to a prostitute, in that the people reject a loving God to pursue false gods and the idols of other nations. But nowhere is the imagery as stark as in this portion of Ezekiel. He uses some of the coarsest and crudest language in the Bible. In Jewish tradition, this chapter of Ezekiel was among the last to be taught to young men because of its potential to offend. But, of course, that is exactly the point.

Ezekiel describes two sisters, Oholah and Oholibah, who represent Samaria and Jerusalem (the capital cities of Israel and Judah). Both women engaged in prostitution from a young age, beginning while they were in Egypt. More recently, however, Oholah (Samaria) had become enamored with the Assyrians. At that time the Assyrian Empire was among the greatest powers in the world. Israel (the northern kingdom) wants to emulate Assyria and copies both their cultural and religious practices.

This instance of prostitution is, in fact, adultery. Assyria turns out to be a cruel lover. The Assyrians destroy Israel in 721 BC, depopulating the land and scattering the population across the great empire (23:9–10).

Ezekiel's audience had come from the southern kingdom of Judah. They had probably heard of Israel's demise; after all, the northern kingdom had virtually disappeared from the face of the earth. It was not hard for the people of Judah to assume that Israel had done something to offend God and that He had dealt with them. But Judah wrongly assumes that since Jerusalem is still standing and they are still around, God is not as angry with them.

Ezekiel declares that God is in fact even angrier with Judah than He had been with the north. Their spiritual lust and prostitution had continued more intensely than ever, even after they witnessed the Lord's furious response to the behavior of the northern "sister." Judah has no excuse for continuing infidelity, but their attitude is portrayed as the lust and fascination of a young woman for a dashing, handsome lover (23:11–21).

Yahweh has finally turned away from His wife in disgust, proclaiming that Judah will face the same end as her northern sister. The lovers to whom she had given herself will be the instruments of her destruction (23:22–35). She will undergo the same foreign invasion and conquest that Israel had suffered a century and a half prior. The bond between Judah and the surrounding nations had never been a satisfying one, yet the severing of that bond will be horrific. Ezekiel's depiction of foreign armies stripping off clothes and fine jewelry of their victims is more literal than symbolic (23:26). In certain chronicles written by conquering nations during this time, the brutality of the treatment of prisoners was a source of pride.

The numerous accusations against Oholah and Oholibah appear all the more heinous in the context of promiscuous seduction (23:36–45). The picture is of women who can't get enough, losing all standards as their loyalties shift from one foreign country to another. Judah's adultery is shameless, and in the Law of Moses the punishment for adultery was death. Unrepentant actions are about to have consequences (23:46–48).

📖 24:1–27

JUDGMENT AND MOURNING TO COME

As Ezekiel completes the section of his writing having to do with the judgment of Judah, he provides yet another date (24:1). The siege on Jerusalem will begin on January 5, 587 BC, but the city won't fall until August 14, 586 BC, so the people there are in for more than a year and a half of turmoil.

Ezekiel had previously cited a proverb indicating that the inhabitants of Jerusalem viewed the city as a cooking pot and themselves as the meat, worthwhile and protected (11:3). God's message in this passage is that, yes, the city might be a cooking pot, but it is a place where the people will be confined and consumed (24:3–12). In this case, the pot is encrusted due to heat applied so long and at such a high temperature that only a scummy residue remains (24:6). Emptying the pot "piece by piece" seems to suggest the depopulation of the city. And no lot is cast, because the casting of lots presumes the Lord's active involvement in the people's lives. Yahweh is no longer accommodating the people's presumption that they have special status before Him.

Based on Ezekiel's earlier personal involvement with his prophecies, it is likely that he acts this one out as well: filling a cooking pot with water, placing choice pieces of meat in it, setting fire beneath it, and so on. The pot would have been heated until the meat burned away and only bones were left (24:5). The visible blood is a witness to Jerusalem's crimes (24:7–8). And like a modern self-cleaning oven, great heat is used to char the remnants on the sides and bottom of the pot until they can be brushed away (24:11–12).

After Ezekiel's parable ends, God abandons the metaphor and makes His point clearly (24:13–14). The Lord's people had failed to become cleansed, but after undergoing this traumatic experience they will be clean again. God's wrath is not an unreasonable response to their persistently lewd conduct.

Ezekiel had acted out a number of his prophecies, including lying on his side for a portion of each day for weeks at a time (4:4–8) and shaving his head (5:1–4). But nothing he had done so far compares to the personal toll the next object lesson requires of him. God tells him his wife will die (24:15–17).

Although not certain, the circumstances appear to be that his wife has died suddenly and unexpectedly. What *is* clear is that her death is Yahweh's doing, despite the fact that Ezekiel loved her very much (24:16). Five traditional (though not biblically mandated) acts of mourning are mentioned: sighing, removing one's turban (normal wear for a priest), going barefoot, covering one's mouth, and eating special (less flavorful) food (24:17). Ezekiel is denied several of these outward traditions. He is permitted his grief, but not the public demonstration of it.

Demystifying Ezekiel

Ezekiel's comment in verse 18 appears to suggest that Ezekiel told his hearers one morning that his wife would die that day, and then she died that evening. But the wording also allows for the possibility that Ezekiel preached that morning as usual, as if nothing were amiss, even though he was aware that his wife would die. Nothing is said of any conversations between husband and wife after receiving the news, or whether Ezekiel may have pleaded for the life of his wife as David had pled for his son after being told that he would die (2 Samuel 12:15–17).

Naturally, Ezekiel's atypical behavior would have aroused curiosity. It would have been not only surprising but also disturbing and insulting for a man to fail to mourn the wife who he delighted in. The prophet's peers sense that the issue has something to do with them, and they finally ask him what it is (24:19). Their question provides the opportunity for him to tell them what God wants them to hear in a context that is bound to arrest their attention.

Jerusalem was the delight of Israel's eyes and God's as well (24:21). The popular theology of the time was that as long as the temple stood, the nation was safe. But when it fell, the people would be too affected to even mourn properly. While Ezekiel has every right to mourn his wife's death, the exiles have little justification to mourn the downfall of Jerusalem. The destruction of their prized city is fair punishment for their horrific crimes against God (24:20–24).

With the fall of Jerusalem, God's judgment is executed. Ezekiel's duty in preparing his people for the event is fulfilled. Therefore, his period of imposed silence comes to an end (3:26–27). Now the prophet, after a six-year ministry of preaching the doom of Jerusalem, is free to speak again and resume a normal life. He will next turn his attention to God's judgment concerning other nations.

Take It Home

It becomes evident from the repeated enumeration of Judah's problems that patterns of sin are hard to break. Their idolatry started in Egypt. They were delivered and led to the promised land, but the sinful habits continued. The easiest bad habits to break are those that are never formed, especially in matters of faith and obedience to God. Can you identify any potentially damaging patterns beginning to form in your life? If so, what can you do at this early stage to prevent even worse problems later in life?

EZEKIEL 25:1–32:32

IMPENDING JUDGMENT AGAINST THE NATIONS

Setting Up the Section

After completing his six-year ministry of preparing the exiles for the fall of Jerusalem, Ezekiel next turns his attention to God's judgment on a number of surrounding nations. Babylon is not included because, at this time, Babylon is the *instrument* of God's judgment. In fact, this section provides a wider sense of the impact of Babylon's imperial designs on the nations of the ancient world.

📖 25:1–7

JUDGMENT AGAINST AMMON

Ezekiel has shown so far that Judah certainly deserves God's judgment, but the surrounding nations are just as guilty of wrongdoings and atrocities. Were they to escape any kind of divine retribution? Certainly not, as Ezekiel will now go on to describe. Many of Israel's enemies watched with smug satisfaction as Jerusalem fell, but God was by no means finished.

The common bond of the nations Ezekiel will next address is that they are all enemies of Israel. The prophesied judgment of these nations would have therefore provided some hope for the people of God.

Ammon is first on the list. It is the lone nation designated for judgment, other than Judah, in the first twenty-four chapters of Ezekiel (21:28–32). Ammon was located east of Israel, across the Jordan River on the fringe of the Arabian Desert. Israel had a longstanding history of conflict with Ammon, beginning when the Israelites were in the wilderness on the way to the promised land. Saul and David both fought the Ammonites.

When Nebuchadnezzar had come into Palestine, it was essentially the flip of a coin that decided whether he conquered Ammon's capital city of Rabbah or Jerusalem (21:21–23). Since God had ordained Judah's punishment, Nebuchadnezzar chose Jerusalem. But rather than heaving a sigh of relief or giving thanks, the Ammonites took joy in seeing the destruction of Judah. *Aha* is the equivalent of a cheer (25:3). They were sure that their ancient foe had been destroyed and would never rise again.

But although Yahweh had acted in judgment against His people, He had not ceased to be their defender. He will punish those who rejoice at the punishment of Israel, no matter how just that punishment is.

The people of the east are Arabs from the desert who will overpower Ammon (25:4). Yahweh is not like the territorial gods they know, conquered when its people are. Ammon will still have to deal with Israel's God, as will every other nation and every other people.

25:8–11

JUDGMENT AGAINST MOAB

Moab, a territory located east of the Dead Sea, between Edom and Ammon, had also been delighted to see Jerusalem fall. Their response was a bit more understandable because they had been dominated politically and militarily by Israel throughout much of their history. Still, they had been aware that God had intervened on Israel's behalf in times past. Their sin was to deny Israel's election, to suppose that Yahweh was unable or unwilling to act on behalf of His people. It isn't surprising, though, that they failed to acknowledge that Israel was unlike any of the other nations. Israel had come to have the same view of herself, motivated by a great desire to be just like those other nations (20:32). Moab, too, will fall to the desert tribes, beginning with its key cities (25:10).

25:12–14

JUDGMENT AGAINST EDOM

Ezekiel does not enumerate the sins of Edom, but other biblical passages provide reasonable clues. Edom's territory was to the east of the Dead Sea near Moab. Israel (descended from Jacob) and Edom (descended from Esau) had been at odds since Genesis 25. The Edomites had refused Moses' appeal to pass through their territory as the Israelites were leaving Egypt (Numbers 20:14–21), and there had been little camaraderie between the two groups in the years and centuries that followed.

It appears that as soon as Judah became preoccupied with Babylon's army, Edomite raiders took advantage of Judah's unprotected southern borders, attacking towns there as well as Jews who were fleeing south to escape the Babylonians. Not enough is known of history between the sixth century BC and the third century BC to determine exactly how Israel was used as the instrument of the Lord's vengeance on Edom (25:14), although the same result was foretold in Obadiah. But we do know that by the fourth century BC, Edom had ceased to exist as a political entity, and its people were no longer a distinguishable population.

Demystifying Ezekiel

In verse 13, the phrase "from Teman to Dedan" is a sweeping geographical term to indicate the entire nation of Edom from the very south to the very north. The Israelite equivalent was "from Dan to Beersheba," although this reference is from north to south.

📖 **25:15–17**

JUDGMENT AGAINST PHILISTIA

The Philistines had given their name to the entire region: *Palestine* is derived from *Philistine*. They lived along the Mediterranean coast (in what is now the Gaza Strip). During Israel's era of the judges and early monarchy, the Philistines repeatedly threatened to dislodge the Israelites as rulers of the promised land. David finally subdued them (2 Samuel 5:17–25). Perhaps as a result of that defeat, their hostility toward Israel never abated. When the Babylonian invasion provided the opportunity to get back at Israel, they took malicious advantage of it (25:15). But they, too, experience the divine vengeance of God. No record exists of Philistine civilization after the second century BC.

Critical Observation

We must remember that Ezekiel is telling these prophecies to Israelites exiled in Babylon, and there is no indication that the messages are ever actually delivered to the peoples addressed by Ezekiel. So it is evident that the Israelites are actually the intended audience. Ezekiel's listeners, and his readers today, can take comfort in knowing that even though persecution borne out of the malevolence of others is an unfortunate reality of life, God is aware of all injustice and will settle the score in His own timing.

📖 **26:1–28:19**

JUDGMENT AGAINST TYRE

Tyre was only one hundred miles from Jerusalem, originally situated on an island in the Mediterranean Sea about six hundred yards off the coast, connected by what was then a narrow man-made causeway. (It has since expanded due to winds and tides to create a peninsula.)

The date of Ezekiel's pronouncement against Tyre (February 3, 585 BC) came several months after the fall of Jerusalem, which would have been approximately the time that Ezekiel and the exiles were hearing the news. At the same time, Nebuchadnezzar was initiating a siege of Tyre. The many nations that will oppose Tyre in 26:3 include the various ethnic groups within the Babylonian army because imperial armies were comprised of soldiers from various conquered peoples.

Tyre's mainland settlements, unprotected by the sea, will naturally be the first to suffer attack (26:7–14). Still, the protective walls will require a siege—in this case, a siege of thirteen years. The final destruction of Tyre will not occur until the time of Alexander the Great.

The word *coastlands* refers to other maritime peoples who will identify with a seafaring and trading city like Tyre (26:15). It is dreadful to consider that if the powerful Tyre can fall, the same can happen to them. The Babylonian appetite for new lands is voracious. Also, Tyrian control of the seas had provided stability. Now there is uncertainty.

As had been true with the fall of Jerusalem, the Babylonian army is the implement of destruction, but Nebuchadnezzar is only fulfilling the will and action of the Lord. Yahweh uses first-person language (26:19-21), and He speaks of more than mere physical death. The Israelites had a doctrine of the world to come. They would have identified a number of phrases as references to judgment and the next life: "down to the pit," "to the netherworld," "never to return to the land of the living," "a horrible end" (26:19-21).

The city itself will never entirely cease to be. It exists today. But it never recovers significance or becomes the great nation-state it once was.

At this point Ezekiel begins a lament for Tyre. In describing the glories of the past, Tyre is likened to a magnificent ship (27:1-11). The description is poetic in its mention of many of the very best products that Tyre shipped throughout the Mediterranean: Lebanon cedars, cypress wood, ivory, and so on. An actual ship would not, for example, have had linen sails (27:7). Tyre's glory is accented by the geographic breadth of its servants (27:10-11) and trade associations (27:12-24). This list is a historic review rather than a current list of allies. Israel, for example (27:17), had been destroyed about a century and a half earlier.

Yet the glory of Tyre will soon come to an end. If Tyre is a ship, she is going to wreck at sea and sink, and her demise will be hard to watch (27:27).

It is interesting to note that the reason for Tyre's fall is not described much in terms of her various sins, although it is clear that the city is guilty of slave trading and pagan practices (27:13). However, Ezekiel's accusations have more to do with a location that is simply wealthy, fat, and sassy. Tyre's prosperity rests on the sea trade that she has come to dominate (27:25-36). She is accustomed to the luxuries of life. And worse than that, she is proud of herself—a theme that Ezekiel will continue to develop.

At this point Ezekiel's prophecy gets a little more personal. He turns his attention to the king of Tyre, although, in an absolute monarchy of the ancient world, the fates of the king and the kingdom were so intertwined as to be virtually indistinguishable. The people tended to admire and support a king who was responsible for the nation's prosperity and greatness, and they would consider an oracle against such a leader to be directed at themselves as well.

In Ezekiel's day, the king of Tyre was Ethbaal II ("Baal is with him"), a clever man who amassed power and wealth as a result (28:4-5). Many people use such worldly wisdom to great advantage, but he isn't as wise as he *thinks* he is (28:1-3). Normally, the Mesopotamian-Syrian states believed a king was *appointed* by the gods but not actually a god himself. Perhaps Ethbaal II is attempting to elevate his status among the people. Or it could be that Ezekiel uses such language to indicate that the king has a far too high opinion of himself—that he is "playing God," so to speak.

Critical Observation

Daniel gets another mention here (28:3; see 14:14). This is not likely the Daniel whose prophecy is recorded in the Old Testament.

The glory of Tyre and the presumed wisdom of its leader will both disappear with the coming of "the terror of the nations" (28:7 NLT)—Babylon. The king, in his arrogance, has now reckoned with Yahweh.

The Phoenicians, like the Israelites, also practiced circumcision, though for different reasons and at a different time of life. For one of their leaders to die at the hands of uncircumcised foreigners was the ultimate indignity (28:8–10). No historical record has been found detailing the fall of Tyre, but it is not unreasonable to assume that after a thirteen-year siege, the king of Tyre would have been executed, if not tortured first, for creating so much trouble for Babylon.

Ezekiel has already related a lament for Tyre (chapter 27) and at this point is directed to shift from a prophecy against the king of Tyre to a lament for him as well (28:11–12). Few biblical laments are as extreme as this one. The king of Tyre is likened to the first angel in the Garden of Eden, magnificently clothed (unlike Adam) in gold and precious stones (28:11–15).

Ezekiel has twice described cherubim (chapters 1 and 10). Here he compares the king of Tyre to those glorious angelic beings. Cherubim were not unfamiliar to the people of Tyre; a number of their ivory carvings of cherubim have been found.

In the ancient Near East, the dwelling of God was often likened to a mountain. The Genesis account of Eden never suggests it is a mountain, but it is so designated by Ezekiel because of God's presence there (28:14). It was there this cherub walked as a creature of power and privilege.

Then, due to his wickedness, he changes. His great position, status, wealth, and power corrupt him and lead to his fall (28:15–19). The Eden imagery continues as the guardian cherub is driven out, and then the language becomes more general—more relevant to Tyre than Eden.

Critical Observation

Many Christians from the third century until this day believe that Ezekiel 28:11–19, in addition to applying to the king of Tyre, is also a reference to the fall of Satan. We know that God created Satan as good, because everything God creates is good. We presume Satan falls into sin prior to the fall of humans because he approaches Adam and Eve as a tempter and a liar. Scripture never provides the reason for his fall or additional details. It is certainly striking that Ezekiel describes the king of Tyre not simply as a glorious human but as a guardian cherub. Others of his descriptions also seem to allow for this interpretation. Whether or not the passage is intended to apply to Satan, it is clear that Ezekiel's theme is an illustration of pride going before a fall.

JUDGMENT AGAINST SIDON

Sidon was the second city to Tyre in Phoenicia. In fact, this is the only place in the Old Testament where the city is mentioned without its tie-in to Tyre, so it seems logical that it would be a partner in this oracle of doom (28:20–23). Sidon would not be spared the same destruction that was in store for Tyre.

A BRIGHT SPOT AMID THE PROPHECIES OF DOOM

This short section of Ezekiel 28 is almost exactly halfway through the portion of his prophecies that concern the grim futures of Israel's enemies (chapters 25–32). It is also the pivot around which the entire section turns. God is dealing with Israel, but these other nations are also being judged so Israel will be freed from their influence, both spiritually and politically. This section paves the way for the third section of Ezekiel (chapters 33–48): Israel's return from exile and the renewal of the life of the people of God in the promised land.

The Israelites in Babylon understood the difficult, and usually permanent, fate of captives. But the Lord will not be prevented from delivering His people and blessing them again in the land, even if it means the destruction of entire nations.

JUDGMENT AGAINST EGYPT

Ezekiel's oracles of judgment against Egypt comprise the final and longest segment of the second section of his book. Of all of Israel's enemies, the Egyptians are by far the most powerful. From the perspective of both Jeremiah and Ezekiel, the Babylonians are working as an instrument to accomplish the Lord's will. Egypt, on the other hand, has resisted Babylon's incursion into Palestine—an action viewed as resistance to God's will. When the Jews remaining in Jerusalem turn to Egypt in hopes of help and deliverance from the Babylonians, it is one further demonstration of their intransigent unwillingness to repent and honor the Lord.

Ezekiel's various oracles against Egypt are stretched across a considerable period of time. Most are dated, but they are not necessarily presented in chronological order. For example, the one beginning in 29:17 is the last of the prophecies (dated 571 BC). The one that follows it (beginning in 31:1) is dated fifteen years *earlier*. Some of the prophecies were spoken prior to the fall of Jerusalem, and others long after.

The first of Ezekiel's prophecies against Egypt is dated January 7, 587 BC. As was true of the king of Tyre, Egypt's Pharaoh had delusions of grandeur and would suffer for them along with his kingdom. It would be difficult to overestimate Egypt's dependence on the Nile. Due to the scarcity of rainfall, all agriculture and plant life depended on the water brought north from the highlands of central Africa by the great river. But Pharaoh, who was so proud of his control of the Nile, is portrayed as a great fish caught in the river and thrown onto the land to serve as food for animals (29:1–5).

Through the centuries, Israel had occasionally sought help from Egypt against her enemies, always in defiance of the warnings of Yahweh. Beseeching Egypt had not helped against the Assyrians, and it will do no good against the Babylonians either. Ezekiel's image is that of a person leaning on a staff, but the staff is a weak reed that quickly gives way under weight (29:6–7).

As a result, God will humble Egypt. The nation won't cease to exist as some of Israel's other enemies, although it will become a small, insignificant kingdom (29:8–16).

Critical Observation

In 29:10, "from Migdol to Aswan" is another usage of locations at extreme ends of a nation to indicate totality (in this case from north to south). Migdol is a delta city. Aswan, the site of the famous modern dam, is in the south, not far from Egypt's border with Ethiopia.

In the next of Ezekiel's dated prophecies concerning Egypt (29:17–21), Babylon is shown as doing the Lord's work, though hardly by her own intention. Still, the reward for her pains is the wealth of Egypt. Not much of the historical record exists for this portion of Egyptian history, but it appears that the Pharaoh had to contribute large amounts of money to Babylon to help fund their siege of Tyre. Meanwhile, Israel begins to regain strength (29:21).

Just as Ezekiel had given a lament for Tyre, so also he relates one for Egypt, a nation that had never before suffered a catastrophic invasion (30:1–26). The Assyrians, at the height of their power, had managed to render Egypt a client state for a time, but Egypt had weathered that storm. However, the Day of the Lord is approaching (30:3). Babylon will invade in 568 BC, crushing the might of Egypt while devastating all her allies (30:4–26). Even after the fall of Babylon, Egypt will remain a Persian colony until 404 BC, and after that she will fall to Alexander the Great in 332 BC.

In a lengthy metaphor, Ezekiel likens Egypt to a great cedar tree of Lebanon (31:1–18). But then, Assyria had also been a great tree, a wonder to behold and without equal. It had then been cut down, never to recover. Egypt, too, will fall and fare only slightly better in the aftermath.

Ezekiel concludes this section with a lament for Egypt's Pharaoh, describing Egypt's fall in the most sweeping terms (32:1–32). Egypt has been a dominant power, but God will soon dominate Pharaoh (32:1–16). The final scene is one of a number of fallen powers, Egypt among them, buried together in the pit in various stages of ignominy and shame (32:17–32).

Take It Home

Ezekiel shows that in a powerful and successful country, it is easy to put one's trust in the wrong things: military might, reputation, wealth, and so on. After Israel and Judah had forsaken God, they longed for help from what seemed to be indestructible nations (Assyria, Babylon, Egypt, etc.). But all those mighty forces came to the same end. As contemporary Christians, it is easy to make the same mistake. Any person or nation who commits the same sins, in defiance of the lessons of human history, will pay dearly. What steps can you take today and in the weeks to come to ensure that your trust and hope are in God alone?

EZEKIEL 33:1–36:38

AFTER GOD'S JUDGMENT OF JUDAH

An Appropriate Response	33:1–33
Sheep and Shepherds	34:1–31
Israel and Edom	35:1–36:38

Setting Up the Section

This section begins the third and final segment of Ezekiel's writings. Most of what he has said so far has been somber. The first section (chapters 1–24) dealt with God's judgment on Judah. The second section (chapters 25–32) covered the judgment of Judah's enemies. With those matters behind, however, his look to the future is hopeful and positive. In the final chapters of his book, he foresees Israel's restoration and prosperity as they again receive the blessings of God.

▥ 33:1–33

AN APPROPRIATE RESPONSE

Ezekiel has already explained that God designated him a watchman (3:16–21), but he reiterates the concept. The logic is clear and unassailable: If a watchman warns of impending catastrophe but the people ignore his warning, they have no one to blame but themselves for the disaster that overtakes them (33:1–9). The watchman is to blame only if he detects the danger but fails to sound the warning.

Ezekiel has been a conscientious watchman. He sounded the warning. In response, the people see that their suffering is a result of their sins, and they are depressed and discouraged about their situation (33:10). Their pessimism is understandable. After all, they had been exiled from their homeland, and Ezekiel had for years been forecasting Jerusalem's catastrophic devastation. But was theirs a state of repentance or simply sorrow?

Under such circumstances it is easy to lose sight of the power of God and His willingness to bless those who trust Him. The Israelites have a hard time believing their lives can become dramatically different, but Ezekiel keeps challenging them to repent and reestablish their hope (33:11). A person's (or a people's) past does not necessarily determine the future. Someone who has lived a righteous life by all appearances will not be excused if later he or she turns away from righteousness to sin. Likewise, a person who has lived a wicked life is not prevented by his or her past from becoming righteous at once by turning away from sin to the Lord (33:12–20).

For a number of years, Ezekiel has faithfully spoken for God, predicting the fall of Jerusalem. In the twelfth year of exile, word arrives that the dreaded event has finally come to pass (33:21–22). Judah, the remainder state of Israel, exists no more. The date of the fall of the city is August, 586 BC, but it would have taken months for the news to travel to Babylon. When Ezra later travels from Babylon to Jerusalem, it takes him more than four months, and that is with an escort along well-maintained roads during a time of peace. A fugitive attempting to remain hidden from Babylonian soldiers might have taken much longer to go the same distance.

Critical Observation

Apparently the second section of Ezekiel (chapters 25–32) interrupts the chronological flow of the book. The Lord had imposed a symbolic silence on Ezekiel (3:26), but the restriction was to be lifted when a fugitive informed the prophet of the fall of Jerusalem (24:25–27). The arrival of that fugitive is announced in 33:21–22, and Ezekiel is finally free to resume ordinary day-to-day speech with other people.

It appears significant that Ezekiel does not use the names of Jerusalem or Judah throughout this section. It is as if the city and the land no longer deserve their names. Indeed, neither the exiles in Babylon nor the people who remained in Judah had a proper perspective on the situation.

Some of the Israelites remained in the area of Jerusalem, even though the city was in ruins. These are the poorest of the Israelites that the Babylonians had three times left behind (2 Kings 25:12), yet they have the mindset that they have managed to outlast the others. They even compare themselves to Abraham: If God had given the patriarch—one man—the land, then certainly a group of them had the right to it. But comparing themselves to the righteous Abraham isn't appropriate. Ezekiel quickly lists a number of their ongoing sins and what the consequences of those sins will be (33:23–29). Jeremiah's account confirms Ezekiel's prophecy: The lives of the people left behind go from bad to worse. An abortive rebellion leads to the flight of many to Egypt and an increase in poverty. When the exiles eventually return from Babylon, the people who had remained in Judah are found eking out a hardscrabble existence.

The exiled Israelites in Babylon don't fare much better. They come to recognize Ezekiel as an authentic prophet of God. He enjoys a newfound popularity as people come to him to hear what God has to say. But God sees through their spiritual facade. The recognition of truth is not always coupled with the willingness to obey. Ezekiel faithfully proclaimed God's truth, but the people saw him as no more than an entertainer and responded in the same way they might to a singer or musician (33:30–32). Eventually, however, they see God's Word come to pass and acknowledge that when Ezekiel spoke they were hearing the words of the Almighty Himself (33:33).

📄 34:1–31

SHEEP AND SHEPHERDS

Ezekiel had previously placed responsibility for Israel's pathetic spiritual condition on its leaders (22:6–12). Here God has him prophesy against the nation's *shepherds*. When contemporary believers hear the word, they tend to think of pastors or ministers, but Ezekiel's hearers would have immediately thought of their *kings*, not prophets or priests. The likening of kings to shepherds was commonplace in the ancient Near East.

The kings of Israel and Judah are compared to shepherds who are glad to benefit from the food and wool available to them yet refuse to take care of the flock that provides those assets (34:1–6). Of the forty-two kings who ruled from Saul to Zedekiah (about 1030 BC until 586 BC), very few were consistently faithful to their responsibility as overseers of the people of God. Another handful were moderately faithful, but most were completely insensitive to the needs of the people as they used the position only to aggrandize themselves. Israel's exile is the direct result of the malfeasance of her kings.

Yahweh is about to take matters into His own hands. He will hold the incompetent shepherds accountable for their unfaithfulness. His primary interest, however, is not to punish the rulers but rather to rescue His sheep from them (34:7–16). Utterly unlike the selfish reigns of Israel's kings, Yahweh will attend to the needs of His people and provide for them. (Ezekiel 34:16 is the mirror opposite of 34:4.)

Yet the problems will continue for a while (34:17–22). Those who are wealthy and powerful—"the sleek and the strong" (34:16 NIV)—will continue to take advantage of the poor and weak people. In fact, the matter will not be ultimately resolved until God provides a new shepherd, one akin to His servant David (34:23–24). This will be a single person who perfectly embodies the kingly ideal.

It may have seemed that the collapse of Judah, the capture of her kings, and the exile of her people to Babylon had signaled the end of God's covenant with the house of David. However, Ezekiel's pronouncement of God's promise reveals that the covenant with David has by no means been revoked. The promise is still in force. David's descendant will again sit on his throne.

With the appointment of this new king, the Lord will establish a covenant of peace with Israel. Ezekiel lists a number of images of blessing and prosperity that the covenant will bestow upon the people of God (34:25–31; see Leviticus 26; Deuteronomy 28). Everything God had promised Israel will eventually be realized.

ISRAEL AND EDOM

Israel and Edom were two mountainous nations that shared a long history of animosity and conflict (Israel tracing its roots to Jacob and Edom going back to Esau). This section of Ezekiel contrasts their respective destinies.

After the fall of Jerusalem, Judah is left with an economy in shambles and a lack of effective government or military. Edom, encouraged by the Babylonians, takes advantage of Judah's vulnerability and invades at that time, taking whatever the Babylonians haven't already removed and annexing portions of the land. It might seem that this particular passage should have accompanied the previous section of judgments against foreign nations (chapters 25–34). However, the promise of Edom's destruction, coming immediately after the destruction of Jerusalem, serves as the background for a prophecy of Israel's restoration.

Mount Seir (35:2) is symbolic of the entire nation of Edom (35:15). The two nations Edom has in its sights are Israel and Judah (35:10). The Edomites are celebrating the desolation of Jerusalem; even worse, they slaughter the Jews they catch fleeing from the Babylonians (35:5–6).

But soon Edom's punishment will fit their crime as they experience similar desolation (35:10–15). Those who use their strength to take advantage of others are rarely popular. When Edom eventually faces the same crisis for which they had ridiculed Israel, the rest of the world takes a perverse delight in their misery.

Demystifying Ezekiel

The entire book of Obadiah (short though it is) is devoted to a similar prophecy against Edom. Obadiah also foretells that the violence of the Edomites will bring God's wrath upon them.

Edom declines steadily under Babylonian, then Persian, then Greek, and finally Roman rule. Its former mountain strongholds are now only tourist stops in southern Jordan.

Just as Mount Seir represents Edom, the mountains of Israel stand for the entire nation (36:1). Ezekiel does not provide a date for this prophecy, but it is clear that it is given after the destruction of Jerusalem while Judah is at the mercy of her enemies. God's message to Israel is just the opposite of the accompanying prophecy to Edom (and other nations). In fact, it was probably hard for many people to believe such a promise, considering Israel's current circumstances: nation and temple in ruins, people in exile, kings dead or imprisoned. So throughout this section, Ezekiel repeatedly punctuates his message with, "This is what the Sovereign LORD says."

Indeed, the news is good. God is renewing the blessings previously spelled out in His covenant with Israel, including increased fertility of the land and the people (36:8–12). The people have done nothing to deserve it. They had defiled Israel, and when God removed them from that defiled land, their continued inappropriate conduct caused other nations to profane God's name (36:16–18). The assumption of Israel's enemies is that Israel's God must not be very powerful if He can't save His people from such indignities.

Yet the Lord loves His people and will deliver them even though Israel has done nothing to deserve His mercy. Ezekiel makes it clear that Yahweh is not rewarding the people for their goodness, because they haven't been good or faithful for a long time. Rather, God is acting to show the holiness of His own name, His faithfulness to His own Word (36:19–23).

God's faithfulness to His Word is seen in the promises of 36:25–27, which are another form of the same promises previously given in Deuteronomy 30:6–8. And as the Spirit of God works among the people, many will respond with deep contrition (Ezekiel 36:31).

Take It Home

The problem Ezekiel is confronting on a national level can also be problematic at a personal level. God's judgment of His people is somber and at times tragic. As other nations witness it, the appropriate response is repentance for their own wrongdoings, but instead they rejoice and celebrate. Do you think people today—even believers—sometimes take joy in the ignominious downfall of their enemies (either nationally or individually)? How might you avoid feeling that same inappropriate satisfaction when a personal enemy has a bad or embarrassing experience?

EZEKIEL 37:1–39:29

DRY BONES AND NEW LIFE

Life Restored to Dry Bones	37:1–14
Restoration and Unification	37:15–28
Judgment against Gog	38:1–39:29

Setting Up the Section

This section contains one of the few passages from the long book of Ezekiel that might be somewhat familiar to the average person. As Ezekiel continues his message of God's redemption of Israel, he is shown in a most emphatic way God's immense power to restore His people. Ezekiel also alerts the people of a king to come who will unite them again, and he delivers a prophecy against the land of Gog.

📄 37:1–14

LIFE RESTORED TO DRY BONES

Although Ezekiel has been prophesying with great regularity, this is the first *vision* he records since chapter 11. The message of chapter 37 essentially repeats what Ezekiel had proclaimed in chapter 36, but in a different way that makes the same point and drives home the message.

God shows Ezekiel a valley with a great many dry bones (37:1–2). The fact that the bones are unburied and baking in the sun suggests a curse concerning those who break the Lord's covenant: "Your carcasses will be food to all birds of the sky and to the beasts of the earth, and there will be no one to frighten them away" (Deuteronomy 28:26 NASB). It is a reminder that Israel has suffered precisely the fate the Lord long ago warned about if she was not faithful to His covenant.

Ezekiel is instructed to walk among the bones, perhaps to see for himself how brittle they are. These bones have had all the skin, flesh, and sinews removed by decomposition and/or scavengers, and they have been bleached in the hot Middle Eastern sun.

Critical Observation

Ancient burial customs tended to require interment twice. The body was first placed in a family tomb on a shelf cut out of the rock for that purpose. Later, when the shelf was needed for another body, the family would place the desiccated bones in an *ossuary*, literally a "bone box." The skeleton would have to be broken up with the bones packed individually. Sometimes many sets of bones were stored in the same ossuary.

The Lord's question to Ezekiel in verse 3 is intended to start the prophet thinking about life after death. Next Ezekiel is instructed to address the long-dried-up bones, to prophesy to them (37:4–6). More specifically, he is told to tell the bones that God is planning to make them live again. The word for *preaching* in this section, often translated as "prophesy" (literally, "to speak for God"), occurs seven times throughout the passage.

The obvious question is: What possible good is it to make such an effort? So much time has passed, and the bones are so dry that they are not even connected to one another. They are loose bones, not intact skeletons. Yet Ezekiel does as he is told (37:7).

Demystifying Ezekiel

In Ezekiel 37:1–14, the prophet writes of *breath*, *wind*, and *spirit* in various contexts. We miss the significance, but his listeners could not have overlooked the clever wordplay because in Hebrew (and later in New Testament Greek) the same word is used to define each of those terms. Ezekiel uses the word ten times in these fourteen verses to emphasize how the breath of God's Spirit allows us to become living spirits and how God's sovereignty is highlighted by the fact that He controls the four winds.

In response to Ezekiel's preaching, the bones not only come together to form complete skeletons but also grow tendons, flesh, and skin (37:7–8). However, they still have no breath until God instructs Ezekiel to prophesy once more, after which the former pile of bones rises to form a vast army (37:8–10).

This vision, as it turns out, is Yahweh's response to the hopelessness and despair of His people. A saying has begun to circulate among the dispirited Jews in Babylon: "Our bones are dried up and our hope is gone; we are cut off" (37:11 NIV). Ezekiel's vision demonstrates that for God's people, hope is never gone.

To reinforce the positive message of the vision, God speaks of opening the graves of His people to restore them to Israel (37:12–14). The image of resurrection and anticipation of a new exodus are brought together to describe what the Lord is going to do for Israel: Israel will be made alive spiritually, and she will be brought back as a people to the promised land. Yet nothing in the world would have appeared less likely when Ezekiel saw this vision and reported it to his fellow exiles in Babylon.

RESTORATION AND UNIFICATION

After the vision of the valley of dry bones, God provides Ezekiel with yet another depiction of Israel's restoration. God instructs him to take two sticks (representing Israel and Judah) and join them together. It is not clear exactly how he does this, but the result is the appearance of a single stick, demonstrating that the nations will again be one.

Demystifying Ezekiel

Israel had previously been the name of the northern ten tribes. Sometimes *Ephraim* was used as a synonym because it was the principal tribe (from which all the northern kings had come) and it covered the geographical area of Samaria, the capital of the northern kingdom. But Israel had been conquered and absorbed into surrounding nations more than a century ago. Judah was all that was left of the original nation of Israel. In the view of all the prophets, including Ezekiel, Judah had inherited the title of *Israel* and remained a divinely chosen people in covenant with Yahweh.

Like the meaning of the valley of the dry bones, this too would have been hard for Ezekiel's audience to understand (37:18–19) and almost too good to believe. God is promising not only a political/social restoration but also spiritual renewal (37:20–24). The phrase, "They will be my people, and I will be their God" (37:23 NIV), reflects God's covenants with Abraham and Moses, and some say it is a succinct way to describe New Testament salvation.

God's people will be united under a single king. He is called David because he will be a leader from the house of David (37:24). Modern believers may recall David's adultery, fall, and the miserable second half of his reign. But David was a man after God's own heart. It was under his reign alone in the history of Israel that the nation was free of idolatry and polytheism—a remarkable achievement in a world where the great number of gods made religion without idols seem a contradiction in terms.

The closing reference to God's dwelling place among the people anticipates a major theme that Ezekiel will develop in chapters 40–46 (37:27–28).

JUDGMENT AGAINST GOG

The nature of biblical prophecy is such that sometimes people can examine the same passages and come up with quite diverse interpretations. This particular section of Ezekiel is one such complicated and potentially confusing section. For example, there was no real political restoration for the Jewish nation as Ezekiel describes in the second half of chapter 37. The exiles return to Judah, to be sure, but never gain true independence again. After Babylonian exile, they remained a tiny client state of a succession of powers: Persia, Greece, the Seleucids, Rome, and the Turkish Empire.

From there Ezekiel moves on to the Gog/Magog section (chapters 38–39) and then the elaborate account of building a new temple (chapters 40–48). Some people approach these passages as unfulfilled prophecies of Israel's eventual restoration as a great nation in the promised land. However, that is not the way the Bible itself treats these prophetic texts.

Ezekiel and numerous other prophets wrote of the future of God's people as a whole—Jews and Gentiles alike. The promised land, never limited to a piece of Canaanite real estate, was ultimately a promise of heaven and eternity.

Demystifying Ezekiel

Continuing through the rest of Ezekiel, a number of presumptions will influence how his visions and prophecies will be interpreted:

1) The covenant that God made with Abraham and renewed with Israel at Sinai is the theological/spiritual arrangement by which modern Christians live today. There has always been, and will always be, but one people of God.

2) The Bible is a single book with a single message about a single people and their single Savior. A failure to see Gentile believers as the object of so much of biblical prophecy inevitably leads people to think that the Old Testament has to do with another people and their situation, not with us and ours. The whole Bible comes alive as we realize it is our family history, our story, and not someone else's.

3) Modern Christians are in the same situation as our ancestors were in the days of Ezekiel: We are awaiting the consolation of Israel and the fulfillment of the new covenant.

4) We have been given a number of anticipations of this ultimate consummation: the return of the Jews from Babylon, the incarnation of the Son of God and His resurrection from the dead, the Lord's changing of individual hearts, the survival of the Jews through the last twenty-five hundred years and the rebirth of their national identity in 1948, and so forth.

Magog, Meshech, and Tubal are three grandsons of Noah (38:1–3; see Genesis 10:2), and the peoples who descended from them were still known to Ezekiel's contemporaries. Magog is thought to have been a land in western Asia Minor, though that is not certain. Meshech and Tubal are two relatively small nations of Cappadocia (present-day Turkey). Ezekiel has already mentioned the latter two locations in passing (27:13; 32:26). Meshech had a warlike reputation due to frequent conflicts with the Assyrians (Psalm 120:5–7). The name *Gog* seems to have been derived from the name of a powerful king of Lydia (western Asia Minor) in the first half of the seventh century BC. So Ezekiel refers to two separate nations with the king from a third—a great force gathering to invade the south sometime in the future.

Gog's great army will be enlarged by mercenary troops from a variety of other nations that span the furthest reaches of the known world, all united to invade the promised land where Israel lives in safety (Ezekiel 38:5–6). Ironically, Gog and his legions will be following Yahweh's orders (38:7–16). Sheba and Dedan are caravan trading nations, one to the east and one to the west, hoping to profit at Israel's expense by buying plundered goods to resell to their trading partners (38:13).

This assault on Israel will be the fulfillment of other predictions made by Old Testament prophets. The description of the Lord putting an end to Gog's aggression is universal and cosmic. The entire earth is involved; all creatures tremble. The account of warfare in Revelation reflects many of the same events as Ezekiel 38:17–23: earthquake (Revelation 11:13), fire and hail raining down from heaven (Revelation 8:7; 20:9), and birds eating the flesh of the enemies of God (Revelation 19:17–21). There is evidence that the beast of Revelation is to be understood as Gog.

Ezekiel 39 is a repeat of Ezekiel 38, but with more emphasis on Gog's destruction than the attack on Israel. It will be total annihilation, with no survivors to bury the dead and even the homelands of the invading armies lay to waste (39:1–6). Ezekiel's reference to "the day" in 39:8 ties in to other biblical prophecies about the Day of the Lord. On that day, God will reverse which side does the plundering and looting (39:9–10). The burial of enemy soldiers will take seven months, but the ritual purification of the land (including removing all bones) will take much longer (39:11–16).

With such an image of the victory God will give His people, it should have been abundantly clear that it isn't for any want of power on Yahweh's part that Israel falls prey to the Babylonians. He is judging His people, but the long-range result will be a restored house of Israel—a transformed and spiritually renewed people living in communion with God and in willing obedience to Him (39:17–29).

Take It Home

Israel's promised turnaround from exiled captives to those being renewed and restored to fellowship with God in their own land is almost too much to believe. Put yourself in Ezekiel's place as he was chosen to deliver such news. Do you think he even comprehended the significance of his message? And note especially his willingness to preach to a valley filled with dry, disconnected bones. Can you relate to trying to encourage someone who perpetually seems unable or unwilling to listen? If so, reread Ezekiel 37:1–14 as a reminder that God's Spirit is powerful enough to reach *anyone*. God's people need to continue to speak faithfully for Him, even in situations where a positive outcome seems unlikely.

EZEKIEL 40:1–46:24

A NEW TEMPLE

Setting Up the Section

The final nine chapters of the book of Ezekiel, beginning with this section, are a great vision of the future of Jerusalem and Israel presented in terms of an idealized temple and promised land.

📖 **40:1–4**

A DIFFERENT KIND OF VISION

Ezekiel has been given some very specific visions to proclaim to the people of God exiled in Babylon, not least among them the fall of Jerusalem and the confident expectation of being freed to return to their homeland. Other visions of his were much more symbolic than specific, such as the valley where a pile of dry bones sprang to life. His vision of a future temple has been interpreted both ways.

Some people consider the closing chapters of Ezekiel a description of an actual temple to be built in Jerusalem at some point in the future. (Its description and measurements do not match any previous temple.) But a number of reasons arise from the biblical text to discourage such a viewpoint. The high mountain position (40:2) suggests the dwelling of God, and we may assume that Ezekiel intends for us to understand that he is looking southward toward Jerusalem (although the city is not specifically mentioned). However, there is no high mountain north of Jerusalem, or anywhere in Israel for that matter.

In addition, the design of the temple is highly stylized or idealized: Its dimensions are dominated by multiples of five, with twenty-five a common number and everything exactly proportioned—it is not unlike the description of the heavenly Jerusalem found in Revelation 21—a description so fabulous it is impossible to visualize.

Demystifying Ezekiel

The date would have been April 28, 573 BC, but of equal significance is the *way* Ezekiel's vision is dated. The fact that it is twenty-five years after Ezekiel's exile may be a subtle reference to the year of Jubilee (40:1). Every fifty years all enslaved Israelites were to be freed (Leviticus 25:8–13). The twenty-fifth year would mark the turning point when people no longer looked back to the catastrophe of the exile but forward to their restoration. The vision also occurs at the first of the year, which invites comparison to Israel's deliverance from bondage in Egypt (Exodus 12:2).

MEASURING THE TEMPLE

One other thing to keep in mind is that Ezekiel's descriptions were not illustrated. His audience had only his words. Modern readers may find the temple section of his writing repetitive or overly detailed, but that was the only way the prophet could attempt to describe the splendor he witnessed. He needed to provide lots of details to help his listeners/readers form appropriate pictures in their minds.

As his celestial host proceeds to measure the temple, Ezekiel records not only the measurements but also a number of observations (40:3–4). Starting at the east gate (40:5–16), they move into the outer court (40:17–19) and its north (40:20–23) and south (40:24–27) gates before continuing to the inner court with its gates and special rooms (40:28–47). Ezekiel, as a priest, is able to enter the Holy Place, but he remains there as the angel goes alone into the Most Holy Place (40:48–41:4). Additional side rooms surround the temple in three layers (41:5–7). The cherubim carved into this temple have only two faces rather than the four that Ezekiel had previously seen firsthand (41:5–26; see 1:10). Finally, Ezekiel is shown the priests' rooms (42:1–20).

This must surely have been an inspiring vision for the people of Israel. As they will eventually discover, the temple they had known is completely gone. When it is reconstructed after the exile, even the foundation has to be rebuilt. Impressive buildings are still a measure of the greatness of a city. The reputation of Paris would be diminished without its Eiffel tower, Notre Dame, and Arc de Triumph. Rome is enhanced by the Coliseum, St. Peter's, the Trevi Fountain, the Spanish steps, and the Pantheon. Jerusalem without the temple was just not the city it should be, and Ezekiel envisioned a marvelous temple indeed.

GOD'S GLORY RETURNS

As Ezekiel's vision continues, he discovers that another attribute of this new temple is its permanence (43:6–7). Israel is still in shock over the loss of their first temple—the one Solomon had built. It will soon be reconstructed by Zerubbabel, but it will also fall. Later Herod enlarges and restores the temple during the time of Jesus. This permutation has the shortest existence of all, destroyed by the Romans only a few years after its completion. The temple Ezekiel describes, however, would be the dwelling place of God forever (43:7).

This is a powerful vision. Ezekiel had previously described the glowing, fiery radiance that indicated the presence of God, and he had heard angels' wings that sounded like the movement of a great army (1:24–28; 43:3).

It is significant that the glory of the Lord enters this new temple through the east gate, for it was from the east gate that His glory had departed in Ezekiel's former vision (10:18–19). A great reversal is taking place as the complete manifestation of God's divine majesty returns to take its place among His people. The filling of the temple with the glory of the Lord (43:5) is a phenomenon previously seen in the days of Solomon (1 Kings 8:10–11) and in one of Isaiah's visions (Isaiah 6:4).

The presence of Yahweh is further confirmed by His voice (Ezekiel 43:6). The reference to the temple as the place for the soles of His feet (43:7) recalls the ark of the covenant in earlier passages as the Lord's footstool (1 Chronicles 28:2). While the ark is the embodiment of the Lord's presence in the old temple and viewed as Yahweh's throne, it is not prominent in this new visionary temple. The temple itself is God's throne and dwelling place. The shift of emphasis away from the ark to God's more widespread presence is also reflected in Jeremiah's writing (Jeremiah 3:16–17).

The nature of the defilement mentioned in Ezekiel 43:7–8 is unclear. Various sources have speculated that the problem might involve the tombs of kings being placed too near the temple (although no evidence of such a practice exists), some kind of cult that worshiped the dead, or memorials being built nearby that detracted from a single-minded focus on Yahweh. Whatever the specific problem had been, it was yet another way Israel had betrayed God's covenant and shown indifference to His holiness.

In this visionary description of the future consummation of salvation, the people of God are still summoned to live in holiness. Even when all is complete, obedience and loyalty to the Lord are expected. The end of history is connected to the responsible actions of the Lord's people.

Ezekiel is challenged to keep the description of the new temple before the people, who are still mourning the fall of Jerusalem's temple (43:10–11). It is the next best thing possible to snapping a photo of what he had seen and showing the snapshot to encourage and strengthen those who saw it. Ezekiel's regular descriptions also remind the people that they had strayed away from God in the first place, creating the problems they eventually faced. However, they are now able to again enjoy God's presence, thanks to His forgiving grace.

📖 **43:13–46:24**

THE FUNCTION OF THE TEMPLE

Unlike the gods of the surrounding territories, Yahweh has no interest in a temple where He can enjoy basking in the glory of His surroundings. Israel's temple had an ongoing function to be the place where people worship the Lord and He fosters holiness among them. Yahweh desires fellowship with His people, which necessitates their purity and righteousness.

Ezekiel next makes a transition from describing the incredible temple to providing regulations that will govern worship. The altar needs to be properly dedicated (43:13–27), and this time the priests will serve faithfully (44:1–31). Interestingly, there is no mention of a high priest in this section, although the prince who abides in the temple with God is mentioned frequently in the material that follows, beginning in 44:3. The priests will not only attend to the temple but also serve as preachers, teachers, and rulers of the people (44:24).

The division of land is summarized in 45:1–8; it will be covered in greater detail in 48:1–22. Great emphasis is placed on justice in the land. The king will rule justly and for the sake of the people, not himself, and private land will be protected from royal confiscation (45:8–12).

The next section (45:13–46:24) specifies the offerings to be made and the feasts to be celebrated in the new temple. They are similar to, but not identical with, the regulations in the Law of Moses. In addition are guidelines for other public services and daily offerings.

Ezekiel's vision is, in a sense, a map of holiness. Every detail serves to emphasize an ideal worship depicted in forms that are understandable and meaningful to his contemporaries. The Lord draws near and invites His people to come near to Him, but He does not cease to be the God of terrible holiness. His people must revere Him accordingly.

Take It Home

It is a common problem for people and/or churches to disregard or minimize the holiness of God. Certainly, God does invite His people to draw near to Him (Hebrews 4:16; 10:22; James 4:8). He is abundant in grace and mercy. Yet as we approach God and come to see Him more clearly, there should be times when, like Ezekiel, we are floored by His glory (Ezekiel 1:28). How would you rate your own awareness and respect for the holiness of God? What experiences have you had when the Lord's holiness was most evident to you?

EZEKIEL 47:1–48:35

THE RIVER MEASURED AND THE TERRITORY DIVIDED

Setting Up the Section

As Ezekiel finishes describing his vision of a future temple, he also concludes his lengthy book. In this section he depicts the river flowing out of the temple and explains how the land is to be divided among the tribes.

📖 **47:1–12**

THE RIVER THAT FLOWS FROM THE TEMPLE

Numerous references to a river of life are found throughout the Bible. The theme begins in Genesis as four rivers flow through the Garden of Eden and continues to the final chapter of scripture that describes a river, clear as crystal, flowing from the throne of God. The latter example, written by John, appears to derive in a substantial way from Ezekiel's description in this passage. All ancient Near Eastern temples faced east, and Israel's was no exception (47:1). The worship was conducted according to completely different principles, of course, but the sanctuary would have looked familiar to that culture. As Ezekiel returns from the kitchens in the outer court of the temple to the sanctuary itself in the inner court, he sees a small stream of water gushing out from beneath the slab of stone at the base of the main doorway.

The east gate had been closed (44:1–2), so the flow of water is diverted to the south side of the gate structure. Ezekiel exits through the north gate (47:1–2). As he watches, his angelic escort does periodic depth checks. After walking about 1000 cubits (a standard Hebrew cubit was 17.5 inches), the water is ankle deep. Another 1000 cubits, and it has become knee deep. Another stretch, and it is waist deep. At the fourth measurement (by that time, well over a mile away from the temple), the water has become an impassable stream—both too deep and too wide to cross (47:3–5). No mention is made of tributaries, so the stream appears to become larger through miraculous effect.

Critical Observation

The physical topography of Israel would have required that a literal river cross valleys and ascend and descend mountain ranges before it could drop several thousand feet to the basin of the Dead Sea. What Ezekiel sees is a miraculous river in a vision.

During Ezekiel's time, as is true today, little life could be found in the Dead Sea. It has no exits, and the water that gathers there is filled with various toxic materials, including salts. But Ezekiel witnesses flowing water that will freshen the sea and soon have it teeming with life. In fact, the Dead Sea will rival the Mediterranean as a popular fishing spot (47:8–10).

Ezekiel begins and ends this section with an emphasis on where the water originated (47:1, 12). He sees fishermen standing on lush lakeshores and casting nets in spots that have for millennia been barren desert wastes. En-gedi and En-eglaim (47:10) were a significant distance apart, emphasizing that the entire lake is fresh and full of fish. Yet the surrounding swamps and marshlands remained salty because salt was a prized commodity. The various kinds of fresh fish would be preserved in the salt. In addition, the water creates a lush habitat for fruit trees (47:12). Ezekiel paints a verbal picture of unlimited abundance.

📖 **47:13–48:35**

THE DIVIDING OF THE LAND

The division of the territory as viewed by Ezekiel is considerably different from the boundaries that God had given Joshua centuries before. The boundaries described are essentially those that Israel possessed during the time of David and Solomon, except that the land east of the Jordan is not included in Ezekiel's vision (47:15–20). This time the division is to be equitable, where originally some tribes had considerably more land than others (47:14).

Another variation is a broadening of who will be entitled to a stake in the land. Under the Law of Moses, aliens could become circumcised and gain membership in the community, yet they were banned from owning land, which relegated them to something of an outsider status. But with the ability for outsiders to join the community *and* possess land, the distinctions between them and the native Israelites are entirely eliminated (47:22–23).

Ezekiel's description of the allotment of the land is so idealized that it ignores the topography of Canaan. Each tribe's designated segment runs east and west, from one side of the promised land to the other. Near the center of those bands is one strip reserved for the city, the sanctuary, the priests, and the prince (48:8–22). Seven tribes will be situated north of that strip (48:1–7), and five tribes south (48:23–28).

A number of intriguing details come to light in Ezekiel's depiction. For one, the sons of Jacob's two wives (Rachel and Leah) are positioned nearest the central reserve and the sanctuary. The children by handmaidens Bilhah and Zilpah are further removed. Another change is the location of Judah, now in the northern section rather than the south.

Demystifying Ezekiel

Judah's move from a southern tribe to a position farther north (48:7) is perhaps a symbol of the overcoming of longstanding animosities between Israel and Judah existing since the kingdom had been divided. Nevertheless, Judah remained closest to the central reserve on the north, and Benjamin on the south.

Still another surprise is that the names of the tribes connected with the twelve gates of the city (48:30–35) do not match the names in the land allotment. The land division is as before, with Joseph being replaced by his two sons (Manasseh and Ephraim) and with Levi omitted (because the Levites were distributed for ministry among the other tribes). But the *gates* include a gate for Joseph and one for Levi, reverting to the twelve original sons of Jacob (Israel).

Finally, we find a great ending to a great book (48:35). The continuing story of the kingdom of God is a story of the presence of the Lord. Because of Israel's unbelief and disobedience, she had forfeited the presence of God. But the new epoch would herald the arrival of Immanuel—God with us—and it would eventually result in His coming to be with His people forever.

Take It Home

The prophetic books have a reputation for proclaiming "gloom and doom," and certainly Ezekiel has much to say about God's judgment. Yet the final chapters of his book are actually quite encouraging. His message to Israel is that the God who had judged them will also restore them to fellowship with Him. What can you learn from Ezekiel that will help you develop a broader understanding of who God is and how He relates to His people?

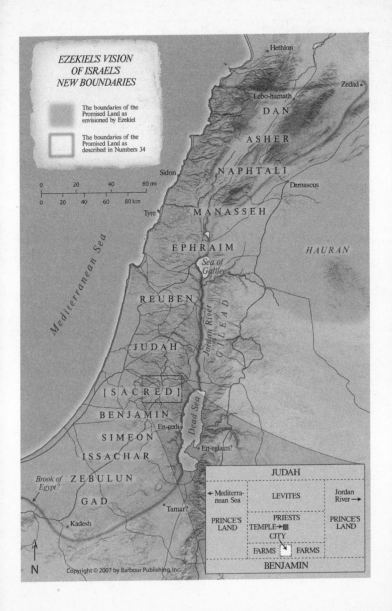

EZEKIEL'S VISION
OF ISRAEL'S
NEW BOUNDARIES

The boundaries of the
Promised Land as
envisioned by Ezekiel

The boundaries of the
Promised Land as
described in Numbers 34

Hethlon

Zedad

Lebo-hamath

D A N

A S H E R

N A P H T A L I

Sidon

Damascus

Tyre

M A N A S S E H

E P H R A I M

Sea of
Galilee

HAURAN

R E U B E N

Mediterranean Sea

J U D A H

Jordan River

G I L E A D

[S A C R E D]

Dead Sea

B E N J A M I N

En-gedi

S I M E O N

En-eglaim?

I S S A C H A R

Brook of
Egypt?

Z E B U L U N

G A D

Tamar?

Kadesh

N

Copyright © 2007 by Barbour Publishing, Inc.

JUDAH

←Mediter-
nean Sea

LEVITES

Jordan
River→

PRINCE'S
LAND

PRIESTS
TEMPLE→■
CITY

PRINCE'S
LAND

FARMS

FARMS

BENJAMIN

CONTRIBUTING EDITORS:

Dr. Robert Rayburn holds a Master of Divinity degree from Covenant Theological Seminary and a doctorate in New Testament from the University of Aberdeen, Scotland. His commentary on Hebrews was published in the *Evangelical Commentary of the Bible.*

Pastor **John Hanneman** is a preaching pastor at Peninsula Bible Church Cupertino. He has been in in the ministry for 30 years and has worked in singles ministry most of that time. He is passionate about training the next generation of Christians. John and his wife, Liz, have three children and three grandchildren.

Rev. Stephen C. Magee, MBA, MDiv is the pastor of Exeter Presbyterian Church in Exeter, New Hampshire. He has preached through all of the Old Testament as part of daily worship at the Exeter Church. He also writes an online devotional series at www.epcblog.blogspot.com.

Pastor **Doug McIntosh** has served Cornerstone Bible Church of Lilburn, Georgia since its beginnings in 1971. Doug is a graduate of Dallas Theological Seminary and serves as a member of the Board of Directors of Wycliffe Bible Translators USA. Doug has also published a number of books through Moody Press and Broadman & Holman.

CONSULTING EDITOR:

Dr. Tremper Longman is the Robert H. Gundry Professor of Biblical Studies at Westmont University. He has taught at Westmont since 1998 and taught before that for 18 years at the Westminster Theological Seminary in Philadelphia. Dr. Longman has degrees from Ohio Wesleyan University (B.A.), Westminster Theological Seminary (M.Div.), and Yale University (M.Phil.; Ph.D.). He has also been active in the area of Bible translation, in particular he serves on the central committee that produced and now monitors the New Living Translation.